ESPERANTO

****

ESPERANTO

THE WORLD INTERLANGUAGE

NEW REVISED EDITION

COMPILED BY

George Alan Connor
Doris Tappan Connor
William Solzbacher
The Very Rev. Dr. J. B. Se-Tsien Kao

THOMAS YOSELOFF   •   New York   •   London

****

FOREWORD

Who uses Esperanto? What makes it ten times easier to learn than the average national language? What can I do with it after I learn it? Would Esperanto be of use to me **now,** in my business, travel, scientific research, or hobbies? To provide authoritative answers to questions, the research and practical experience of several experts have been assembled and condensed into this encyclopedic handbook on interlanguage.

This is really **six books in one.** Many other books would be required to cover the same ground. Much of this material is entirely new in its approach to the problem. For those who wish to learn and apply the living interlanguage Esperanto, all the necessary materials are included. The "Guide Book" section, with classified directory to Esperanto agencies and activities throughout the world, is a unique and valuable feature.

The first two editions of this book received high praise and wide circulation in the United States, Canada, and all over the world. Completely revised and up-to-date, the third edition should be able to satisfy all legitimate needs of the user even better.

Each of the **four authors** has made some contribution to each part of the book. Altogether, they have had actual experience in the use of Esperanto in more than fifty-five countries throughout the world. One has represented the United States Government at a World Congress of Esperanto. Another has professionally organized the translation services of more than thirty international conferences.

The librarian who is asked for "a comprehensive book on international language" will have it in this volume. Busy newspaper and magazine editors will have a handy and complete reference book. The school principal and the language teacher will find solid information, high-lighted with examples of the latest teaching methods. Men and women in every walk of life should find here what they want to know about the increasingly important linguistic aspects of the problem of international understanding.

It is the sincere hope of the authors that most readers will use this book for **learning** Esperanto, in addition to learning about Esperanto. Anyone who studies the textbook carefully will be ready to read books and magazines in Esperanto. Correspondence with foreign lands may be started even before the course is completed. Learners should apply their new knowledge to the furtherance of people-to-people interchange, to the end that mankind may become literate in world communication.

CONTENTS

Part 4—Guide Book for the Practical Esperantist

Classified Esperanto Directory

Part 5—Esperanto-English Dictionary

Part 6—English-Esperanto Dictionary

LANGUAGE AND INTERLANGUAGE

****

Inteligenta persono lernas la Interlingvon Esperanto rapide kaj facile. Esperanto estas la moderna, kultura, neŭtrala lingvo por ĝenerala interkomunikado. La Interlingvo estas simpla, praktika solvo de la problemo de interkompreno.

THE TIME IS RIPE FOR INTERLANGUAGE

LANGUAGE barriers cause misunderstanding and countless difficulties in the world. They make us speechless when we should be articulate, dependent on guesswork and makeshift methods when we should be able to stand firmly on our own feet, backward and ineffective when we should be in the lead. Two Presidents of the United States have expressed themselves forcefully on this subject.

In addressing the graduating midshipmen of the United States Naval Academy in Annapolis, on June 4, 1958, President Dwight D. Eisenhower said: "We are, indeed, poor linguists. We are too much handicapped because so many of our people have failed to become knowledgeable in a language other than ours. Success in this will do much to improve human understanding in a world of great cultural diversity, and thus to strengthen our relationships with other peoples. This is one indispensable step towards a peaceful world."

Ten years earlier, President Harry S. Truman said in an interview published in the **New York Times Magazine:** "Getting to know other nations and their getting to know us is necessary for international friendship and cooperation. One of the chief obstacles that stand in the way is the difference in language . . . It is hard to hold conversations through interpreters, for though translations may be literal, nevertheless the intended meanings may be unintentionally distorted."

The Congress of the United States decided that it was time to do something about this when it passed the National Defense Education Act of September 2, 1958, authorizing a multimillion-dollar program for "increased or improved instruction in modern foreign languages" through direct grants to institutions of learning and through financial assistance to state education departments.

The language problem has many facets. Its implications in education, science, business, and politics are innumerable. There has been a growing awareness of the fact that increased emphasis on foreign language study, though useful and urgent, will not suffice, but that for worldwide use a practical, neutral, and easy-to-learn world interlanguage is necessary. Furthermore, such a means of communication is not only desirable, but is already in existence and has stood the test of time. The facts about Esperanto, well established by experiment and experience, are finding growing recognition both at the grass roots and among the world's leaders.

In 1959, on the occasion of the one-hundredth anniversary of the birth of Dr. L. L. Zamenhof, author of Esperanto, a Sponsoring Committee for a campaign to promote the increased study and wider application of Esperanto was formed. It included the President of Brazil (Juscelino Kubitschek), former Presidents of France (Vincent Auriol) and Switzerland (Enrico Celio), the former Secretary General of the United Nations (Trygve Lie), the Speakers of the Belgian and the Polish Parliaments, the Prime Ministers of Belgium, New Zealand, and Poland, former Prime Ministers of France and the Netherlands, the Foreign Ministers of Australia, Brazil, Guatemala, Norway, and Uruguay, the Ministers of Education of Brazil, Ceylon, Denmark, Guatemala, Norway, Poland, Sweden, and Yugoslavia, Cabinet Ministers and former Cabinet Ministers from countries mentioned above as well as from Austria, Finland, the German Federal Republic, Great Britain, and Hungary, three Nobel Prize winners (for Physics, Literature, and Peace, respectively), and other outstanding leaders in many fields from all over the world.

At the Pan American Union in Washington, on July 3, 1958, the Secretary General of the Organization of American States, Dr. José Antonio Mora, of Uruguay, received an Esperanto delegation for the presentation of a statement in favor of Esperanto signed by the Presidents of 49 important Brazilian organizations. He was also handed a memorandum recalling past support for Esperanto by Inter-American organizations and leaders, beginning with the First Pan American Science Congress at Santiago de Chile which in January 1909 unanimously adopted a resolution stating that it "recommends Esperanto as a neutral international language which deserves an important place in the programs of instruction of the American nations." The memorandum pointed out that the first Director General of the Pan American Union, the late Dr. John Barrett, served as President of the Sixth Universal Esperanto Congress in Washington (1910) and as President of the Esperanto Association of North America. The governments of Brazil, Costa Rica, Ecuador, Guatemala, Honduras, Mexico, the United States, and Uruguay as well as a number of European and Asian governments were officially represented at the Universal Esperanto Congress in Washington.

A resolution in favor of Esperanto was adopted by UNESCO (the United Nations Educational, Scientific, and Cultural Organization), at its General Conference in Montevideo, on December 10, 1954. Introduced by Mexico, seconded by Switzerland, slightly amended at the request of Great Britain, the resolution "takes note of the results obtained by Esperanto in the field of international intellectual relations . . . recognizes that these results correspond with the aims and ideals of UNESCO, authorizes the Director General to follow current developments in the use of Esperanto in education, science, and culture." The resolution also notes that "several Member States have announced their readiness to introduce or expand the teaching of Esperanto in their schools and higher educational establishments, and requests these Member States to keep the Director General informed of the results obtained in this field."

The UNESCO resolution, which resulted in increased support for Esperanto by governments, intergovernmental organizations, and public opinion, was passed in reply to a petition which had been presented to the United Nations on August 2, 1950, and which the Secretary General of the U.N. had referred to UNESCO. The petition, signed by 895,432 individuals and by 492 organizations with a membership of almost 15½ million, urged the United Nations, "in view of the worldwide use of Esperanto, the only auxiliary language which has had appreciable success," to help "spread the use of this language in every possible way, for example, by encouraging its teaching in schools where teachers are available, and developing its use in travel, international commerce, and correspondence."

And what about the linguists? someone might ask. The late Edward Sapir, one of the founding fathers of modern linguistics, wrote as long ago as 1933 in his article, "Language," in the **Encyclopaedia of the Social Sciences:** "The logical necessity of an international language in modern times is in strange contrast to the indifference and even opposition with which most people consider its possibility. The attempts so far made to solve this problem, of which Esperanto has probably had the greatest measure of practical success, have not affected more than a very small proportion of the people whose international interests and needs might have led to a desire for a simple and uniform means of international expression . . . The opposition to an international language has little logic or psychology in its favor. The supposed artificiality of Esperanto . . . has been absurdly exaggerated . . . The lack of interest in the international language problem, in spite of the manifest need for one, is an excellent example of how little logic or intellectual necessity has to do with the acquirement of language habits . . ."

Fortunately, the opposition and indifference mentioned by Sapir have been receding in later years. Public opinion polls in many countries have shown considerable awareness of the need for a world interlanguage. In the United States a nationwide Gallup Poll, organized shortly after the end of World War II, showed that 71 per cent of the American people believed that an international language should be taught in the schools of all countries. A statewide poll in Minnesota produced 74 per cent affirmative answers to the question, "Do you believe a universal or common language which all countries could understand is practical and should be encouraged?" Of those answering "yes," 76 per cent indicated they would be willing to learn the international language if it were not English. For those with a college education, the positive answers ran as high as 90 per cent. For the age group of 21 to 29, irrespective of schooling, the percentage was 88. Such figures prove that the American people—just like people elsewhere in the world—have become language-conscious and that the time is ripe for decisive action in favor of Esperanto as a means of communication and understanding.

In a speech delivered at the **New York Herald Tribune** Forum, former Senator William Benton, at that time Assistant Secretary of State in charge of cultural relations with the rest of the world, declared: "We must hope that we shall need to invest less of our resources in military power as we invest more of our thought and attention in the task of mutual understanding. **In an atomic age, understanding, not bombs, is the last, best hope on earth.**"

LANGUAGES UNITE AND DIVIDE

"SPEECH, which sets man apart from the rest of creation and is his greatest social asset, serves paradoxically to separate him from most of his fellow humans. What amounts to a binding tie inside the family, the tribe, and the nation, acts as a barrier between those groups and others constituted a short distance away." This quotation from a lecture by Professor José Martel, of the College of the City of New York, and President of the New York Language Teachers' Association, shows the essence of the language problem. Men are not much better than deaf-mutes when they meet humans belonging to a different language group. To bridge the gap from one language group to another, a bridge language, an Interlanguage, is needed.

It is difficult to say how many languages there are in the world. The French Academy has established a list of 2,796. The number of languages of real literary and practical importance is, of course, much smaller, and may be put at approximately 120. There are only about seventeen languages whose speakers number over twenty-five million people. They are, numerically speaking, in approximately the following order: Chinese, English, Hindi-Urdu, Russian, Spanish, Japanese, German, French, Bantu (many dialects), Bengali, Portuguese, Italian, Javanese, Polish, Arabic, Indonesian-Malay, Telugu.

Out of these, Professor Mario A. Pei, of Columbia University, chooses eight which he calls "key languages": "The man who has some practical acquaintance with English, French, German, Spanish, Portuguese, Italian, Russian, and Japanese is, roughly speaking, in a position to make his way around the world. If to this knowledge he adds a smattering of Arabic, Chinese, Malay, and Dutch, and the ability to identify a few other tongues, so that he can distinguish between Polish and Czech, Swedish and Danish, Finnish and Hungarian, at least in their written form, his linguistic education, for purely utilitarian purposes, is completed" (**The World's Chief Languages**, p. 15).

Professor Pei calls these languages "key languages" because they are understood by a relatively large number of persons outside the countries where they are indigenous. They have obtained "international" standing either by being superimposed on other countries by imperial and colonial powers, or by being widely studied because of their economic, literary, social, and scientific importance. By concentrating on what is essential from a practical point of view, and by using streamlined methods of language study, it is possible to learn several or all of Professor Pei's "key languages" to an extent sufficient for limited purposes.

Language study is, and will undoubtedly remain, of great importance for many groups of persons. But there is "language study" and "language study": An infinite number of variations are possible between what Lancelot Hogben and Frederick Bodmer (in **The Loom of Language**) call "the perfectionist school" (meticulous study of grammar and literature) and what they call "the nudist school" (direct method, without grammar and "rules"). Learning to read, write, and speak Chinese is almost a lifetime job for a Westerner. At an International Service Seminar in Pennsylvania, however, a young Chinese Ph.D. offered to teach anyone to converse in Chinese on simple everyday topics in six weeks. For some people this may be all they want or need. Efficient techniques for this have been developed during the war for the Army Specialized Training Programs and the Area Studies of American universities.

A press correspondent in Athens should know Greek; a correspondent in Berlin should be familiar with German (and nowadays also with Russian). An American firm specializing in exports to Brazil should engage staff members knowing Portuguese. Firms in many countries have employees who know English, and their American, British, or Canadian business partners profit from this. But what if the market is to be expanded so as to include outlets where no English-speaking staff is available? What if an American firm having no Turkish-speaking personnel has to compete on the Turkish market with British, German, or Swedish firms who do engage Turkish-speaking clerks? What if a middle-sized manufacturer needs exports not just to one or two countries but all over the world?

People in many countries have been learning foreign languages, but unfortunately the languages learned are not everywhere the same. One of the authors of this book once made a lecture and study tour through Central and Southeastern Europe, giving talks in Esperanto, German, French, Italian, and Hungarian. At times he had to use what little Russian, Ukrainian, Polish, Rumanian, and Serbo-Croatian he knew. Often he did not succeed in making himself understood or in understanding others. But only once on that two-month trip did he have an opportunity to talk English, with a Member of the Rumanian Parliament. English is not much good in that part of the world, where French, German, and Russian used to be studied most.

A great many languages are used as, what one might call, "regional interlanguages." Arabic, Malay, and Swahili are in this position. In the India of today, people have to know both English and Hindi in addition to their mother tongue if they want to prosper. In some parts of the Congo, they have to learn Swahili and French in addition to their native speech.

Political considerations, sympathies and dislikes, often exercise a favorable or unfavorable influence on the study and use of certain languages. In Central European countries, where German used to be widely taught, Russian is now taking its place. In the schools of Eastern Germany, Russian is replacing English. In India, the nationalist movement tries to make Hindi the national tongue. Progress is slow. Even when nationalist leaders from different parts of the country met for anti-British discussions, they had to talk English. Some of them, however, are fanatically determined to change this. As to Ireland, the **Washington Merry-Go-Round** once told the story of Michael McWhite, Delegate of Eire to the League of Nations, who always used French in his Geneva speeches, explaining this allegedly by saying: "I can't speak my own language, and I'll be damned if I'll speak English."

Language learning is here to stay, but there is a limit to what even specialists can learn, and a majority of human beings have little or no talent for becoming linguists. The need for a neutral Interlanguage, as a bridge between language groups and also as a bridge over national prejudices and sensibilities, becomes more urgent every day.

Naturally, there are many people who would like their native tongue to become the international language. They would enjoy the privileged position which this would give them. But others are not willing to accept such discrimination. National feelings and jealousies are strong, and it does not look as if they were going to die out soon.

An eminent linguist, Dr. Björn Collinder, Professor of Finno-Ugrian Languages at the University of Upsala, Sweden, stated this in an article on "The World Language Problem," published in a Swedish teachers' journal: "A national language cannot become the world language without crushing the other languages. This possibility is naturally out of the question. . . . When Latin was the language of the educated people, of the Catholic Church, and of diplomacy, the situation was entirely different. No nation had the right to schoolmaster the others when the verbal or written use of Latin was concerned. . . . What we need now is a simplified Latin, a rationally streamlined language, conserving the Latin-Greek vocabulary which is already international, and at the same time so simple and regular that anyone may learn it in elementary school. Fortunately we have such a language: **Esperanto.** . . . If the world were not governed by as little wisdom as it is, Esperanto would already have been introduced in the schools of all lands, and the world language problem would be solved."

INTERNATIONAL CONFERENCES
AND ORGANIZATIONS

THERE was a time—Professor Collinder referred to it in the article just quoted—when Latin was the universal language, at least in the Western world. Important documents and speeches, instruction in the universities, discussions and transactions of learned societies were handled in this tongue, even when it had ceased to be spoken in everyday life. In the Hungarian Parliament, Latin was the language used until deep into the nineteenth century. As early as 1662, however, England's "Royal Society" replaced Latin by English in its deliberations. About thirty years later the French Academy of Sciences followed this example, adopting French as its official tongue.

Then came the time when French, the most logical, polished, and elegant of European languages, became the medium of international

[9

diplomacy. The prestige of French literature and civilization was so great that in many countries the upper classes cultivated the study of French, engaged French governesses for their children, and talked French among themselves, particularly when they did not wish to be overheard by their servants.

At many of the earlier international conferences it was taken for granted that only delegates knowing French would attend. If someone did not know French well enough to speak it in public, he was expected to keep quiet. If he happened to be a very important person, he could speak in his own language and have his statement translated into French by an interpreter. This was, however, the exception, not the rule. There are still a number of international organizations at whose conferences French is the only official language. For one six-year period between the two wars, Professor Herbert N. Shenton, of Syracuse University, gave their number as sixty-nine. They include such organizations as the Academy of International Law, the International Bureau of Weights and Measures, the International Aeronautic Federation, and the International Red Cross. To an ever increasing extent, however, English and German, and to a lesser degree Italian and Spanish, challenged the position of French, and since World War II, Russian has been claiming and obtaining equal status in a number of organizations.

When the League of Nations was founded at the Versailles Peace Conference, a "battle of the languages" was fought. Clemenceau wanted French to be the only official language while Woodrow Wilson insisted on equal status for English, and Baron Sonnino of Italy clamored for Italian to be treated with the same consideration as English. Later great efforts were made to obtain official standing for Spanish, the mother tongue of a third of the nations represented in the League. Eventually French and English were made official, with equal rights. Rule 16 of the Rules of Procedure adopted by the First Assembly of the League of Nations read as follows:

1. Speeches in French shall be summarized in English, and vice versa, by an interpreter belonging to the Secretariat.

2. A representative speaking in another language shall provide for the translation of his speech into one of these two languages.

3. All documents, resolutions, and reports circulated by the President or Secretariat shall be rendered in both French and English.

4. Any representative may have documents circulated in a language other than French and English, but the Secretariat will not be responsible for their translation and printing.

5. Any Member of the League or any group of Members may require that all documents and publications shall be regularly translated into and printed and circulated in a language other than French or English but shall in such case defray all the necessary expenses.

A similar arrangement was made for the International Labor Organization of the League of Nations. At ILO conferences the number of delegates with little or no linguistic training was, however, much greater than at the assemblies of the League, so that gradually German was recognized for almost all purposes as a third official language, and Spanish, to a somewhat lesser degree, as a fourth. Both the League and the ILO were compelled to handle more than two dozen languages in their correspondence and other activities.

While the League of Nations was able to manage with two official languages, the United Nations has had to use five: English, French, Spanish, Russian, Chinese. Since it is physically impossible to use all of them for every purpose, English and French have been given a privileged position as "working languages." The U. N. Security Council adopted (May 16, 1946) the following Rules of Procedure:

38. Chinese, English, French, Russian, and Spanish shall be the official languages of the Security Council, and English and French the working languages.

39. Speeches made in either of the working languages shall be interpreted into the other working language.

40. Speeches made in any of the three other official languages shall be interpreted into both working languages.

41. Any representative may make a speech in a language other than the official languages. In this case he shall himself provide for interpretation into one of the working languages. Interpretation into the other working language by an interpreter of the Secretariat may be based on the interpretation given in the first working language.

42. Verbatim records of meetings of the Security Council shall be drawn up in the working languages. At the request of any representative a verbatim record of any speech made in an official language other than the working languages shall be drawn up in the original language.

43. All resolutions and other important documents shall forthwith be made available in the official languages. Upon the request of any representative, any other document shall be made available in any or all of the official languages.

44. Documents of the Security Council shall, if the Security Council so decides, be published in any language other than the official languages.

Other U.N. organs have substantially the same rules. In the General Assembly the advocates of Spanish succeeded at an early date in making it a third working language, and the increased use of simultaneous interpretation (the Filene-Finlay Speech Translator) has made possible more translations into Russian and Chinese. The U. N. Secretariat, however, has consistently pointed out that it is costly to give additional tongues the status of working languages. In his Annual Report for 1947, Secretary-General Trygve Lie declared: "The uncertainty of some of the rules of procedure of the various organs concerning interpretation and translation into non-working official languages, and the reporting in these languages, has at times made it difficult to deal with such work with the best despatch. . . . The Secretary-General was obliged to make it clear to the Economic Commission for Europe that, until and unless the General Assembly voted the necessary credits, he would not be able to give effect to a decision by the Commission to employ a third working language in addition to the two recommended by the Assembly to the other organs of the United Nations."

Simultaneous interpretation has greatly facilitated U.N. operations and has resulted in saving time for the Delegates. On the other hand it has imposed heavier burdens on the Secretariat staff.

At private international conferences, the three-language system (French-English-German) is widely used, and many organizations permit, in addition to these, Spanish, Italian, Dutch, or Esperanto.

The language difficulties at all international conferences are enormous. The selection of participants is strongly influenced by linguistic considerations. Many otherwise perfectly qualified persons refrain from attending conferences because they feel that their knowledge of foreign languages is inadequate. Many organizations send delegates who are good linguists, though their other qualifications are sometimes only second-rate.

A great variety of devices has been used to overcome the language obstacle. Speeches are often secured in advance, translated into different languages, mimeographed, and distributed among the delegates. Sometimes members are seated according to language groups and asked, after each speech, to withdraw into neighboring rooms where translations in several languages are given simultaneously. Obviously, discussions and proceedings are very slow with these translations, because the whole conference has to wait for the translator who is slowest. Sometimes simultaneous translation is impossible, as for instance in a case experienced by one of the authors of this book, when a speech was delivered in Russian, then at first translated into German, and only afterward from German into English, French, and Esperanto, because only one of the interpreters was able to translate from the Russian directly. Other delays are due to the fact that people talking in a foreign language with which they are not thoroughly familiar are likely to need more time for making themselves clear. Their speeches become stammering, longwinded, repetitious, hard to follow, consuming the nerves as well as the time of their fellow delegates. It is an art to express oneself briefly, forcefully, and concisely, even in one's own language.

The most important technical device invented for the facilitation of international conferences is the Filene-Finlay Speech Translator, sometimes called "the earphone system." It has been used at the International Labor Organization since 1929, at the Nuremberg War Crimes Trials, in the Belgian Parliament, and, since 1946, at the United Nations. Originally proposed by Mr. Edward A. Filene, the Boston philanthropist, it was worked out by a British scientist, Professor Gordon Finlay, tested on a limited scale at the 1926 International Labor Conference, and further developed in the following years. Interpreters for different languages are placed in glass-enclosed booths and talk into microphones while the speaker is delivering his speech. The seats of the delegates are equipped with earphones connected with the translators' microphones. By pressing one of four or five buttons, a delegate can choose the language in which he wishes to hear the speech. By turning a small knob, he can also regulate the strength of reception.

This system, of course, has its limitations and disadvantages. H. N. Shenton mentions some of them (in **Cosmopolitan Conversation,** Columbia University Press): "The most serious obstacles . . . lay in the physical and nervous limitations of translators, be they of ever so high a type and training. It proved exceedingly difficult for the interpreters to carry on under the conditions imposed by the new device. . . . It is also a more intense strain to listen to speeches through the machine than it is to listen to the interpreter directly, a common experience with most telephonic devices, of course." Mistranslations slip through more easily than with other systems under which there are always a few persons in the audience who have understood the original speech and can check the translator and obtain rectifications when serious mistakes occur. It is also rather disconcerting to see a speaker talking and gesticulating while hearing through the earphone a translation not of what he is saying but of what he said a while ago.

On a limited scale the system has been used by the U. N. since

October 1946. In October 1947, the General Assembly began to use radio sets developed by IBM (International Business Machines), embodying the Filene-Finlay patents. Secretary-General Trygve Lie pointed out in a special report on Simultaneous Interpretation (U. N. Document A/383, Sept. 3, 1947) that "all meetings cannot physically use simultaneous interpretation, since only four of the larger rooms are equipped."

Another important factor is the high cost of the Filene-Finlay system. Many organizations cannot afford it. Theoretically the number of languages in which simultaneous translations are possible is unlimited. Practically, however, only four or five, at the utmost six, languages can be used. No international conference is rich enough to make arrangements for such potential needs as translations from Polish into Chinese, from Italian into Norwegian, or from Portuguese into Bulgarian. In fact, therefore, the Filene-Finlay system, even under the most efficient management, is unable to eliminate the monopoly of a few major languages.

It is no help at all outside the assembly hall. At most international conferences, personal contacts between delegates from different countries are more important than speeches (which could easily be printed and sent out by mail) and official discussions. It is a sad but, unfortunately, a quite common experience to see delegates take their meals and spend their leisure hours in the company of colleagues from their own countries. It may be thrilling for Mr. Smith, of New York City, to meet Mr. Murphy, of Chicago, and Mr. Miller, of Toronto, at a conference in Copenhagen, but on such an occasion it would undoubtedly be more important for him to spend some time with Mr. Hansen, of Copenhagen, Dr. Kowalski, of Warsaw, and Professor Huber, of Zurich.

Neither the Filene-Finlay Speech Translator nor any other system of translations can overcome the basic inequality between delegates speaking their mother tongue and those who have to express themselves in a language not their own. In a lecture on the "Inferiority Complex in Language," Professor José Martel discussed this important fact which he called "the strongest argument against the use of an organic language . . . as an instrument of international communication." Professor Martel concluded: "For members of different groups to communicate freely and without mutual embarrassment, it might be better to use some language which is not organic to either of the speakers. That, of course, is the reason for the development of a neutral Interlanguage as an easy second tongue for both."

Esperanto is this neutral and easy Interlanguage. According to extensive tests made by Professor Edward L. Thorndike, of Columbia University, "the achievement in the synthetic language will probably be from five to fifteen times that in a natural language, according to the difficulty of the latter." The use of Esperanto, either as sole conference language or as sole translation language (all languages permitted, but translations made only into Esperanto), solves the language problem of international conferences—if delegates are willing to make the relatively small effort of learning the Interlanguage. The League of Nations Secretariat described, in its report on Esperanto (1922), a conference, held at League of Nations headquarters in Geneva, where only Esperanto was spoken: "We have witnessed the case of the International Conference of Educational Authorities at the Secretariat of the League of Nations in which the debates were in Esperanto. We were much struck by the ease and rapidity with which delegates from all countries expressed their ideas and understood each other; moreover, the discussions were not interrupted by translations. As many as thirty-two speakers were heard at the same meeting and an amount of work was done in three days which might have taken ten days to accomplish in an ordinary conference using several official languages."

One of the conferences where Esperanto was the sole translation language was the Inter-Religious Conference for Peace, held at The Hague in 1928 with about 450 delegates from many lands. When invitations were sent out, every notice contained the announcement that Esperanto would be the only language of interpretation. "The majority of delegates," says a report printed in **Cosmopolitan Conversation**, "on their arrival had quite forgotten that statement about Esperanto. When they expressed surprise . . . (they were) referred to the printed notice, and they seldom made any further comment or inquiry but just set to in the most natural way to study the little keys obtainable at the Conference. By the end of a few hours most of the audience seemed to get used to the strange, simple, easily understood medium of interpretation. General contentment was expressed as well as approbation and congratulation." One participant made this comment on the effectiveness of the system used: "We found it most restful to have only one language of interpretation, in addition to its being a good time-saver. The audience grows used to one common medium, and everyone seems to experience considerably less mental fatigue than when submitted to the usual process of repetition of speeches in at least two, and often three, different languages." One of the organizers commented on the fact that no one talked about Esperanto: "It was just a living language, of practical service, and accepted and appreciated as such."

The use of Esperanto as sole translation language is, of course, not as time-saving as its use as the only conference language. It is, however, the logical system for the transition period, as long as Esperanto is not universally used in international relations. It requires only a minor effort for an educated person to learn to **understand** Esperanto while some practical experience is needed for **speaking** it fluently.

Why then, someone may ask, has Esperanto not been generally introduced as a translation language at international conferences? A partial answer may be found in a statement made by a representative of the American Council of the Institute of Pacific Relations after the Shanghai Conference of the Institute, in 1932: "The case for the use of an auxiliary language seems to be a strong one. . . . Most educated Japanese and Chinese do manage to acquire a fairly fluent use of English, French, or German. . . . I suppose that the same people could also learn Esperanto. . . . Quite frankly, the much greater difficulty seems to me that the more or less aged statesmen, bankers, and educators who constitute so large a proportion of our participants simply cannot be persuaded to make any personal effort at all to acquire a new medium of expression" (**Cosmopolitan Conversation**, pp. 444-5).

It is difficult to persuade some people, in particular those whose mother tongues have been enjoying the privileged position of official languages at conferences, to make a personal effort, even if it is small in comparison to the advantages which can be obtained. Progress will necessarily continue to be gradual. But the experience gained in approximately 1,150 international conferences at which Esperanto has been used in one form or another will make future progress easier and faster.

NATIONAL LANGUAGES
IN "BASIC" DISGUISE

ONE of the most striking instances of the recognition of the need for a world language was Mr. Winston Churchill's speech at Harvard University in 1943, when he said: "It would certainly be a great convenience for us all to be able to move freely about the world—and to find everywhere a medium, albeit primitive, of intercourse and understanding." He was advocating English for the rôle, via the easy-dosage method of "Basic English." His speech was a clear recognition of the need for an auxiliary tongue, coupled with the pleasant thought: **my** language. Basic English, worked out by Professor C. K. Ogden, of Cambridge, England, and first published in 1930, is neither the first nor the only project of its kind. During the first World War, in 1915, a Munich Professor, Dr.

Adalbert Baumann, worked out WEDE (Welt-Deutsch, Universal German), a simplified form of German with phonetic spelling, to be used in a German-dominated postwar world. Similar blue-prints were published at one time or another for a simplification of French, Spanish, and Italian, as well as for simplified Latin and Greek, so as to make them fit for use as auxiliary languages. Linguistic imperialism was the admitted or subtle background of most of these projects. The "battle of the languages" is frequently but one specialized front in the struggle for national prestige and spheres of influence. According to I. A. Richards' **Basic English and Its Uses,** Rudolph Hess, shortly before his flight to England, "announced at a party conference that when the Nazis had won, English would become 'a minor Germanic dialect of no world importance'. . . ." Professor Richards comments: "His utterance contrasts well with Bismarck's view that the most significant event of the nineteenth century was the acceptance of English as the language of North America."

At about the same time that C. K. Ogden published **Basic English,** Professor Zachrisson, of Upsala, Sweden, proposed his "Anglic," which is English with semi-phonetic spelling. His project was based on the idea that irregular spelling and difficult pronunciation are among the greatest handicaps of English. Unfortunately, such spellings as "internashonal asoesiaeshon" make words difficult to recognize for people in other countries.

Basic English (the word "Basic" is sometimes explained as meaning British-American-Scientific-International-Commercial) is essentially a reduced vocabulary and a system of defining things and ideas by means of this minimum word list. Thus a beefsteak becomes "a cut from the back of a male cow kept on the fire long enough with the right things"; "to sell" becomes "to take money for"; a pear is "an apple-like fruit round at one end and pointed on the other." The **New York Times Magazine** recently printed an article, "One Language for One World," by Lee McCabe, ending with "several phrases taken at random from the Army's guides for soldiers stationed overseas, and the same phrases as they would appear in Esperanto . . . and Basic English." Basic English did not fare well at all in this comparison. Take, for instance, phrase 7: "This watermelon tastes good." Basic English: "This large green fruit with the form of an egg and a sweet red inside has a good taste." Esperanto: "La akvomelono gustas bone." The 12 phrases used as examples total 73 words in English, 61 in Esperanto, 158 in verbose and clumsy Basic English.

In an article entitled "Basic—as a Linguist Sees It," Professor Mario A. Pei, of Columbia University, declared: "I oppose Basic English on the following grounds: 1. It is an unsatisfactory means of expression for the normal English speaker; 2. It is fundamentally misleading in its claims and methods; 3. It presents greater difficulty to the average foreign learner than does ordinary English."

David M. Earl, in the magazine **American Esperantist**, in a report on his experiences as a teacher of Basic English, said: "It is not a solution to the problem of choosing a world auxiliary. We, as Esperantists, would do well to stress this attitude: that Basic can be no rival to Esperanto because it is essentially a **method of introducing English,** not an entity in itself. Although this opinion may not be accepted by Ogden, it is clearly stated by Dr. Richards in his book, **Basic English and Its Uses:** 'We should be poor servants of the future if in spreading the English language we impaired it. Happily the very constitution of Basic English makes it an influence tending in the other direction. It is no rival to or substitute for an ampler English, where the use of that is feasible. It is an introduction and an exploratory instrument' (pp. 6-7)."

It seems that Basic English has found no other practical uses than to serve as an introduction to English for foreigners, and to teach a relatively small number of English-speaking people how to express themselves with a limited vocabulary. No international conference has ever been held in Basic English, and we know of no business firm or international organization prepared to correspond in Basic.

THE QUEST FOR A
UNIVERSAL LANGUAGE

THE World Interlanguage Esperanto did not fall out of the blue sky as something no one had ever thought of. It came as the fulfillment of a dream which hundreds of men and women had dreamed through the ages. When reading the eleventh chapter of Genesis, Christians and Jews thought with melancholy of the world, as it was before men tried to build the Babel tower, when "the whole earth was of one language and one speech." Good old Homer, who knew how troublesome the language problem is, sang: "Many tongues are spoken by humans, but one by the gods."

Saint Hildegard of Bingen, the learned abbess, seems to have been the first to work out, in the twelfth century, a "new language," the "Lingua Ignota." In England, Bishop Wilkins, brother-in-law of Oliver Cromwell, published a plan for a "philosophical language," in which scholars everywhere could express themselves logically and perfectly.

In France, the great philosopher, René Descartes, in a letter to Abbé Mersenne in 1629, described his ideas about a universal language: "That language would have only one kind of conjugation, declension, and word structure. The changes in verb and word construction would have to be effected by affixes added to the beginning or end of the root-word." This sounds almost like a blueprint for Esperanto. The German philosopher, Leibniz, worked on a language which would be "an algebra of thought." When Diderot and d'Alembert edited their famous Encyclopédie, they could not ignore the many efforts made for the establishment of a "philosophical," "artificial," or "universal" language. The French Secretary of the Treasury, Faiguet, wrote an article on "Nouvelle Langue" for their Encyclopedia. His basic idea was to supply the learned academies of Europe with a means of intercommunication. Thomas More, in his Utopia, speaks of a "rational language," and Comenius advocated "a new, perfect language . . . which will be incomparably easier to learn than any natural language."

Most of these projects were a priori languages, invented artificially, and in many cases their authors combined the quest for a universal language with attempts to invent a system of "pasigraphy," codes and signs for an absolutely logical expression of thoughts in writing. None of these projects got beyond the blueprint stage, and only very few inventors went to as much trouble as Saint Hildegard, who worked out a vocabulary.

The first synthetic language which penetrated into practical use was Volapük. It stands about half-way between the a priori language projects and the a posteriori language, Esperanto. Volapük's author was a Catholic priest, Monsignor Johann Martin Schleyer, of Konstanz, Germany. He worked out a grammar which was absolutely regular, though rather cumbersome. The vocabulary consisted of words taken from English, German, and Latin, but considerably mutilated. Volapük itself is a compound of two English words: "vol" (world) and "pük" (speech), and thus means "world speech" (the "a" indicates the genitive). "Compliment" became "plim," "animal"—"nim," "year"—"yel." Although the language was difficult to learn and had many other faults, it soon won hundreds of thousands of followers. About thirty periodicals were published in it, and approximately 300 clubs in different countries were devoted to its study and diffusion. The movement organized three international Congresses at which, however, little Volapük was spoken. Reading and writing it was a thrilling hobby for many, speaking it fluently went beyond the capacity of even its inventor. Volapük's fall was faster than its rise. At the Paris Congress, in 1889, nine years after the first appearance of the language, a quarrel broke out between Monsignor Schleyer, who regarded the language as his private property, and the Volapük Academy, of which Professor Auguste Kerckhoffs of Paris was President, which wanted far-reaching reforms. The end of Volapük was hastened by the progress of Esperanto which appeared in 1887 and was immediately considered by many as infinitely superior. Many Volapükists went over to Esperanto. On the other hand, Volapük's fiasco slowed down the early development of the Esperanto movement because many people were deeply disillusioned and despaired of the possibility of a neutral auxiliary language. Fifteen years of slow progress were needed to overcome the inertia and skepticism of public opinion. The last Volapük Congress was held in 1889, the first Esperanto Congress in 1905.

There were, of course, always a number of skeptics predicting that Esperanto would go the way of Volapük. Esperanto has, however, weathered all storms and stood the test of time. In sixty years of steady though sometimes slow progress, it has become, to use the words of Professor Edmond Privat, of the University of Neuchâtel, Switzerland, "the living language of a living people." It is today the only living Interlanguage, rendering considerable services in many fields, and ready to serve on a much larger scale.

The project makers have, however, not given up their pastime. There were several hundred blueprints before Esperanto came, and there have been several hundred more since Dr. L. L. Zamenhof published his **Lingvo Internacia.** Only one of them, "Ido," a "reformed" Esperanto, succeeded temporarily in winning followers and obtaining some practical use. Even in its heyday, however, it never had more than 5 per cent of the followers of "classical" Esperanto. Ido has now disappeared, but the lessons of its history are still of interest.

Ido was marketed as the language recommended by a Delegation for the Adoption of an International Auxiliary Language, founded at the Paris World's Fair in 1900. The Delegation had the support of influential academic circles and secured within a number of years the "affiliation," at least nominally, of 310 societies of all kinds and of 1,250 scientists and scholars. The Secretary and Treasurer of the Delegation, Couturat and Leau, two Paris Professors, published a voluminous **History of Universal Language.** It was hoped that some universally recognized authority, for instance the International Association of Academies, would be willing to select the best international language. When this body refused to do so, a circular was sent out to the affiliated organizations, asking for suggestions as well as for the appointment of a Committee. Out of seventy-four replies received, fifty-seven were in favor of Esperanto. A Committee of Twelve was elected, but only three of these members were able to attend meetings; six others, who were able to attend, were "co-opted." Then matters happened behind the scenes, and eventually the Committee (three elected and six co-opted members) "decided to accept in principle Esperanto" but with "certain modifications, on the lines indicated by the conclusions of the report of the Secretaries and by the project 'Ido,' if possible in agreement with the Esperanto Language Committee." The project "Ido" was the work of the Marquess Louis de Beaufront, a leading French Esperantist, whom Dr. Zamenhof had appointed as his personal representative to the Delegation. A storm broke loose. The Honorary President of the Delegation, Professor Foerster (Germany), one of the Vice Chairmen, Professor Baudouin de Courtenay (Russia), and many others resigned. Most of the societies and scholars who had given their names to the Delegation refused to support the new language which was more "natural-looking" than "unreformed" Esperanto but was much more difficult to learn and had a number of other disadvantages. A report of the Paris Chamber of Commerce, printed as an appendix to the League of Nations Report on "Esperanto as an International Auxiliary Language," said of Ido: "This so-called perfection was only a further complication, which has delayed the development of Esperanto by causing confusion in the public mind." Ido lived until about 1930 when the movement began to disintegrate rapidly.

Of other language projects, the most important have been: "Esperantido" and "Esperanto II," by Professor René de Saussure, Switzerland; "Latino sine Flexione" ("Latin Without Flections"), by Professor Giuseppe Peano, Italy; "Occidental," by Edgar de Wahl, Estonia; "Novial," by Professor Otto Jespersen, Denmark; "Interglossa," by Professor Lancelot Hogben, England. None of these has penetrated into practical use. There have also been repeated efforts to set up new International Committees to "study" the question, but the experiences of the "Delegation" should be a warning. The International Auxiliary Language Association in the United States, Inc. (IALA), which started out with the statement that it had "no intention of developing or promoting any new language" and that its function was merely to "serve as a neutral clearing house for study and information," eventually also joined the ranks of the project makers and produced Interlingua, a system designed for passive rather than active use. At times it received intensive promotion. The 1922 League of Nations Report commented on such efforts: "A study of the history of the proposed reforms such as Ido and Esperantido, which are in many points contradictory, leads to a fear that if a new committee of theorists met today, such as the committee which proposed Ido in 1907, it would propose further modifications which in their turn would be criticized at the end of a few years, and so on indefinitely. It is in the interest of the world to have one auxiliary language, not two or three, and, from a practical point of view, there is less risk in taking one of which some experience has been gained and which has already attained some tradition and a guarantee of lasting unity."

THE GENESIS OF ESPERANTO

THE American Philosophical Society, of Independence Square, Philadelphia, became interested in the Interlanguage problem when Volapük was at the height of its fame. On October 21, 1887, this Society (which was founded by Benjamin Franklin, and of which Thomas Jefferson was President for eighteen years) appointed a Committee to Examine into the Scientific Value of Volapük. This Committee, later renamed Committee on International Language, consisted of Henry Phillips, D. G. Brinton, and Monroe B. Snyder. On November 18, 1887, it reported that it did not consider Volapük a satisfactory solution of the problem. It expressed, however, its strong belief in the desirability of a constructed Interlanguage: "The English language is a jargon of marked type and illustrates what was stated by W. von Humboldt early in this century, that from such crossings and mingling of tongues are developed the most sinewy and picturesque examples of human language. This consideration shows that in adopting or framing a universal language we need not hesitate to mould it from quite diverse linguistic sources" (**Proceedings of the American Philosophical Society,** Vol. XXV, p. 3). The Committee then outlined the conditions which, in its opinion, a constructed auxiliary language ought to fulfill: It should be based on "elements from the Aryan languages, English, French, German, Spanish, Italian, and Russian." The spelling should be phonetic, and each letter should always represent the same sound, easily pronounceable for all peoples. The vowels should be restricted to the basic five—a, e, i, o, u. The grammar should be simple and "consonant with the types of grammar of the Aryan languages."

After these outlines had been presented to the Society, the Committee received from Warsaw a book in French by **Doktoro Esperanto,** presenting a language corresponding almost exactly to the conditions outlined in the report. The Committee expressed its great satisfaction with the **Lingvo Internacia** ("International Language") proposed by Dr. Ludwik Lazar Zamenhof (whose pen name was Dr. Esperanto) and stated: "The plan of Dr. Zamenhof is especially to be recommended in this respect (the formation of the vocabulary) and may be offered as an excellent example of sound judgment. It is remarkable and pleasant to see how easy it is to acquire. . . ."

Henry Phillips, Secretary of the American Philosophical Society, translated Dr. Zamenhof's book into English, added an **English-International Vocabulary,** and had the whole published in 1889 by Henry Holt & Co., in New York, under the title, **An Attempt at an International Language, by Dr. Esperanto.** Before investing so much time and effort, however, the American scholar made a practical test which he described in a footnote on page 13: "The Translator wrote a letter in this language to a young friend who had previously never seen or heard of it, enclosing the printed vocabulary. He received an answer in the same tongue, with no other aid. This was a crucial test."

Before Mr. Phillips' book was published, the American Philosophical Society discussed the report and supplementary reports of its Committee at several meetings and adopted the following resolution: "Resolved that the President of the American Philosophical Society be requested to address a letter to the learned bodies with which this Society is in official relations and to such other societies and individuals as he may deem proper, asking their cooperation in perfecting a language for learned and commercial purposes, based on the Aryan vocabulary and grammar in their simplest forms, and to that end proposing an International Congress, the first meeting of which shall be held in London or Paris." In January, 1889, "Mr. Horatio Hale was requested to prepare a historical digest of schemes for a universal language, to be printed and distributed by the Society in advance of the meeting of the Congress it proposes to convene."

Unfortunately the Congress did not materialize. One of the reasons was that Mr. Phillips fell ill. His death, in 1895, deprived the early Esperanto movement of its first pioneer in the Western Hemisphere.

Dr. Zamenhof put a great deal of hope in the Congress to be called by the American Philosophical Society. He also put great confidence in another device: Mr. Phillips' book, like all early publications on Esperanto, had on its last pages eight copies of a form which was to be filled in, signed, and mailed to Warsaw: "I, the undersigned, promise to learn the international language proposed by Dr. Esperanto if it is shown that ten million people have publicly made the same promise." Mass advertising was not yet well developed in those times, and Dr. Zamenhof's meager means were entirely inadequate to secure ten million signatures. In reality, the Interlanguage made tremendous progress not because of people promising to learn it but because of people actually learning and using it.

Ludwik Lazar Zamenhof was born at Bialystok, Poland (then Russia), on December 15, 1859. His father, Dr. Mark Zamenhof, was a

Professor of Languages and obtained some fame as author of a comparative book of proverbs in Russian, Polish, French, and German (later extended to include Latin, Hebrew, and Esperanto). The family was Jewish, strongly oriented toward "assimilation." The language ordinarily spoken in the home was Russian, but Polish and Yiddish were also heard frequently, particularly when there were visitors. Young Ludwik learned Latin, Greek, German, French, English, and Hebrew in school. In his early youth he was deeply impressed by the tensions between the four language groups inhabiting Bialystok (Poles, Russians, Germans, Jews) and dreamed of a common language which would aid unification. For a while, he thought that a revival of Latin or Greek, or a philosophical a priori language, might be the solution. He got on an entirely different track, however, when in the fifth class of secondary school he started to learn English. "I was struck by the simplicity of its grammar," Dr. Zamenhof later told a friend. "I realized then that complicated forms of grammar are not essential. . . . So I began to simplify, discarding unnecessary forms. I saw the grammar gradually melt away under my hands until it occupied only a few pages. . . ." But the vocabulary continued to bother young Zamenhof. One day, however, he noticed the identity of endings in such Russian words as **shveytsarskaja** (janitor's room) and **konditorskaja** (confectionery). He noticed that in many languages words are derived from others by the use of prefixes and suffixes. This gave him the idea that an even more extensive and absolutely regularized use of such prefixes and suffixes in a constructed Interlanguage would make it possible to obtain great richness and clarity of expression with a vocabulary many times smaller than that of any national tongue.

By 1878, when he was 19 years old, he thought that his language was ready. He told his classmates in school about it. They became very enthusiastic, and the birth of the new language was celebrated by a banquet. But matters did not get much further, and Zamenhof soon noticed that his project needed a great deal of polishing. He began to translate from different languages into his "new," constructed Interlanguage, and made changes whenever he met with difficulties. He also began to write directly in the "international" tongue, and to develop a simple, easy, and elegant style. He tested the language thoroughly for nine years and published it only in 1887. The "First Book" appeared in Russian on August 3. Editions in Polish, French, German, English, Hebrew, Bulgarian, and Swedish followed in rapid succession.

In the meantime, L. L. Zamenhof had completed medical studies at the Universities of Moscow, Vienna, and Warsaw, and had become an oculist. The necessity of working for a living interfered considerably with his activities for the **Lingvo Internacia,** which soon was called, after the pseudonym under which he published it, "the Esperanto language," or simply "Esperanto." A number of enthusiastic followers in different lands started to correspond with Dr. Zamenhof in the language, and he began to accept "subscriptions" for a monthly book list, at thirty kopecks (fifteen American cents) a year.

In 1889 the World Language Club of Nuremberg, Germany, abandoned Volapük and rallied to Esperanto. In cooperation with Dr. Zamenhof, it began publication of a monthly magazine, **La Esperantisto.** It lasted until 1895 when the Russian censorship forbade its entry into the Czarist Empire because it printed an article by Count Leo Tolstoy, who had become an enthusiastic promoter of Esperanto. The magazine was forced to discontinue publication because almost two-thirds of its paying subscribers lived in Russia. In the same year, however, the Esperanto Club of Upsala, Sweden, started publication of a new magazine, **Lingvo Internacia.** Its editor, Valdemar Langlet, was the first to make an extensive trip through a number of countries (Finland, Russia, Turkey, Rumania, Austria-Hungary, Germany), visiting Esperantists everywhere and demonstrating how easy international conversations become by means of the neutral Interlanguage.

Esperanto Clubs meanwhile were organized in different cities, beginning with St. Petersburg, Upsala, Moscow, Sofia, Munich, Malaga, Freiburg, Soissons, Warsaw, Helsinki. Books on and in Esperanto were published. Progress was hastened considerably when in France a magazine for the promotion of the language, **L'Espérantiste,** was started in 1898 and a number of famous French university professors, members of the Academy of Sciences, and renowned writers joined the movement. Men like General Sébert, Professor C. Bourlet, Professor Th. Cart, Professor Grosjean-Maupin, President Boirac of Dijon University, etc., soon became the outstanding leaders in the movement. The first Universal Esperanto Congress was held at Boulogne-sur-Mer, France, in 1905. The knowledge and practical use of the Interlanguage rapidly spread around the world, and Esperanto journals were sprouting like mushrooms.

In the English-speaking countries, the first pioneers were Mr. Henry Phillips and Mr. Richard Geoghegan, an Irishman who became acquainted with Esperanto when he studied languages at Oxford University. His English translation of Zamenhof's first book was published in Warsaw in the same year when Mr. Phillips' book appeared in New York. Mr. Geoghegan worked a great deal for Esperanto in England and in the United States, where he was for a while a British Consul. He died at Fairbanks, Alaska, in October, 1943, 77 years old and still working hard for Esperanto.

In England, the **Review of Reviews** gave considerable publicity to Esperanto, and its founder and editor, William T. Stead, became one of the founders of the London Esperanto Club. At present Great Britain has one of the best organized Esperanto movements in the world.

In the United States, there was little organized Esperanto activity after Mr. Phillips' death. At about 1906 the **North American Review** and the **Christian Endeavor World** began to advocate the study and use of Esperanto in a systematic way, and several daily newspapers published Esperanto lessons by Professor Grillon of Philadelphia. In October, 1906, the journal **Amerika Esperantisto** was started at Oklahoma City, in 1907 the **American Esperanto Journal** at Boston. The Esperanto Association of North America (EANA) held its first Annual Congress at Chautauqua, New York, in 1908. Annual American Esperanto Congresses have been held regularly since then, with the only interruption in 1943-45, because of war conditions. Two Universal Congresses of Esperanto have been held in the United States: the sixth in Washington, D. C., in 1910, and the eleventh in San Francisco, in 1915.

The first Esperanto magazine in the Western Hemisphere, edited in Esperanto, French, and English, was **L'Espérantiste Canadien**, founded by Father F. X. Solis, of the Seminary of St. Hyacinthe, Quebec, in 1901. It became **La Lumo** in 1902 and discontinued publication in 1904. In recent times, Canadian Esperantists have joined the ranks of the Esperanto Association of North America which has held five of its Congresses in Canada: Montreal 1919, Toronto 1922, 1934, and 1948, and Neuville, Quebec, 1958.

THE STRUCTURE AND EVOLUTION OF ESPERANTO

ESPERANTO is a **constructed or extracted**, not an **artificial** language. It is based on the elements of the most important European tongues, reduced to a minimum by strict regularization and an ingenious system of prefixes and suffixes, which are also taken from natural languages. There are, of course, some artificial elements in Esperanto, for instance the verb endings (**helpas**—"helps", **helpis**—"helped", **helpos**—"will help", **helpus**—"would help"), and some semi-artificial elements, for instance the regularized table of correlatives. But there are also artificial and semi-artificial words and "code words" in English and every other language, e. g., "Wacs," "Waves," "fob," AM, PM, SOS, AAA, AFL-CIO, etc.

Phonetic spelling is one of the most important features of Esperanto. Every letter of the alphabet corresponds to one—and only one—sound, and vice versa. This requires the use of accented letters of which there are six in Esperanto: ĉ, ĝ, ĥ, ĵ, ŝ, ŭ. There has been some criticism of the Esperanto "supersigns." The simple fact is that the unaccented Latin alphabet is inadequate for the representation of the sounds of any language. English, which, of course, cannot be spelled phonetically, is one of the very few languages which has no accented or additional letters. Spanish has 6, French 11, German 4, Polish 9, Czech 14, Hungarian 9, Turkish 9. It should be noted that the Latin alphabet for the Turkish language was introduced by Kemal Atatürk as late as 1928 and that it was found impossible to do without accented letters.

The fact that Esperanto is an agglutinative language, i. e., that it consists of root-words which form compounds without undergoing any changes, makes it easy to learn and also particularly attractive for those whose mother tongues are non-European or non-Aryan. It also makes it possible for anyone to understand anything written in Esperanto without having studied it before, if a vocabulary or one of the small Esperanto "Keys" (which exist in 39 languages) is enclosed. In his "First Book," Dr. Zamenhof illustrated this by the following sentence: "I do not know where I left my stick; did you not see it?" Supposing that a German wanted to write this to an English-speaking person, he would translate it from German into Esperanto as follows, dividing the words into their elements by hyphens: **"Mi ne sci-as, kie mi las-is mi-a-n baston-o-n; ĉu vi ĝi-n ne vid-is?"** The English-speaking addressee turns to his Esperanto "Key" and reads as follows:

mi	= I	I
ne	= no, not	not
sci-	= know . . . . } know
-as	= ending of present tense of verb . . . .
kie	= where	where
mi	= I	I
las-	= leave . . . . } left
-is	= ending of past tense of verb . . . . .
mi-	= I . . . .
-a-	= ending of an adjective (nom. case) . . } my
-n	= ending of the objective case . . . . .

[27

baston-	= stick	
-o-	= ending of noun (nom. case)	} stick
-n	= ending of the objective case	
ĉu	= whether; asks a question	whether
vi	= you	you
ĝi-	= it (nom. case)	} it
-n	= ending of the objective case	
ne	= no, not	not
vid-	= see	} saw (did see)
-is	= ending of past tense of verb	

The above, translated into literal English, is: "I not know where I left my stick; whether you it not saw?" This is perfectly comprehensible. Someone may say: "But if the German had written this sentence in his own language and I had found a German dictionary, I could just as easily have made out his meaning." Now the following is the German for this sentence: "Ich weiss nicht, wo ich meinen Stock gelassen habe; haben Sie ihn nicht gesehen?" On referring to the German dictionary, he would find: ICH=I, WEISS=white, NICHT=not, WO=where, ICH=I, MEINEN=to think, STOCK=stick, GELASSEN=composed, calm, HABE=property, goods, HABEN=to have, SIE=she, her, it, they, them, you, IHN=(not in the dictionary), NICHT=not, GESEHEN=(not in the dictionary). Therefore the sentence would read: I white not where I to think stick composed property; to have she (blank) not (blank)." It would be rather difficult, Dr. Zamenhof comments, to gather the meaning of this.

The Esperanto grammar, consisting of sixteen rules without exceptions, is so simple that it can be mastered within a few hours, and also the system of prefixes and suffixes is easy to understand. It obviously requires some practice to apply the rules of grammar and word derivation correctly and fluently, but the effort needed is incomparably less than that of learning a national tongue.

The Esperanto vocabulary consists to a very large extent of words which are internationally known. An English-speaking person is likely to recognize between 70 and 75 per cent of the Esperanto words, once he is familiar with the phonetic spelling of the Interlanguage and with the rules of grammar and word derivation.

Some critics consider an Esperanto text from the point of view of immediate comprehensibility for polyglots who have not studied the Esperanto grammar and the rules for the formation of words. Such immediate comprehensibility is not claimed by Esperanto. Facility of reading, writing, and speaking not only for polyglots, but for everybody, after a study of the grammar, prefixes, and suffixes, is the criterion.

"Natural appearance" has been necessarily sacrificed in Esperanto when it conflicted with phonetic spelling and facility of learning. Some critics have, for instance, expressed regret about the fact that the "ph" and "th" in Greek words have been replaced by "f" and "t." They object to such stems as **fotograf**. They ignore, however, that the overwhelming majority of languages, outside of English and French, have the phonetic forms. "Photography," for instance, is **fotografia** in Italian, Spanish, and Portuguese, **fotografiet** in Swedish, Danish, and Norwegian, **fotografija** in Russian, Serbo-Croatian, and Bulgarian, as well as in Lettish, Lithuanian, and Albanian, **fotografja** in Polish, **fotografie** in Czech. In German and Dutch both forms ("ph" and "f") are used, and modern usage tends toward generalization of "f." One writer found the Esperanto words **kafo** ("coffee") and **nacio** ("nation") "mutilated." A comparison with a majority of word forms in other languages reveals, however, that these are widely-known forms.

Words which do not exist internationally were selected by Dr. Zamenhof mainly from the Romance languages, to a lesser extent from the Germanic languages, and in a very few cases from the Slavic languages, and from classical Latin and Greek. Purely Slavic words which have no similar forms in other languages can be counted on the fingers: eĉ, ĉu, po, krom, nepre, prava, klopodi, svati, vosto, kolbaso, bulko, pilko, ŝelko, kaĉo, barĉo, kartavi. Greek words (in addition to "international" words in philosophical, medical, and technical terminology) are **kaj** and **pri**, classical Latin are **sed, tamen, post, hodiaŭ, kvankam**. Many German words which Dr. Zamenhof chose are widely understood in Slavic and other countries. **Kelnero** (waiter), for instance, is a German word which has penetrated into one Romance language (Rumanian), two Germanic languages (Dutch and Norwegian), at least three Slavic languages (Polish, Serbo-Croatian, Bulgarian) as well as Lithuanian and Estonian. Another Esperanto word of German origin, **farbo** (paint) exists in Polish, Czech, Serbo-Croatian, Dutch, Swedish, Danish and Estonian. These examples may suffice to show that even some of the words which may not seem to us particularly suitable have a great degree of internationality.

No national language is either entirely "finished" or "perfect." Nor is Esperanto. Its vocabulary and style are being continuously developed in practical use. The **Fundamento de Esperanto**, containing the sixteen rules of grammar and the basic vocabulary, is considered by Esperantists as the basis of the language and the living guarantee of its unity and continuity.

The Esperanto Academy **(Akademio de Esperanto)** and its predecessor, the **Esperantista Lingva Komitato,** have from time to time recognized new words for which a need was felt and which had succeeded in penetrating into considerable use. The Seventh Official Supplement to the **Universala Vortaro** was published by the **Akademio** in December 1958. About 150 technical dictionaries (for medicine, chemistry, biology, engineering, aviation, astronomy, music, philosophy, theology, etc.) have been worked out.

Modern life continuously brings new words into everyday use, most of them formed artificially from Greek and Latin roots. They are, of course, simply taken over into Esperanto. On the other hand, certain words and usages in Esperanto are becoming obsolete. The letter **h**, for instance, is being increasingly replaced by **k**. Words such as **svati** ("to make a match," "to find a wife for someone") are hardly used any more. In Zamenhof's time, it was a very important word in Eastern and Central Europe. In the meantime, the "boy meets girl" problem has everywhere passed out of the hands of mothers, uncles, and aunts. The time may come when the Esperanto Academy will officially declare **svati** and several other words as "obsolete." Evolution, without loss of unity and continuity, makes Esperanto a living language. Long practical use has demonstrated the genius of Zamenhof. In almost every case there is a relevant reason for the choice he made, even if some words and word forms may look a bit strange to people seeing them for the first time. The grammatical structure and basic vocabulary of Esperanto have been thoroughly tested in more than seventy years of practical use and are found to be sound and adequate. The vocabulary is being constantly developed in accordance with modern needs, and minor changes are possible within the framework of the **Fundamento.** There is no need for anyone to try to do Dr. Zamenhof's work all over again.

THE LIVING FACT OF ESPERANTO

ESPERANTO makes its claims not as a mere project which may, at some later time, solve the language problem in international relations, but as a going concern and a living fact which is at this very moment rendering significant services to men and women in every field of human endeavor. The League of Nations Report on Esperanto stated that, at the time of its publication (1922), about 4,000,000 Esperanto textbooks had been sold and that about 700,000 adults had learned the language in evening classes, and 100,000 children at school. Taking into consideration further progress as well as the fact that a majority of Esperanto students learn the language by self-study, an objective observer will conclude that several million persons have learned the Interlanguage. Perhaps one million persons use Esperanto occasionally while several hundred thousand use it with some degree of regularity. Only a minority of these, about 80,000, are members of Esperanto organizations.

Important international organizations which have published descriptive booklets, folders, or other informative materials in Esperanto include the United Nations (UN), the United Nations Educational, Scientific, and Cultural Organization (UNESCO), the International Labor Organization (ILO), the World Health Organization (WHO), the World Meteorological Organization (WMO), the Intergovernmental Committee on European Migration (ICEM), and the International Association for Social Security. UNESCO has issued illustrated posters with Esperanto text, lists Esperanto translations in its **Index Translationum,** and has paid considerable attention to the language in its publications on technical translating, scientific abstracting, and interlingual scientific and technical dictionaries.

At United Nations Headquarters in New York an Esperanto Club for members of the Secretariat was founded on September 10, 1958, following two Esperanto classes attended by staff members from 13 countries. The first President of the Club was a Belgian.

The use of Esperanto in radio and television has been steadily increasing. Early in 1959 regularly scheduled Esperanto shortwave broadcasts originated in Austria, Brazil, Bulgaria, Guatemala, Italy, Morocco, Switzerland, and Venezuela. They numbered 96 a month. Regularly scheduled medium-wave radio broadcasts originated in Austria, Brazil, France, Guatemala, the Netherlands, Spain, Venezuela, and Yugoslavia. Occasional programs and interviews in and about Esperanto were numerous in countries all over the world, including the United States and Canada, on both radio and television.

In the history of radio, Esperanto has played an important rôle. On May 5, 1924, for instance, a broadcast in Esperanto from station WOR, Newark, N. J., by Mr. J. D. Sayers, President of the New York Esperanto Society, was received in Tokyo by Mr. Hiroshi Ando, an engineer of the Imperial Laboratories. This reception over 9,000 miles constituted a record at that time.

At the request of the League of Nations the International Telegraphic Union in 1926 recognized Esperanto as a "clear language" in international communications and as such not subject to expensive code rates.

The Esperanto literature consists at present of approximately 8,450 books, including the Bible, many classics, numerous scientific books, as well as modern fiction (Erich Maria Remarque, Upton Sinclair, Edna Ferber, Axel Munthe, Knut Hamsun, Selma Lagerlöf, Sholem Asch, G. K. Chesterton, Agatha Christie, H. G. Wells, etc.) and books on geography, history, politics, economics, biography, religion, and philosophy. The practice of permitting scientific articles and reports in Esperanto as well as in other languages has been spreading in scholarly, scientific, and technological periodicals. More than sixty scholarly journals publish summaries in Esperanto. Most of them appear in countries whose national languages are not widely studied abroad, e.g. Japan, Brazil, the Netherlands, Denmark, Sweden, Norway, Finland, and Yugoslavia. The Esperanto press consists of about 135 periodicals published in more than 30 countries.

While Japan ranks first in the quantity and variety of scientific publications in Esperanto, especially in medical science, meteorology, mathematics, and engineering, Brazil holds first place when it comes to government support. The Brazilian Government Institute of Geography and Statistics accepted Esperanto officially as its auxiliary language on July 18, 1938. It has used Esperanto in many of its publications, including the Statistical Year Book of Brazil and the Brazilian Geographical Review. In 1939 the National Council of Statistics made the study of Esperanto compulsory for the professional staff of statistical institutes. In 1941 one of the authors of this book was invited to come to Brazil and teach Esperanto to the statisticians. Fifty-five staff members, 23 of them employees of the Statistical Services of the various Brazilian States, the others Federal employees in Rio de Janeiro, were enrolled in Esperanto classes that year. Several Brazilian States have, in addition, passed laws or decrees on the use of Esperanto. The Statistical Department of the State of Santa Catarina, for instance, decided in 1945 to add summaries in French, English, and Esperanto to all its publications. In 1946 it decided that "all correspondence with foreign countries will be in Esperanto, with the exception of communications addressed to the overseas diplomatic and consular missions of Brazil and those going to countries where Portuguese is spoken."

Esperanto has been used in one form or another at more than 1,150 international congresses and conferences. Every year an estimated 12,000 to 14,000 persons attend international conferences or summer schools at which Esperanto is the only or principal language used. Some of these are organized by Esperanto societies, others are not. In recent years the organizers and sponsors of international conferences and summer schools using Esperanto have included the European Association of Peoples Colleges, the Swedish Institute for Cultural Relations with Foreign Countries, and the Danish International Student Committee.

World travelers who circled the globe, using nothing but Esperanto in all countries visited, include Mr. Donald E. Parrish and Mr. Joseph R. Scherer, both of Los Angeles, California.

Sermons in Esperanto have been preached by clergymen of all faiths, including Catholic and Orthodox bishops and priests, Protestant ministers, and rabbis. Five Popes and many bishops have blessed the Catholic Esperanto movement. The YMCA, the Christian Endeavor movement, and other Christian groups have used Esperanto. Buddhist, Shintoist, Moslem, Theosophist, Baha'i, Spiritualist, and other religious organizations are using the Interlanguage. So are political groups of all tendencies.

The labor movement found in Esperanto a language easy enough to be learned and fully mastered by simple workers as well as labor leaders. Labor union organizations in European, Asian, and Latin American countries and also—though not yet on any considerable scale—in the United States (e.g. the International Ladies' Garment Workers' Union) have organized Esperanto classes.

The International Red Cross Conference of 1921 adopted a resolution urging "all Red Cross organizations to encourage the study of the auxiliary language, Esperanto, and especially in the junior sections, as one of the most powerful means of attaining mutual understanding and cooperation in the sphere of the Red Cross." The motion was presented by Dr. Wang of China and supported in the discussion by delegates from Argentina, Germany, Poland, Yugoslavia, and Switzerland.

Hundreds of Chambers of Commerce, Trade Fairs, Railroad, Steamship, and Air Transport Companies have been using Esperanto in advertising and correspondence. In 1931 the Presidents of 112 French Chambers of Commerce passed a resolution in support of Esperanto. In Great Britain over fifty Chambers of Commerce adopted resolutions favoring the Interlanguage.

In 1921, twenty-one members of the French Academy of Sciences issued a manifesto calling Esperanto "a masterpiece of logic and simplicity" and urging scientists to use it. Shortly afterward sixteen other prominent signatures were added.

In 1958 a Committee of European Mayors, including the Mayors of Vienna, Cologne, Mainz, Dijon, The Hague, Bologna, Turin, Verona, Lund, Uppsala, and Nottingham, polled the Mayors of 16 European countries outside the iron curtain about their views on the language problem and Esperanto. Asked whether in their opinion Esperanto might provide the solution of the language problem, 545 answered "yes," 95 "no," and 29 expressed no opinion. An even larger number of Mayors, 586 came out in favor of a thorough examination of the potential advantages of Esperanto by the Council of Europe.

Rotary Clubs also use Esperanto. In 1933, for instance, "the Paris Rotary Club cooperated with other European Rotary Clubs in maintaining an international summer camp for children in Switzerland. Children from nearly every nation in Europe were in attendance at this camp, and it was found necessary to adopt Esperanto as a means of communication. In about three weeks, the report says, the children were able to jabber Esperanto and get along with one another famously" (Report at the Inter-

[33

national Service Committee of Rotary International, 1933). There is a Rotary Esperanto Fellowship (Rotaria Esperanto-Amikaro), whose aims are "to aid in advancing the sixth object of Rotary International by means of the international auxiliary language Esperanto. To further and to fulfill the cause of REA, Rotary Clubs should have at least one member who can use Esperanto both in interpreting and correspondence."

There have been numerous international youth camps organized by the Esperanto Youth Organization and the Scout Esperanto League. Esperanto is also used, together with other languages, at the World Jamborees of the Boy Scouts. At one held at Gödölö, near Budapest, Hungary, in 1933, Esperanto interpreters were posted at the bank, the ticket office, the post office, and other places. Esperanto guides were available. Among some delegations, for instance those from France, Czechoslovakia, Norway, Spain, Portugal, Japan, and Trinidad, the proportion of Esperanto-speaking members was 10 per cent or more. On various occasions large groups of scouts gathered around roaring campfires for Esperanto community singing.

An increasing number of educators and linguists have advocated the use of Esperanto as a "general language", i.e., as a basis for the study of other tongues.

In the United States and Canada, the Esperanto movement has been much weaker than in European countries, the Far East, and Brazil, because the need for an Interlanguage was not felt with the same acuteness. Now that the United States is playing a rôle of ever increasing importance in world affairs and is host to the United Nations, it is both desirable and necessary that this should change.

Esperanto is being used by hundreds of thousands of people all over the world in a great variety of fields. It is already of tremendous practical use and well worth any investment of time, effort, and money. Those learning it acquire a key to the world, an instrument of great practical value, a treasure of cultural enrichment, and make at the same time a modest, but very real contribution to the cause of international understanding and world peace.

PRACTICAL TEXTBOOK
OF ESPERANTO

LESSON I (UNUA LECIONO)
ALPHABET AND PRONUNCIATION

Every letter of the Esperanto alphabet has one sound only, always the same. There are no silent letters. Spelling and pronunciation are matters of extreme simplicity in Esperanto. This phonetic excellence is achieved by the use of a few accented letters (which closely approximate the basic symbols of the International Phonetic Alphabet). Every word is pronounced as it is spelled. To name the letters simply add -o to the consonants: a, bo, co, etc.

The Esperanto alphabet consists of twenty-eight letters: a, b, c, ĉ, d, e, f, g, ĝ, h, ĥ, i, j, ĵ, k, l, m, n, o, p, r, s, ŝ, t, u, ŭ, v, z. The letter ĥ is used infrequently, with the value of Scottish ch as in loch. It is being generally replaced by the symbol and sound of k. The letter ĥ is not used in this textbook. There is no q, w, x, or y in Esperanto.

VOWELS

Esperanto vowels are pronounced approximately as follows:

a   is pronounced like a in father   **tablo** (table)
e   is pronounced like e in obey (without the y sound)   **teo** (tea)
i   is pronounced like i in machine   **vino** (wine)
o   is pronounced like o in show (without the w sound)   **koro** (heart)
u   is pronounced like u in rule   **gusto** (taste)

Note that the Esperanto vowels are not double sounds (diphthongs) as in English. The Esperanto e and o are heard in the Italian re, do, as sung by a good singer on a prolonged note. In English, pure e and o hardly exist. The good Esperanto speaker learns to pronounce the vowels as pure vowel sounds without the English diphthongal glide sounds.

CONSONANTS

Esperanto consonants are pronounced as in English, except:

c   is not sounded like s or k, but like ts in wits: **paco** (peace)
ĉ   is pronounced like ch in church: **ĉambro** (room)
g   is always like g in gift: **glaso** (glass)
ĝ   is pronounced like g in gem: **ĝermo** (germ)
j   has the international phonetic sound of y in yes: **jaro** (year)
ĵ   is pronounced like s in leisure: **ĵurnalo** (journal)

r is rolled more than in English, being always clearly pronounced.

s is always like **s** in sun: **soldato** (soldier)

ŝ is pronounced like **s** in sugar: **ŝultro** (shoulder)

ŭ is the consonantal **u**, similar to English **w**, but used only after the vowels **a** (**aŭ**) and **e** (**eŭ**) to form diphthongs which are pronounced as single glide sounds with one impulse of the voice

aŭ is pronounced like au in sauerkraut: **aŭtomobilo** (automobile)

eŭ has no equivalent in English—it is the Esperanto **e** plus the Esperanto **u** pronounced rapidly together with one impulse of the voice, like **ayw** in wayward: **leŭtenanto** (lieutenant)

ACCENTUATION OR STRESS

The **accent** or **stress** in Esperanto words is always on the next-to-the-last syllable: **sinjoro** (sin-JOR-o), **sinjorino** (sin-jor-IN-o), **universo** (u-ni-VERS-o), **historio** (his-to-RI-o). Note that each vowel constitutes a syllable. Always pronounce each syllable clearly and separately in Esperanto. As a general rule in Esperanto pronunciation, remember that there is greater use of lips and facial muscles than in English. Sounds are placed forward in the mouth, not back in the throat. All sounds must be clearly spoken. Esperanto is the **interlanguage** for **all peoples,** so one of its first principles must be clarity.

WORDS FOR PRONUNCIATION PRACTICE

To be pronounced aloud, and correctly accented. Be careful with the accent in words ending with **-io,** and remember that each vowel is a separate syllable. You can probably guess the meanings of most of these words without a dictionary.

lampo	ŝipo	ĝardeno	kanario
suno	ĉokolado	jubileo	karaktero
letero	centro	omnibuso	Ameriko
idealo	individuo	jargono	Aŭstralio
telefono	familio	entuziasmo	Eŭropo

LESSON II (DUA LECIONO)

YOU MEET AN ESPERANTIST

Here are some expressions needed when you meet Esperantists, on the street, in the club, in your class. Practice the words and phrases out loud—the class responding in unison. Go through them several times until you know the words and greetings by heart. In some instances, aids to literal understanding will follow the English translations. You are given a fairly large number of words in this beginning lesson, so that you can carry on a simple conversation in Esperanto from the very start. Wear a green star emblem—symbol of Esperanto—and begin speaking!

Sinjoro, S-ro (Mister, Mr., sir, gentleman)

Sinjorino, S-ino (Mistress, Mrs., lady, madam)

Fraŭlino, F-ino (Miss)

ĉu (whether—introduces a question)

vi (you—singular and plural)

parolas (speaks, is speaking)

Ĉu vi parolas Esperante? (Do you speak Esperanto?)

jes (yes)

mi (I)

iomete (a little)

Jes, mi parolas iomete. (Yes, I speak a little.)

Pardonu! (Pardon!)

ne (no, not)

komprenas (understand)

Pardonu, mi ne komprenas. (Pardon, I do not understand.)

tro (too)

rapide (fast, rapidly)

mi petas (please—I beg)

Ne tro rapide, mi petas. (Not too fast, please.)

Saluton! (Hello!, How do you do?, Greetings!)

kiel (how)

fartas (fare)

Kiel vi fartas? (How are you?—How do you fare?)

sano (health)

Kiel vi sanas? (How are you?—How is your health?)

Bone! (Good!, Fine!, OK)

Dankon!, Mi dankas! (Thanks!, I thank you!)

mateno (morning)

Bonan matenon! (Good morning!)

tago (day)

Bonan tagon! (Good day!)

vespero (evening)

Bonan vesperon! (Good evening!)

ĝis (until)

revido (re-seeing)

Ĝis revido! (Until we meet again!—until re-seeing)

Adiaŭ! (Goodbye!)

vidas (see, is seeing)

ke (that—conjunction)

sur (on)

la (the)

jako (jacket)

estas (is, am, are)

verda (green)

stelo (star)

Mi vidas, ke sur la jako estas verda stelo. (I see that on your jacket is a green star.)

klubo (club)

kunvenas (meets, is meeting)

hodiaŭ (today)

La klubo kunvenas hodiaŭ vespere. (The club meets this evening.)

nun (now)

iras (go, is going)

al (to)

Mi nun iras al la klubo. (I am now going to the club.)

kiu (who)

kio (what—what thing)

de (from, of)

en (in)

Usono (United States of North America)

Mi estas de Usono. (I am from the United States.)

prezidanto (president)

delegito (delegate)

profesoro (professor)

instruas (teaches, is teaching)

instruisto (teacher)

universitato (university)

[39

La profesoro instruas en la universitato. (The professor teaches in the university.)
muziko (music)
muzikisto (musician)
li (he)
ŝi (she)
ni (we)
S-ro Melo, la muzikisto, estas Esperanto-delegito. (Mr. Melo, the musician, is an Esperanto delegate.)

NOTES ON GRAMMAR

1. Notice the words **sinjoro, universitato, delegito, jako**—they are all names of things or persons (nouns). All nouns in Esperanto end with the letter **o**.

2. Perhaps you noticed also that **sinjoro** (Mr.) and **sinjorino** (Mrs.) are alike except for the ending syllable (suffix) -in- for the Mrs. The suffix -in- forms the feminine counterpart of words in Esperanto. So, if **fraŭlino** means Miss, then **fraŭlo** would be the word for bachelor! If **frato** is brother, sister would be . . . . ? If **koko** is a rooster, a hen would be . .? If **patro** is father, then mother in Esperanto is . . . . ?

3. There is no **a** or **an** (indefinite article) in Esperanto: **stelo** means star or a star, and **artisto** means artist or an artist. As for **the** (definite article), it is always **la** in Esperanto: **la profesoro, la fraŭlino, la stelo.**

4. The little word **ĉu** introduces a question, when no other question word such as **kio** (what) or **kiu** (who) is used. To form a question, all you do is to begin the regular statement with **ĉu**: **Vi parolas Esperante,** (You speak Esperanto). **Ĉu vi parolas Esperante?,** (Do you speak Esperanto?) Try these sentences: **Are you a delegate? Are you the president? Do you teach in the club?** But note that **Who is the president?** is **Kiu estas la prezidanto?**

5. The words **estas, iras, komprenas, vidas** all express action or condition (verbs). In Esperanto we notice that these words all have the ending -as when we speak of what is happening in the present time (present tense). All verbs in the present tense in Esperanto have the ending -as. This form is the same for all persons and numbers: **Mi estas** (I am). **Vi estas** (You are). **Li estas** (He is). **Ŝi estas** (She is). **Ni estas** (We are). **Ĝi estas** (It is). **Ili estas** (They are).

Special Note: The English verb forms **is going, am going, are going** are all rendered in Esperanto by just the simple present tense of the verb **iras.** Never use **estas** with another -as verb. Do not say **mi estas iras**, but simply **mi iras** (I am going).

6. **No** in Esperanto is **ne**. **Ne** is also placed before the verb to form a negative statement: **Mi ne parolas rapide** (I do not speak rapidly). **Mi ne komprenas** (I do not understand).

7. In Esperanto, as in English, the suffix **-ist-** means a person professionally or regularly connected with what is expressed by the root-word: **muziko** (music), **muzikisto** (musician); **instruas** (teach), **instruisto** (teacher); **arto** (art), **artisto** (artist).

CONVERSATION

American Miss in Paris meets Young Man with a Green Star

Fraŭlino: Pardonu, sinjoro, ĉu vi parolas Esperante? Mi vidas, ke sur la jako estas la verda stelo!

Sinjoro: Bonan vesperon, fraŭlino! Jes, mi estas Esperantisto. Vi bone parolas Esperante.

Fraŭlino: Mi parolas iomete. Mi estas de Usono.

Sinjoro: Esperantistino de Usono? Bone! Bone! S-ro Petit estas la Esperanto-delegito en Parizo . . .

Fraŭlino: Pardonu, sinjoro, ne tro rapide, mi petas. Mi ne komprenas.

Sinjoro: Ho, jes . . . Mi parolas tro rapide, ĉu ne? S-ro Petit estas la delegito en Parizo. S-ro Melo estas la prezidanto de la klubo. La klubo kunvenas hodiaŭ vespere. Profesoro Durand parolas. Li estas bona Esperantisto. Li instruas en la Universitato Sorbonne . . .

Fraŭlino: Pardonu . . . mi ne komprenas. Ĉu vi instruas en la Sorbonne?

Sinjoro: Ne . . . ne mi, fraŭlino . . . la Profesoro Durand . . . kiu estas Esperantisto . . . li instruas en la Sorbonne.

Fraŭlino: Pardonu . . . kiu estas vi, sinjoro?

Sinjoro: Ho, mi estas S-ro Bontono. Mi estas muzikisto! Mi vidas, ke vi estas muzikistino, ĉu ne?

Fraŭlino: Jes, mi estas instruistino de muziko.

Sinjoro: Bone, fraŭlino! Mi iras al la kunveno de la Esperanto-klubo. Nun . . . ni iras al la kunveno! Ĉu bone?

Fraŭlino: Jes . . . jes! Mi dankas, sinjoro.

NOW, YOU MAKE THE CONVERSATION

Go back to the words and phrases at the beginning of the lesson. Make sure that you know them well. Then work out the following conversation. Be sure to practice it orally without reference to written work. In a class, assign parts for practicing this conversation. The persons should stand up before the class, and speak as smoothly and naturally as possible. Put some acting into it! The teacher may read out the English instructions. Encourage free conversation without hems and haws!

1. You walk over to a stranger, beg his pardon, and ask if he speaks Esperanto.

2. He says yes, he does a little bit.
3. You say, you speak a little. You ask if he is the delegate in Paris.
4. He says no, he is a teacher at the university.
5. You say you don't understand, not too fast, please.
6. He repeats.
7. You say you are going to an Esperanto meeting.
8. He says he is going to the university. The Esperanto meeting is this evening, isn't it? (ĉu ne?)
9. You say yes, and the president is Mr. Melo.
10. He says, oh yes, thanks you, and says goodbye.
11. You reply, until we meet again in the meeting.

LESSON III (TRIA LECIONO)

COUNTING—MATH IS EASY IN ESPERANTO!

1	unu	31	tridek-unu
2	du	32	tridek-du
3	tri	40	kvardek
4	kvar	50	kvindek
5	kvin	60	sesdek
6	ses	70	sepdek
7	sep	80	okdek
8	ok	90	naŭdek
9	naŭ	100	cent
10	dek	200	ducent
11	dek-unu	300	tricent
12	dek-du	301	tricent-unu
13	dek-tri	330	tricent tridek
20	dudek	335	tricent tridek-kvin
21	dudek-unu	1000	mil
22	dudek-du	million	miliono
23	dudek-tri	billion	biliono
30	tridek	1947	mil naŭcent kvardek-sep

The entire numeral system of Esperanto is built up from the first ten numerals, plus words for hundred, thousand, million, etc. Try forming the following numbers, and pronouncing them: 24, 35, 46, 57, 68, 79, 19, 55, 400, 980, 345, 1887.

Hints on pronunciation: There are no silent letters in Esperanto. Therefore, in the combination kv in kvar, kvin, both letters are clearly sounded—but with one impulse of the voice: **kvar**. Don't put in any extra vowel sounds, such as **ka-var, ka-vin!** Also watch the word **ses**—remember the **e** in **obey!**

MATEMATIKO

7+4=11	(sep plus kvar estas dek-unu)	Now add these: 10
20—5=15	(dudek minus kvin estas dek-kvin)	14
18÷6= 3	(dek-ok per ses estas tri)	38
2×2= 4	(duoble du estas kvar)	80

The suffix **-obl-** is used for multiplication.　　　　La sumo estas ....

Make up other mathematical problems, using the Esperanto numerals. If someone is studying with you—or if you are in class—take turns giving answers to various problems.

LESSON IV (KVARA LECIONO)

HOW TO FIND YOUR WAY

Attention: Among other things, you will learn to find your way with the Esperanto plural in this lesson. There are a number of words ending with **-aj** and **-oj.** The approximate sounds of these endings may be heard when pronouncing the English words **my boy.**

kie (where)
fervojo (railway, railroad)
stacio (station)
Kie estas la fervojo-stacio? (Where is the railroad station?)
rekte (directly)
antaŭ (in front of, before)
Rekte antaŭ vi. (Directly in front of you.)
bona (good)
restoracio (restaurant)
Kie estas bona restoracio, mi petas? (Where is a good restaurant, please?)
estas (there are—impersonal usage)
restoracioj (restaurants)
Estas du restoracioj. (There are two restaurants.)
granda (large, big)

kaj (and)
luksa (luxurious)
Unu estas granda kaj luksa. (One is large and luxurious.)
la alia (the other)
malgranda (small)
sed (but)
pura (clean, pure)
La alia estas malgranda sed pura. (The other is small but clean.)
malsata (hungry)
Ĉu vi estas malsata? (Are you hungry?)
nu! (well!, so!)
soifa (thirsty)
ankaŭ (also)
Nu, jes, kaj mi estas soifa ankaŭ. (Well, yes, and I am thirsty also.)

[43

strato (street)
avenuo (avenue)
kvardek-dua (forty-second)
Tre bone! Estas restoracio en Kvardek-dua Strato. (Very well! There is a restaurant on Forty-second Street.)
hotelo (hotel)
proksime (near)
Ĉu estas hotelo proksime? (Is there a hotel near?)
kia (what kind of)
Kia hotelo ĝi estas? (What kind of a hotel is it?)
moderna (modern)
Ĉu ĝi estas moderna? (Is it modern?)
kun (with)
Kun bonaj litoj? (With good beds?)

mola (soft)
komforta (comfortable)
Kaj kun molaj komfortaj litoj? (And with soft comfortable beds?)
Kompreneble! (Of course!)
ili (they)
Kompreneble! Ili estas tre komfortaj. (Of course! They are very comfortable.)
Bone! Kie estas la hotelo? (Good! Where is the hotel?)
ĉe (at)
angulo (corner)
Ĉe la angulo. (At the corner.)
necesejo (toilet, W. C.)
Kie estas necesejo, mi petas? (Where is a toilet, please?)
Dekstre! (To the right!)

NOTES ON GRAMMAR

1. Words such as **good, soft, comfortable,** which describe something or somebody (adjectives), all end with the letter **a** in Esperanto: **bona, mola, komforta, moderna, luksa.** The adjective may be placed before or after the noun, but general usage is before the noun. The question word **kia,** that asks **what kind of,** also ends in **a: Kia hotelo?** In the number system, the words **first, second, third,** etc., also modify something: **first book, third street.** Therefore these "ordinal" numbers are formed in Esperanto by adding **a** to the simple "cardinal" numbers: **unu** (one), **unua** (first); **tri** (three), **tria** (third); **dek-kvar** (fourteen), **dek-kvara** (fourteenth). Pronoun adjectives, showing possession, are also formed by adding **a** to the simple pronoun: **mia** (my), **via** (your), **lia** (his), **ilia** (their).

2. A word that tells manner, circumstance, time, place or degree, is an **adverb.** In Esperanto, adverbs are either "primary", such as **ankaŭ, nun, tro, jes,** which have no distinctive ending; or "derived" from root-words, such as **bone, rekte, rapide.** Note that all derived adverbs in Esperanto end with **e. Kie** asks the question **where,** so it also carries the sign of the adverb. Now you understand why the **e** ending is used in **mi parolas Esperante.** How do you speak? **Esperante** (in Esperanto). The same with: **Mi parolas angle** (I speak English), **france** (French), **hispane** (Spanish). Adverbs are more widely used in Esperanto than in any other language. Your ability to use adverbs will show excellent Esperanto form!

3. The syllable **mal** attached to the beginning of a word (prefix), gives

44]

a direct opposite meaning to a word: **granda** (large), **malgranda** (small); **komforta** (comfortable), **malkomforta** (uncomfortable); **sata** (satisfied, have enough of), **malsata** (hungry); **dekstre** (to the right), **maldekstre** (to the left). You will also find this prefix **mal** showing up with nouns and verbs. So watch for them!

4. The plural (more than one) in Esperanto is formed by adding **j** to the noun **o** ending: **lito, litoj; sinjoro, sinjoroj**. The pronunciation of **oj** is similar to the **oy** in **boy**. The accent remains on the next-to-the-last syllable: **LIToj, sinJORoj, sinjorINoj**. The adjectives that describe these plural nouns also take the plural ending **j**: **bonaj litoj, modernaj sinjoroj**. The **aj** has the sound of **ai** in **aisle**.

GENERAL NOTE

If you have kept your mind alert, with a sharp eye on the text thus far, you can begin to see the essential character and make-up of Esperanto. The vocabulary consists mainly of root-words: **lit-, klub-, est-, dank-**. To the root-words, endings are added to form various kinds of words or parts of speech. By the use of prefixes and suffixes we can build up a whole series of new words and meanings from a basic root:

bona	good	**instruo**	instruction
bono	the good	**instrua**	instructive
bone	well	**instruas**	teaches
malbona	bad	**instruisto**	teacher
malbone	badly	**instruistino**	woman teacher

The root-words may also be combined together, as in English, to form compound words: **fer-vojo** (iron-way, railroad), **fervojo-stacio** (railroad station), **dank-letero** (letter of thanks).

These characteristics make Esperanto flexible and easy to learn. They tremendously cut down the number of separate words one must learn. Try your hand at making up new words from old ideas. It's good practice, and what's more, fun!

CONVERSATION

Mr. Adams goes into an information office to ask a few questions. He sees a clerk wearing the green star and says:

S-ro Adams: Bonan tagon, sinjoro! Vi parolas Esperante, ĉu ne?

Informisto: Jes, sinjoro. . . .

S-ro A.: Mi petas, ĉu estas bona restoracio proksime?

Inform.: Jes, estas du restoracioj en la strato proksime. La restoracio "Ritz" estas granda kaj luksa. Ĝi estas rekte antaŭ la hotelo "Granda." La alia estas malgranda restoracio, sed bona, pura kaj moderna.

S-ro A.: Tre bone! Kie ĝi estas?

Inform.: Ĉe la angulo de Kvardek-dua Strato kaj Oka Avenuo—iomete maldekstre de la "Ritz."

S-ro A.: Mi dankas . . . ankaŭ, mi petas . . . ĉu la hotelo "Granda" estas bona?

Inform.: Kompreneble! Ĝi estas tre moderna, kaj kun bonaj, molaj, komfortaj litoj.

S-ro A.: Kie ĝi estas?

Inform.: Ĝi estas en la "Avenuo de la Verda Stelo" proksime al la fervojo-stacio.

S-ro A.: Ho, bone . . . Mi iras al la stacio nun. Mi dankas . . . adiaŭ, sinjoro.

Inform.: Pardonu . . . sinjoro . . . ĉu vi estas malsata nun?

S-ro A.: Nu, jes, mi estas malsata . . . kaj tre soifa ankaŭ . . . kaj vi?

Inform.: Mi ankaŭ. Mi iras kun vi al la restoracio.

S-ro A.: Tre bone! Sed . . . mi parolas Esperante tre malbone. . . .

Inform.: Ho, ne, sinjoro . . . vi tre bone parolas. Ĉu estas aliaj Usonaj Esperantistoj kun vi?

S-ro A.: Ne . . . mi parolas Esperante, sed la aliaj parolas angle. Ili iras al kunvenoj, sed ne komprenas. . . Mi iras al Esperantistaj kunvenoj . . . en la universitato . . . al la kluboj . . . kaj mi tre bone komprenas. Mi ne parolas rapide, sed mi bone komprenas. . . .

(So, S-ro Adams and the Informisto both go out together for some lunch.)

SELECT THE BEST PHRASE

Here are several situations, given in English, for which phrases in Esperanto are added. After each situation, read the phrases out loud, and then select the one best suited to the English statement.

I You meet S-ro Adams one bright morning, greet him and ask if he is going to the club:

   1. Bonan vesperon, S-ro Adams, ĉu la klubo estas proksime?
   2. Bonan matenon, S-ino Adams, la klubo kunvenas hodiaŭ, ĉu ne?
   3. Bonan matenon, S-ro Adams, ĉu vi iras al la klubo?

II He answers yes, but that now he is going to a restaurant:

   1. Jes, sed mi nun iras al la stacio.
   2. Jes, sed nun mi iras al la restoracio.
   3. Jes, sed nun mi iras al kunveno en la restoracio.

III You ask him if he is very hungry:
1. Ĉu mi estas tre malsata?
2. Ĉu vi estas tre malsata?
3. Ĉu la sinjorino estas malsata?

IV He says yes, and thirsty too, is there a restaurant near:
1. Jes, kaj soifa ankaŭ . . . ĉu estas restoracio proksime?
2. Jes, kaj soifa . . . ĉu la restoracio estas proksime?
3. Jes, kaj soifa ankaŭ . . . ĉu vi iras al la restoracio?

V You say, yes, there is a good restaurant at the corner of Fortieth Street and Eighth Avenue:
1. Jes, estas bona restoracio ĉe la angulo de Kvara Strato kaj Oka Avenuo.
2. Jes, la restoracio estas bona ĉe la Kvardeka Avenuo kaj Oka Strato.
3. Jes, estas bona restoracio ĉe la angulo de Kvardeka Strato kaj Oka Avenuo.

VI He says that's fine, he is now going to Fortieth Street:
1. Bone! Mi iras al Kvardeka Strato.
2. Bone! Mi nun iras al Kvardek-kvina Strato.
3. Bone! Mi nun iras al Kvardeka Strato.

TRANSLATION
Translate the Following Sentences into Good Esperanto.
Be sure that the adjectives "agree" with the nouns.

The beds are large and soft, but not modern. They are in the big hotel near the railroad station. Railroad stations are dirty. There are good restaurants in the station. Of course, the "Ritz" hotel is luxurious, large and modern. The other hotel is modern also, but small. Are the streets and avenues in the United States clean? I am going to Paris, to the big meeting of the Esperanto clubs.

LESSON V (KVINA LECIONO)

YOU WANT TO BUY SOMETHING

tio (that—that thing)
Kio estas tio? (What is that?)
deziras (desire, want, wish)
Kion vi deziras? (What do you want?)

cigaro (cigar)
cigaredo (cigarette)
Mi deziras cigaredojn kaj cigaron.
  (I want cigarettes and a cigar.)

Jen! (Here is!, Here are!, Look!, Behold!)

Jen ili estas! (Here they are!)

havas (have, has)

alumetoj (matches)

Ĉu vi havas alumetojn? (Do you have matches?)

kiom (how much, how many)

kostas (cost, costs)

Kiom ili kostas? (How much do they cost?)

nur (only)

cendo (cent)

Ili kostas nur dudek-kvin cendojn. (They cost only twenty-five cents.)

multe (much, a lot)

multekosta (expensive)

Ili estas multekostaj! (They are expensive!)

fakte (in fact)

malmultekosta (inexpensive, cheap)

Fakte, ili estas malmultekostaj. (In fact, they are cheap.)

ĉar (because)

objekto (object, thing)

mankas (is lacking, are lacking)

Ĉar multaj objektoj mankas. (Because many things are lacking.)

pli (more—quantity)

Kion pli vi deziras? (What more do you wish?)

ekzemple (for example)

nova (new)

radio-aparato (radio, radio apparatus)

dika (thick, heavy)

mantelo (coat)

horloĝo (clock, timepiece, watch)

eĉ (even)

domo (house)

Ho, mi deziras multon! Ekzemple, mi deziras novan radio-aparaton, bonan dikan mantelon, novan horloĝon, kaj eĉ novan domon! (Oh, I want a lot! For example, I want a new radio, a good heavy coat, a new clock, and even a new house!)

vendas (sell, sells)

Ĉu vi vendas ilin? (Do you sell them?)

bedaŭras (regret, regrets, is sorry)

Ne, mi bedaŭras, sinjoro, mi ne havas ilin. (No, I am sorry, sir, I do not have them.)

simpatias (sympathize)

Nu, mi simpatias kun vi! (Well, I sympathize with you!)

Here are some other things to buy:

biciklo (bicycle)

aŭtomobilo (automobile)

pantalono (trousers)

vestoj (clothes)

foto-aparato (camera)

dento-broso (toothbrush)

Hints on pronunciation: In Esperanto each letter is clearly sounded. In the combinations nk, as in **mankas**, and kz, as in **ekzemple**, pronounce the letters separately: man - - - kas, ek - - - zem - - - ple.

NOTES ON GRAMMAR

1. In the sentence **mi deziras cigaron**, you no doubt noticed the -n on the word **cigaro(n)**. If we analyze this sentence, we find that **mi** is the actor of the sentence (the subject), **deziras** is the verb indicating what the actor does (he wants, he desires), and **cigaron** is the object of his desire (what he wants). In order to distinguish the subject of the sentence from the object, in Esperanto the letter **-n** is added to the end of the

object word. So find the person or thing directly affected by the action, and you have the object of the verb! The use of the ending -n permits the utmost freedom of word-order in Esperanto, because all languages do not say things the way we do in English. It is perfectly good Esperanto to change the words around and say, la cigaron mi deziras, or even la cigaron deziras mi. The meaning is the same, and the simple device of putting -n on the object word makes it crystal clear. Note that the object pronouns also take the -n: min, vin, lin, ŝin, ĝin, nin, ilin—Mi vidas lin, kaj li vidas min. (I see him, and he sees me.) In this respect English does something similar, but uses various endings and even complete changes in the words, instead of the one simple device -n as in Esperanto: I, me; he, him; she, her; we, us; they, them.

2. We saw before where adjectives **agree** with their nouns in the plural (in number), and so they also take the -n to show that they belong to (modify) the object noun or pronoun: bonan radio-aparaton, novajn vestojn, etc. Now you will understand why we said: Bonan vesperon!, It means: (I wish you) a good evening! Bona vespero! would merely mean: (It is) a good evening! Incidentally, this device is very convenient if you don't want to wish someone a "good evening"—just leave off the -n's!

3. Notice the new "question word" Kiom? (How many, how much?) You will notice, too, that all the question words so far have begun with the letters Ki-, and each ending indicates its meaning. You will also find as you go along that there is a corresponding set of "pointing out" words (demonstratives), which will all begin with the letters Ti-. Watch for them!

KIu?	who, which (identity)	TIu	that (person, certain one)
KIo?	what (thing)	TIo	that (thing)
KIa?	what kind of (quality)	TIa	that kind of (quality)
KIe?	where (place)	TIe	there (place)
KIel?	how (manner)	TIel	thus (manner)
KIom?	how many, how much (quantity)	TIom	that many, so much (quantity)

4. Special: Note the ease in forming adjectives, nouns and adverbs from verbs, and vice versa. Any root-word can take one of the Esperanto endings, if the final product makes logical sense! simpatias (sympathizes), simpatia (sympathetic), simpatio (sympathy), simpatie (sympathetically).

CONVERSATION
S-ro Adams Goes Into a Store to Buy Some Smokes
S-ro A.: Bonan tagon, fraŭlino! Ĉu vi havas bonan cigaron? Malbona sinjoro deziras bonan cigaron!

F-ino: Jes, sinjoro, ni havas multajn cigarojn, sed ili kostas multe ankaŭ. Unu cigaro kostas dudek-kvin cendojn.

S-ro A.: Kiom? Dudek-kvin cendojn kostas unu malgranda, malpura, malbona cigaro! Ili estas tro multekostaj! Ĉe la alia angulo de la strato, unu cigaro kostas nur dek-kvin cendojn. Mi iras al ĝi!

F-ino: Pardonu, sinjoro . . . mi petas . . . komprenelbe al vi . . . nu . . . la cigaroj kostas nur dek-kvin cendojn!

S-ro A.: Tre bone . . . mi dankas vin . . . kaj ĉu vi havas alumetojn?

F-ino: Jes, sinjoro . . . kaj al vi ili estas tre malmultekostaj . . . nur du cendojn.

S-ro A.: H-m-m-m . . . tre bone! Ĉu vi vendas aliajn objektojn? . . . Ekzemple . . . Kio estas tio? Kiom ĝi kostas?

F-ino: Tio estas nova, moderna, luksa horloĝo. Ĝi kostas okdek dolarojn!

S-ro A.: Bone, mi deziras ĝin . . . kaj mankas al mi multaj objektoj. . . . Mi deziras novan, luksan aŭtomobilon, kaj grandan, modernan domon!

F-ino: Mi bedaŭras, sed ni ne havas ilin!

S-ro A.: Ha-ha! Kompreneble ne! Bone . . . Mi deziras kvin cigarojn, alumetojn, kaj la horloĝon . . . Jen estas okdek-kvin dolaroj! Vi estas bona vendistino! Adiaŭ!

F-ino: Ho, sinjoro . . . Mi dankas! . . . Dankon! . . . Dankon!

(And S-ro Adams goes out, leaving her the extra $4.23.)

NOW, YOU MAKE THE CONVERSATION

Act out the above skit, making your own sentences and conversation. Change the items wanted, using cigarettes, toothbrushes, cameras, coats, houses, etc.

QUIZ—DIRECT OBJECT -N ENDING

Complete the following sentences, by adding the -n ending on the words which need it. Remember, the -n shows the object that receives the direct action of the verb.

Mia frato vendas horloĝoj . La fratino komprenas vi bone . La patro havas du grandaj domoj . Cigaro mi ne deziras , sed mi petas cigaredo . Kiaj cigaredoj vi deziras ? Kiom ili kostas ? Ili kostas dudek - unu cendoj . Kio vidas la muzikisto ? Li instruas Esper-anto . Mi ŝi vidas , sed ŝi mi ne vidas . Kiu estas la prezidanto ? La instruistino iras al la klubo . Bona vespero , fraŭlino .

LESSON VI (SESA LECIONO)

WHAT DO WE EAT?

manĝi (to eat)
Mi deziras manĝi. (I wish to eat.)
iom (some)
da (of—quantity)
supo (soup)
fiŝo (fish)
pano (bread)
viando (meat)
bifsteko (beefsteak)
terpomoj (potatoes)
legomoj (vegetables)
ovoj (eggs)
salato (salad)
frukto (fruit)
deserto (dessert)
Mi deziras iom da fiŝo. (I want some fish.)
Ankaŭ, mi deziras manĝi bifstekon kaj salaton. (Also, I wish to eat a beefsteak and a salad.)
bonvolu (please—be so good as . . .)
menuo, manĝokarto (menu, bill of fare)
Bonvolu doni al mi la menuon. (Please give me the menu.)
trinki (to drink)
glaso (drinking glass)
biero (beer)
vino (wine)
dolĉa (sweet)
freŝa (fresh)
akvo (water)
kafo (coffee)
lakto (milk)
teo (tea)

taso (cup)
Mi deziras trinki glason da biero. (I wish to drink a glass of beer.)
preferi (prefer)
Mi preferas tason da teo. (I prefer a cup of tea.)
tute (entirely, at all)
ŝati (to like, to care for)
Ho, mi tute ne ŝatas teon! (Oh, I don't care for tea at all!)
almenaŭ (at least)
povi (to be able to)
Mi povas trinki almenaŭ dek glasojn da biero! (I can drink at least ten glasses of beer!)
permesi (to permit)
Tion mi ne permesas. (That, I do not permit.)
absolute! (absolutely!, positively!)
nek . . . nek (neither . . . nor)
Mi trinkas nek bieron nek vinon. (I drink neither beer nor wine.)
pli bona (better)
plej bona (best)
ol (than—conjunction)
Akvo estas pli bona ol vino. (Water is better than wine.)
el (out of, of)
ĉiuj (all)
Sed lakto estas la plej bona el ĉiuj. (But milk is the best of all.)
kalkulo (check, bill, reckoning)
Fraŭlino, mi petas la kalkulon. (Miss, the check please.)
trinkmono (tip)

NOTES ON GRAMMAR

1. In the word **trinki** (to drink) the **-i** indicates the infinitive ending of the verb (formed in English by the preposition **to**). The infinitive is used when a verb refers to an action without stating that it is actually performed: **paroli** (to speak), **vendi** (to sell), **iri** (to go), **esti** (to be).

2. The word **da** in the sentence **mi deziras glason da biero** translates **of** after an expression of quantity. **Da** connects a measurement with that which is measured: **glaso da lakto, taso da teo, kulero da sukero** (a spoonful of sugar). **Da** is also used in expressions like: **Kiom da mono vi havas?** (How much money do you have?), **Kiom da pano vi deziras? Da** is the preposition which emphasizes **quantity**.

3. For showing degrees of comparison, Esperanto uses the words **pli** (more) and **plej** (most), without exception. English does not have a regularized form of comparison, sometimes using **more** and **most**, and in other instances using entirely different word forms. Note the following: **bela** (beautiful), **pli bela** (more beautiful), **plej bela** (most beautiful); **bona** (good), **pli bona** (better), **plej bona** (best). In comparisons made with **pli**, the connecting word **ol** (than) is used: **Bostono estas pli granda ol Portlando.** The preposition **el** (out of) is used when referring to the group or class out of which the greatest degree (superlative) is selected: **Nov-Jorko estas la plej granda el la tri urboj.** (New York is the largest of the three cities.) Adverbs also form the "comparative" and the "superlative" in the same way: **La biciklo iras rapide, la aŭtomobilo iras pli rapide ol la biciklo, kaj la aeroplano iras la plej rapide el la tri.** Can you figure out what **less beautiful** and **least beautiful** would be in Esperanto? You're right!—**malpli bela** and **malplej bela!**

4. Hint on pronunciation: In the word **ĉiuj** (all), the stress in pronunciation is on **ĉi-** (the next-to-the-last syllable), and the last syllable **-uj** is pronounced like the **-uj-** in **hallelujah**. Now all together: **ĉiuj!**

CONVERSATION

**S-ro Adams and S-ro Martel meet two other friends,
S-ro Petit and S-ro Hanson, in a restaurant.**

Noto: S-ro Adams estas usonano; S-ro Martel, hispano (Spaniard); S-ro Petit, franco (Frenchman); S-ro Hanson, svedo (Swede).

S-ro Adams: Bonan tagon, sinjoroj, kiel vi fartas?

S-ro Hanson: Tre bone, sinjoro, kaj vi. . . ?

S-ro Adams: Ankaŭ bone . . . sed mi multe soifas. Mi deziras grandan glason da akvo.

S-ro Petit: Ho, sinjoro, akvo ne estas bona! Vino estas pli bona! . . . Fraŭlino, mi petas, ni deziras vinon.

S-ro Adams: Jen estas S-ro Martel, kiu estas hispano . . .Kion vi preferas trinki, S-ro Martel?

S-ro Martel: Mi preferas vinon. Kaj mi ankaŭ deziras manĝi.

Fraŭlino: Ĉu vi deziras tutan manĝon, sinjoro?

S-ro Martel: Jes, kompreneble. Ni hispanoj ŝatas manĝi multon.

S-ro Hanson: Pardonu, sinjoro, ne pli ol ni, la svedoj! Mi ankaŭ deziras manĝi kun vi. Kion vi havas por manĝi hodiaŭ, fraŭlino? Kie estas la menuo?

Fraŭlino: Jen ĝi estas! . . . sinjoro.

S-ro Martel: Mi deziras unue supon, . . . kaj poste viandon. Nu, bifsteko estas bona!

Fraŭlino: Mi bedaŭras, sinjoro, sed ni ne havas bifstekon . . . Ni havas nur fiŝon.

S-ro Petit: Mi ankaŭ deziras manĝi . . Fiŝo estas tre bona. Sed, mi tre soifas, fraŭlino. Mi povas trinki almenaŭ dek glasojn da vino!

Fraŭlino: Sinjoro, tion mi absolute ne povas permesi!

S-ro Petit: Ĉu ne? Nu, mi petas nur unu grandan glason.

Fraŭlino: Jes, sinjoro. Ĉu vi deziras terpomojn kaj salaton kun la fiŝo?

S-ro Adams: Jes, fraŭlino, bonvolu . . . Kaj ankaŭ mi deziras bonan, freŝan panon.

S-ro Petit: Fraŭlino, ĉu vi ankaŭ trinkas vinon?

Fraŭlino: Ne, sinjoro, mi trinkas nek vinon, nek bieron . . . nur lakton.

S-ro Hanson: Kompreneble ni ankaŭ ŝatas lakton, ĉu ne, sinjoroj? Sed biero estas pli bona.

S-ro Petit: Pardonu, sinjoro, sed al ni francoj vino estas la plej bona! Kaj jen, sinjoroj, mi trinkas je via sano! Saluton!

NOW, YOU MAKE THE CONVERSATION

1. You go into a restaurant, greet the waitress, and ask what they have to eat today.
2. She replies, good day, here is the menu . . . , there is soup, fish and salad.
3. You ask if they have beefsteak.
4. She says, no, only fish today, and asks if you wish wine first.
5. You say, no, you prefer water, and ask her to please give (to) you some tea with the fish and potatoes.
6. She says that the coffee is better than the tea today. Do you prefer coffee?
7. You say, yes, please.

NEW WORDS FROM OLD IDEAS

Can you figure out the English for the following Esperanto words:

vespermanĝo	vinkarto	maldolĉa	malpermesi
matenmanĝo	tetaso	maldika	kunmanĝas
matenmanĝas	malŝatas	malnova	la tuto

QUIZ—MATCHING SENTENCES

Find the English sentence that corresponds to the Esperanto, and change the number so that they may be placed in the proper order. In scoring, give yourself one for each correct answer. Score: 12-15 excellent; 8-11 good; below 7 poor.

1. Adiaŭ.
2. Mi dankas vin.
3. Kiu estas la bela fraŭlino?
4. Kie estas la restoracio?
5. Fraŭlino, la teon, mi petas.
6. Kiom da biero vi deziras?
7. Dolĉa vino, maldolĉa persono.
8. Ni povas almenaŭ manĝi fiŝon.
9. Kiom kostas la mantelo?
10. Ni havas nek supon nek salaton.
11. Je via sano!
12. Ĉu la akvo estas freŝa?
13. Estas dudek litoj en la hotelo.
14. Ĝi kostas cent dolarojn.
15. Kiom da trinkmono vi donas?

1. Who is the beautiful girl?
2. We have neither soup nor salad.
3. Miss, the tea, please.
4. Sweet wine, sour person.
5. How much does the coat cost?
6. I thank you.
7. Goodbye.
8. There are 20 beds in the hotel.
9. Where is the restaurant?
10. How much of a tip do you give?
11. How much beer do you wish?
12. It costs one hundred dollars.
13. Is the water fresh?
14. We can at least eat fish.
15. To your health!

LESSON VII (SEPA LECIONO)

TELLING TIME

kioma (which—out of the many)
horo (hour)
Kioma horo estas? (What time is it?—Which hour is it?)
Estas la sesa horo. (It is six o'clock. —It is the sixth hour.)
post (after)
mezo (middle)
tagmezo (noon)
posttagmezo (afternoon)
Estas la oka vespere. (It is eight in the evening.)
tempo (time)
por (for—purpose, aim)
Estas tempo por manĝi. (It is time to eat.)

iĝas (becomes, comes to be—also used as suffix -iĝ-)
ellitiĝi, el-lit-iĝi (to get out of bed —to become out of bed)
je (at—with expressions of time)
kutime (usually, customarily)
Mi kutime ellitiĝas je la sesa. (I usually get out of bed at six.)
frue (early)
levi (to raise)
si (himself, herself, itself, themselves —reflexive pronoun)
Li levas sin je la sesa. (He gets up at six.—He raises himself at six.)
Ŝi levas sin je la deka. (She gets up at ten.)

kiam (when)
komenci (to begin something)
kinofilmo (motion-picture, movies)
Kiam komenciĝas la kinofilmo?
(When do the movies begin?)
for (forth, away)
foriri (to go away, leave)
vagonaro (train)
Kiam la vagonaro foriras? (When
does the train leave?)
veni (to come)
alveni (to arrive, to come to)
kvarono (a fourth, a quarter)
Estas kvarono post la deka. (It is
a quarter past ten.)
duono (a half)
Estas duono post la tria. (It is half
past three.)
tri kvaronoj (three quarters)
Estas la sepa kaj tri kvaronoj. (It
is seven and three quarters.)
minuto (minute)
antaŭ (before)
**Estas la sepa kaj kvardek-kvin
minutoj.** (It is seven forty-five.)

Estas kvin minutoj antaŭ la naŭa.
(It is five minutes before nine.)
akurate (exactly, punctually, at the
right time)
baldaŭ (soon)
proksimume (about, approximately)
Estas proksimume la kvina. (It is
about five.)
ankoraŭ (yet, still)
Ne estas ankoraŭ la dua. (It is not
yet two.)
funkcii (to function, work)
Mia horloĝo ne funkcias. (My watch
does not work.)
sufiĉe (enough, sufficient)
Ni havas sufiĉe da tempo. (We have
enough time.)
hieraŭ (yesterday)
promeni (to take a walk)
parko (park)
**Hieraŭ mi promenis en la parko ĝis
la oka. Je la naŭa mi iris al la
kunveno.** (Yesterday I walked in
the park until eight. At nine I
went to the meeting.)

NOTES ON GRAMMAR

1. Notice that in Esperanto **kioma** (which out of the many) is used to
ask the question **Kioma horo estas?** The answer **always** calls for the **-a**
ending on the name of the hour: **Estas la tria horo.** (It is the third hour,
It is the third hour.) There are various ways of giving the time in Esperanto, just as in English: **Estas kvarono post la oka, Estas la oka kaj
kvarono, Estas la oka kaj dek-kvin minutoj.** They all mean 8:15. Of
course, in countries where the twenty-four hour system of telling time is
used, Esperanto merely conforms to that system. 1:00 p.m. is then **la
dek-tria horo.**

2. You have already met a number of words like **sur, al, kun, en, ĉe,
por** which show some relation between a noun or pronoun and some other
word in the sentence (prepositions): **La verda stelo estas sur la jako.
La hotelo estas ĉe la angulo. Mi iras kun vi.** In Esperanto each preposition
has a definite meaning. But it sometimes happens in translating that none
of the definite prepositions fits the meaning. In such cases national languages use a preposition fixed by tradition and usage, often different in

[55

each language. In Esperanto the indefinite preposition **je** is used. **Je** has no definite meaning of its own, but is translated into each language according to the preposition which that language uses. In phrases indicating time of day, quantity, measure, etc., **je** is generally used: **Mi manĝis je la kvara. Je kioma horo vi iris al la stacio? Mi vendis ĝin je 25 cendoj.**

3. In Esperanto, fractions are formed from the cardinal numbers (**unu, du, tri,** etc.) by the use of the **suffix -on** plus the appropriate noun, adjective or adverb ending: **duono** (one-half), **triono** (one-third), **Triona parto de ses estas du.** (A third part of six is two.) **Li nur duone manĝis la viandon.** (He only half ate the meat.)

4. Perhaps you have noticed, that in all English sentences beginning **There is . . . , There are . . . , It is . . .** , used in a general introductory way with no actual **it** in mind, Esperanto simply uses the verb **estas: Estas la naŭa** (It is nine o'clock). **Estas tempo por manĝi** (It is time to eat). **Estas multaj personoj en la restoracio** (There are many people in the restaurant).

5. Simple past action (past tense of the verb) is expressed in Esperanto by the verb ending **-is: Hieraŭ mi vendis ĝin** (Yesterday I sold it). **Mi havis du cendojn, sed nun mi ne havas eĉ unu cendon** (I had two cents, but now I do not have even one cent). This rule is applicable to all verbs in Esperanto, without exception.

6. When we speak about a person doing something for himself (third person) such as washing, dressing, shaving, Esperanto uses a special word **si** which means **himself, herself, itself, themselves,** depending on who is the subject. **Si** is a reflexive pronoun, because it **always** refers back to the subject of the verb: **Ŝi levis sin je la deka** (She arose—raised herself—at 10 o'clock). **Li lavis sin** (He washed himself). **Ili vestis sin rapide** (They dressed themselves quickly). Remember that **si** is never used in the subject of the sentence, because it must always **refer back** to the subject. Notice the difference between **li lavis sin** (he washed himself) and **li lavis lin** (he washed him—someone else). But, for **myself, ourselves, yourself** (first and second persons) the ordinary pronouns **min, nin, vin** are used without getting into complications! **Mi lavis min** (I washed myself), **vi lavis vin** (you washed yourself), **ni lavis nin** (We washed ourselves).

CONVERSATION

S-ro Adams is waiting at the station to meet F-ino Parker
He asks the porter:

S-ro A: Pardonu, sinjoro, kiam alvenas la vagonaro de Parizo?

Portisto: Akurate je la dek-naŭa kaj dek-kvin minutoj!

S-ro A.: H-m-m, nun estas la dek-sepa kaj duono. Estas sufiĉe frue. Bone, mi povas promeni en la parko iom da tempo. Kaj je la dek-naŭa kaj dek minutoj mi povas veni al la stacio. Nu, ĉu mia horloĝo bone funkcias? Jes, estas nun la dek-sepa kaj dudek-unu minutoj. Mi esperas, ke la vagonaro ne estas malfrua. Mi deziras iri al la kino kun la fraŭlino.

(While he walks in the park he thinks over the day's activities.) Hodiaŭ matene mi ellitiĝis tre frue, . . . proksimume je la sesa. Estis absolute tro frue por mi! Kutime mi ne levas min ĝis la deka. Hodiaŭ mi matenmanĝis je la sepa, tagmanĝis je la dek-dua, kaj ĝis nun mi ne vespermanĝis. Nu . . . estas sufiĉe da tempo por manĝi iom nun. Mi estas tre malsata, ĉar mi manĝis nur supon, iom da pano, kaj salaton je tagmanĝo.

(Li iras al malgranda restoracio kaj petas grandan vespermanĝon. Sed li nur duone manĝis la viandon, kiam li vidas, ke estas la dek-naŭa kaj dek-tri minutoj! Li parolas:) Fraŭlino! Fraŭlino! Rapide! Rapide! La kalkulon! Pardonu . . . sed la vagonaro alvenas kaj mi ne estas ĉe la stacio . . . Jen estas trinkmono por vi . . . Adiaŭ! Ĝis revido! Adiaŭ . . . Estas malfrue! (Kaj S-ro Adams foriras rapide.)

QUIZ—HOW DO YOU SAY IT?

Prepare to give the following sentences orally in Esperanto. Practice until you can say the Esperanto instantly and smoothly.

1. Good morning, Mr. Petit. How are you?
2. Very well, thank you, and you?
3. I don't understand you.
4. He does not speak Esperanto.
5. I am from the United States.
6. How is your mother today?
7. I want some good cigarettes and matches.
8. Here is the menu!
9. Pardon me, where is the railroad station?
10. We are going to the movies.
11. When does the train arrive?
12. At what time did you eat breakfast?
13. She spoke to her father.
14. She washed her clothes yesterday.
15. She got up yesterday morning at 6:15 o'clock.
16. Many things are lacking now.
17. How much does a new automobile cost?
18. The bicycle is old, but sufficiently good.

19. Better early than late.
20. What kind of toothbrush do you want?
21. I sold the radio for fifteen dollars.

LESSON VIII (OKA LECIONO)

MAKING A SOCIAL CALL

hejmo, hejme (home, at home)
Ĉu estas la hejmo de S-ro Paŭlo?
  (Is this Mr. Paul's home?)
Envenu! (Come in!)
Kun plezuro! (With pleasure!)
kiu (which—which certain . . .)
lando (country)
De kiu lando vi estas? (From which
  country are you?)
Kanado (Canada)
de Usono, de Kanado (from the
  United States, from Canada)
ĝoji (to be glad, to be happy)
renkonti (to meet—someone, something)
amerikano (an American)
Mi tre ĝojas renkonti amerikanojn.
  (I am very happy to meet Amer-
  icans.)
nord-amerikano, sud-amerikano (a
  North-American, a South-Amer-
  ican)
interesi (to interest)
Ameriko multe interesas min.
  (America interests me a lot.)
pri (about, concerning)
interesiĝi pri (to be interested in)
Mi multe interesiĝas pri via lando.
  (I am much interested in your
  country.)
riĉa (rich)
vojaĝi (to travel)
tra (through)
Eŭropo (Europe)
Mi nun vojaĝas tra Eŭropo. (I am
  now traveling through Europe.)

Azio, Aŭstralio, Nov-Zelando, Mek-
  siko, Brazilo, Argentino (Asia,
  Australia, New Zealand, Mexico,
  Brazil, Argentina)
per (by, by means of)
ŝipo (ship)
Ĉu vi vojaĝis per ŝipo? (Did you
  travel by ship?)
kelkaj (some, a few)
fojo (a time, an instance)
kelkfoje (sometimes)
aeroplano (airplane)
aŭtobuso (autobus)
azeno (donkey, ass)
Kelkfoje per aeroplano, kelkfoje per
  aŭtobuso, kaj kelkfoje per azeno!
  (Sometimes by airplane, sometimes by bus, and sometimes by
  donkey!)
plaĉi al (to be pleasing to)
Ĉu mia lando plaĉas al vi? (Does
  my country please you?)
meti (to put)
ĉapelo (hat)
tablo (table)
Metu vian ĉapelon sur la tablon.
  (Put your hat on the table.)
Ni iru! (Let us go!)
ĝardeno (garden)
Ni iru en la ĝardenon. (Let us go
  into the garden.)
agrabla (pleasant, agreeable)
Estas pli agrable! (It is more pleasant!)
rigardi (to look at)
Rigardu! (Look!)

infano (child)
jam (already)
tie (there, that place)
La infanoj jam estas tie. (The children are already there.)
familio (family)
do (so, therefore)
Do, vi havas familion! (So, you have a family!)

knabo (boy)
aĝo (age, time of life)
jaro (year)
La knabo estas la pli aĝa; li havas dek jarojn. (The boy is the older; he is ten years old.)
sidi (to sit)
Sidiĝu, mi petas. (Sit down, please.)

NOTES ON GRAMMAR

1. The ending -u on the Esperanto verb shows the command, request (imperative), or wish form of the verb: Envenu! (Come in!); Estu hejme! (Make yourself at home!); Rigardu la tablon! (Look at the table!), Metu vian ĉapelon sur la tablon! (Put your hat on the table!); Ni iru! (Let us go!); Estu feliĉa. (Be happy, May you be happy.) The polite request, of course, needs Mi petas . . . or Bonvolu . . . Note that the infinitive form is always used after bonvolu: Bonvolu rigardi la infanon.

2. The suffix -iĝ- attached to the end of a word gives the meaning becomes, or the coming into existence of the act or condition expressed in the root: sidiĝi (to become sitting, to sit down, to take a seat), interesiĝi (to be interested, to become interested, to take an interest), ellitiĝi (to get out of bed). Notice that iĝi is also used as a separate verb, meaning to become: Mi iĝis Esperantisto. (I became an Esperantist.)

3. You probably noticed the -n on the words ĝardeno and tablo in the sentences: Ni iru en la ĝardenoN. Metu vian ĉapelon sur la tabloN. Both of these instances show action towards a certain object: into the garden, onto the table. Esperanto also uses the -n ending to indicate direction towards where the preposition itself does not show direction (accusative of direction). The -n is also added to kie (where) to express direction towards: kien (whither), Kien vi iras? (Whither are you going?) Notice well the difference in the sentences: Ni iru en la ĝardenon (Let us go into the garden), and Ni iru en la ĝardeno (Let us go [about] in [inside] the garden). However, if a preposition already showing direction towards is used, such as al or tra, then the -n ending is not necessary: Ni iris al la kino, Ni vojaĝis tra Eŭropo. In this, as in all other rules in Esperanto, the purpose is to achieve precision, clarity, and understanding for all peoples, and all language groups.

4. Notice that the word kiu is used before a noun when some certain, specific thing is referred to (pronominal adjective): De kiu lando vi estas? (From which country are you?) Kiu infano estas pli aĝa? (Which child

is the older?) **Kiu** also takes the plural ending **-j** before plural nouns, and the **-n** ending before object nouns: **Kiuj parkoj estas la plej belaj? Kiun ĝardenon vi vidis? Kiujn landojn vi ŝatas?** Pronunciation hint: Remember that the two letters **-uj** are pronounced like the **-uj-** in **hallelujah**. You might compare it also to the **o-i** in the English **who is** glided together.

5. Where in English we use the **-'s** to show possession, Esperanto uses the word **de** (of): **La hejmo de S-ro Paŭlo** (Mr. Paul's home, the home of Mr. Paul). **La taso de la knabo** (The boy's cup). Esperanto **always** uses this form.

CONVERSATION

S-ro Adams goes to visit at the home of the Esperanto delegate:

S-ro A.: Bonan tagon, sinjoro! Ĉu S-ro Paŭlo estas hejme?

S-ro P.: Mi estas S-ro Paŭlo. Mi vidas, ke vi estas Esperantisto. Envenu, sinjoro!

S-ro A.: Dankon, sinjoro, kun plezuro.

S-ro P.: De kiu lando vi venas?

S-ro A.: Mi venas de Usono.

S-ro P.: Mi multe interesiĝas pri via bela, riĉa lando.

S-ro A.: Ho, en mono mi ne estas riĉa, sed en plezuro mi estas tre riĉa, ĉar mi nun vojaĝas tra via bela lando.

S-ro P.: Mi tre ĝojas, ke mia lando plaĉas al vi. Ĉu vi renkontis en mia patrolando riĉajn personojn kaj belajn objektojn?

S-ro A.: Ne, sinjoro . . .

S-ro P.: Ĉu ne, sinjoro? Mi tre bedaŭras . . .

S-ro A.: Ne . . . sinjoro, mi renkontis nur **interesajn** personojn, **belajn** fraŭlinojn, **purajn** hotelojn, kaj **rapidajn** aŭtomobilojn!

S-ro P.: Ha-ha . . . jes, mi komprenas! Ĉu vi renkontis multajn Esperantistojn?

S-ro A.: Sufiĉe multajn . . . En la kluboj kaj kunvenoj, kaj eĉ sur la stratoj.

S-ro P.: Nu, ni iru en la ĝardenon kaj sidiĝu tie. Estas pli agrable. Bonvolu meti vian ĉapelon sur la tablon. Jen, sinjoro, en la ĝardeno estas S-ino Paŭlo, mia edzino (wife), kun miaj du infanoj.

S-ro A.: Ha . . . do, vi havas familion! Kiom da jaroj havas la infanoj?

S-ro P.: La knabo, Johano, havas dek jarojn; la knabino, Betino, havas ses jarojn. Ili ankaŭ parolas Esperante.

S-ro A.: Tre interese!

S-ro P.: Saluton, Johano kaj Betino! Rigardu kiun mi havas kun mi! Estas S-ro Adams de la granda, bela, interesa lando Usono.

(And the young ones start asking S-ro Adams all kinds of questions.)

NOW, YOU MAKE THE CONVERSATION

1. You go to visit a friend. The wife opens the door, and you ask whether Paul is home.
2. She says, no, but he will arrive soon.
3. You ask when did he go out.
4. She says after breakfast, at ten o'clock, but please come in and sit down.
5. You say, with pleasure, and go in.
6. She says, put your coat on the table.
7. You ask how the children are.
8. She says, very well, thank you, the younger one is now in the park.
9. You ask if they speak Esperanto.
10. She says, oh yes, they are good Esperantists. The boy, who is ten years old, goes to the Esperanto meetings. They meet Esperantists from many countries.
11. You say, very interesting!

(Just then your friend comes in and you continue the conversation as you please.)

NEW WORDS FROM OLD IDEAS

From the words, prepositions, prefixes and suffixes already learned, you should be able to make up compound words in Esperanto for the following English expressions. For example: **to come in** is **enveni; beer glass** is **bierglaso,** etc.

to dislike	to put on (a hat, etc.)	to see through
ugly	fish salad	to go through
triple	hometown	century
disagreeable	water glass	one time (one instance)
poor	to contain (have in)	dentist
teacup	to go out	assemble (put together)

TRANSLATION

Translate the following sentences into Esperanto. Watch for places where the -n must be used to indicate **direction towards!** Remember the use of the reflexive **si,** and the Esperanto manner of showing possession with **de:**

Yesterday, I went to Mr. Paul's home. He was not at home, but the children were. They put their little airplanes, automobiles, and ships on the table, and looked at my green Esperanto star. I put the star on the boy's jacket, and that greatly pleased him (plaĉis al). He put his hat on his mother's new table, and joyfully spoke with me. He is eight years old. I am much interested in children. I have six children! It is a big family, but an interesting family.

LESSON IX (NAŬA LECIONO)

DOING THE TOWN

viziti (to visit)
preta (ready)
ekskurso (excursion)
Ĉu vi estas preta por la ekskurso? (Are you ready for the excursion?)
porti (to carry)
Kunportu mantelon! (Take a coat with you!)
Estas sufiĉe malvarme. (It is quite cold.)
Kien ni iru unue? (Where shall we go first?)
devi (to have to, must)
ŝanĝi (to change)
banko (bank)
mono (money)
Mi devas ŝanĝi iom da mono en la banko. (I must change some money at the bank).
landkarto (map)
vidindaĵoj (the sights, things worth seeing)
Kiajn vidindaĵojn vi havas? (What attractions do you have?)
nacia (national)
muzeo (museum)
palaco (palace)
reĝo (king)
diversaj (various, divers)
historia (historical)
katedralo (cathedral)
Estas la nacia muzeo, la palaco de la reĝo, la katedralo, kaj diversaj historiaj lokoj. (There is the national museum, the King's palace,

the cathedral, and various historical places.)
poste (afterwards)
Poste ni iros al la parko. (Afterwards we shall go to the park.)
kial (why—what reason)
tien (thither, to there)
kafejo (café, coffee shop)
Ni iros tien, ĉar estas interesa kafejo tie. (We shall go there, because there is an interesting café there.)
danci (to dance)
dancejo (dancing-place)
Ankaŭ estas dancejo. Ĉu vi ŝatas danci? (Also there is a dancing-place. Do you like to dance?)
Gesinjoroj! (Ladies and Gentlemen!)
aŭskulti (to listen)
Gesinjoroj, aŭskultu la belan muzikon! (Ladies and Gentlemen, listen to the beautiful music.)
juna (young)
junulo (a youth)
gejunuloj (young people)
sekvi (to follow)
La gejunuloj sekvas la Usonan kutimon pri "sving-muziko." (The young people follow the United States custom of swing-music.)
internacia (international)
lingvo (language)
Muziko ankaŭ estas internacia lingvo, ĉu ne? (Music also is an international language, isn't it?)
fari (to do, to make)

morgaŭ (tomorrow)
Kion ni faros morgaŭ? (What shall we do tomorrow?)
veturi (to drive in a vehicle, to travel)
ekster (outside)
kampo (field)
kamparo (country-side, collection of fields)
Ni veturos ekster la urbon al la bela kamparo. (We shall drive outside the city to the beautiful country-side.)
naĝi (to swim)
lago (lake)
arbo (tree)
arbaro (forest, woods, collection of trees)
Ni naĝos en lago, ni promenos en la arbaro. (We shall swim in a lake, we shall walk in the woods.)

NOTES ON GRAMMAR

1. Future action is expressed in Esperanto by the **-os** ending on the verb root: **Ni iros al la parko** (We shall go to the park). **Kion ni faros morgaŭ?** (What shall we do tomorrow?)

2. There are a lot of new suffixes in this lesson—enough to increase your vocabulary by at least 50 new words!

a. **-ind-** suffix means **worthy of, deserving of** whatever is indicated by the root: **vidi** (to see), **vidinda** (worth seeing); **fari** (to do), **farinda** (worth doing); **bedaŭri** (to regret), **bedaŭrinde** (worth regretting, regretfully).

b. **-aĵ-** indicates some **real or concrete thing,** made from or having the quality of the root: **vidindaĵo** (something worth seeing), **belaĵo** (something beautiful), **manĝaĵo** (something to eat, a food), **ovaĵo** (something made from eggs, an omelet), **interesaĵo** (something interesting).

c. **-ej-** suffix denotes a place, specially used for or characterized by the idea implied in the root: **dancejo, kafejo, trinkejo.**

d. **-ar-** suffix denotes a collection of similar objects or beings: **kamparo** (collection of fields, countryside), **arbaro** (a forest), **homaro** (humanity, mankind).

e. **-ul-** suffix denotes a **living being** characterized by the root: **junulo** (a young person), **bonulo** (a good person, a good fellow), **riĉulo** (a rich person), **milionulo** (millionaire).

All of these suffixes may be used as separate words: **inda** (worthy), **aĵo** (a thing), **ejo** (a place), **aro** (a collection).

3. The prefix **ge-** denotes persons of both sexes considered together: **gesinjoroj** equals **sinjorinoj kaj sinjoroj**; **gejunuloj** equals **junuloj kaj junulinoj**; **geknaboj** (boys and girls); **gepatroj** (father and mother, parents); etc.

4. Note the new question word **kial** (why, for what reason). It follows the system for all question words beginning with **ki-**. The ending **-al** shows cause, reason: **Kial vi ne parolas?** (Why do you not speak?)

5. This lesson introduces several little words that point out an object, person, place, or direction. They all begin with **ti-** which is the cue to all demonstratives in Esperanto: **tio** (that thing), **tiu** (that person, that certain one), **tie** (there, that place), **tien** (thither, that direction). **Tial** would mean: (for that reason, so, therefore).

6. Note the use of the adverb form in the sentence: **Estas sufiĉe malvarme** (It is quite cold). We learned before that such phrases as It is . . . , There are . . . , are translated into Esperanto merely by the use of the verb **esti**. The word that modifies this verb, therefore, has the adverbial ending, not the adjectival, because there is actually no noun or pronoun described. Example: **Estas agrable** (It is pleasant). **Estas kutime** (It is customary). **Estas tre varme** (It is very warm).

CONVERSATION

S-ro Martel and S-ro Petit offer to act as guides for F-ino Parker on a sight-seeing tour. They meet her early.

S-ro M.: Ĉu vi estas preta por la granda ekskurso, fraŭlino?

F-ino P.: Ho, jes, sinjoroj, mi tre ĝojas pri la ekskurso!

S-ro P.: Kunportu vian mantelon, fraŭlino, ĉar vespere estos sufiĉe malvarme.

S-ro M.: Kien ni iru unue?

F-ino P.: Nu, kiajn vidindajojn vi havas?

S-ro M.: Ni havas multajn, ekzemple estas la bela nacia muzeo kun interesaj historiaj objektoj.

S-ro P.: Kaj la malnova palaco de nia reĝo. Ĉu tio interesas vin?

F-ino P.: Tre multe! Sed, pardonu, sinjoroj, unue mi devas iri al la banko por ŝanĝi iom da mono.

S-ro M.: Tion vi ne devas fari, fraŭlino! Ni havas sufiĉe da mono.

S-ro P.: Kompreneble, fraŭlino! Ni estas tre riĉaj—ĉar vi estas kun ni!

F-ino P.: Ha, vi bele parolas, sinjoro! Nu, mi estas preta por iri al diversaj lokoj.

S-ro M.: Bone . . . unue ni iros al la katedralo, poste al la muzeo, kaj post tio al la parko.

S-ro P.: Kial al la parko?

S-ro M.: Ĝi estas tre bela parko . . . Mi ŝatos promeni en ĝi kun la fraŭlino—kaj kun **vi**—kompreneble! Ni iros tien, ĉar ankaŭ estas interesa kafejo tie, kaj bona dancejo. Ĉu vi ŝatas danci, fraŭlino?

F-ino P.: Mi tre ŝatas danci, sinjoro.

S-ro P.: Ho, jes, en Eŭropo la gejunuloj tre ŝatas danci kaj aŭskulti al tiu sving-muziko de Usono.

F-ino P.: Tre interese! Mi vidas, ke la muziko ankaŭ parolas internacian lingvon!

S-ro M.: Nu . . . ni iru!

QUIZ—ANSWERING QUESTIONS

After studying the above conversation read the following questions aloud, and see if you can answer them orally—and correctly!

1. Kiuj estas pretaj por fari ekskurson?
2. Kien ili iros?
3. Kial S-ro Martel deziris iri al la parko?
4. Kian muzikon la gejunuloj ŝatas?
5. Kiujn vidindajojn la tri gesinjoroj vidos?
6. Kial la fraŭlino devas kunporti mantelon?
7. Kiel parolis S-ro Petit?
8. Kie dancos la gesinjoroj? Kie ili trinkos?
9. Kien la fraŭlino devis iri unue?
10. Kial la du sinjoroj estis riĉaj?

NOW, YOU MAKE THE CONVERSATION

If you are studying by yourself, pretend that you are two people and try to carry on a lively conversation using the outline below. In class, assign parts to a number of different people and vary the outline as you wish. You may also write up this exercise, but the oral practice is the most important.

You meet a friend and start discussing what you plan to do tomorrow, such as: going out into the country, what you wish to see, how you will travel, what time you plan to leave, whether you should take a coat, whether you wish to walk through the woods, go swimming in the lake, go to a dance, listen to some music somewhere, when you want to go to dinner, where, what you will want to eat and drink, and when you plan to go home, etc.

WRITE YOUR OWN STORY

Write a short essay on: **Kio estas la plej interesa vidindajo proksime al mia hejmo?** Try to use the words and phrases you have already learned, before turning to the dictionary for help. This will be a good opportunity for you to go back and review the words and sentences already given. You'll be surprised what ideas for your topic you may get from them!

[65

LESSON X (DEKA LECIONO)

LA VETERO—THE WEATHER

You are planning to make a visit to the country—weather permitting. So you ask the hotel clerk:

Kia vetero hodiaŭ? (How's the weather today?—What kind of weather today?)

opinii (to think, to opine, to have an opinion)

pluvi (to rain)

Mi opinias, ke pluvos. (I think it will rain.)

esperi (to hope)

Mi esperas, ke ne. (I hope not.)

S-ro Martel diris, ke li venos je la deka. (Mr. Martel said that he would come at ten o'clock.)

ĉielo (sky)

malhela (dark)

Nu, la ĉielo estas tre malhela. (Well, the sky is very dark.)

nigra (black)

nubo (a cloud)

kolekti (to collect, to bring together)

kolektiĝi (to collect together, to come together—to become collected)

Nigraj nuboj kolektiĝas. (Black clouds are collecting.)

vento (wind)

ventego (a high wind, a storm)

ŝajne (seemingly, apparently)

certe (certainly)

pluvego (hard rain, downpour of rain)

Ŝajne ni havos ventegon, kaj certe pluvegos. (Apparently, we shall have a storm, and it will certainly rain hard.)

pluv-ombrelo (rain-umbrella)

necesa (necessary)

Pluvombrelo estos necesa. (An umbrella will be necessary.)

alie (otherwise)

malseka (wet)

malsekiĝi (to get wet, to become wet)

Alie vi malsekiĝos. (Otherwise you will get wet.)

porti (to wear)

pluv-mantelo (raincoat)

Mi portas bonan pluvmantelon. (I am wearing a good raincoat.)

kaŭĉuko (rubber)

ŝuo (shoe)

bezoni (to need)

Vi ankaŭ bezonos kaŭĉukajn ŝuojn. (You will also need rubbers—rubber shoes.)

koto (mud)

Estos tre kote. (It will be very muddy.)

fulmo (lightning)

tondro (thunder)

fulmotondro (thunder storm)

timi (to be afraid of)

Mi timas fulmotondron. (I am afraid of a thunder storm.)

resti (to remain, to stay)

ĉi tie (here)

Do, estos pli bone resti ĉi tie. (So, it will be better to stay here.)

ĉesi (to cease, to stop)

Ĝis la pluvo ĉesos. (Until the rain stops.)

La sezonoj en Esperanto: (The seasons in Esperanto:)

printempo (spring)

somero (summer)

aŭtuno (autumn)

vintro (winter)

La monatoj de la jaro: (The months of the year:)

Januaro	Aprilo	Julio	Oktobro
Februaro	Majo	Aŭgusto	Novembro
Marto	Junio	Septembro	Decembro

NOTES ON GRAMMAR

1. In indirect or reported speech such as: **He said that he would come, She said that she was afraid of the storm,** Esperanto uses the tense of the verb that was originally used by the speaker in direct speaking. Thus **He said that he would come at ten** is translated **Li diris, ke li venos je la deka,** because the person actually said: **Mi venos je la deka** (I will come at ten). The same is true of **Ŝi diris, ke ŝi timas la ventegon.** The person in direct speech said: **Mi timas la ventegon** (I am afraid of the storm). Notice that Esperanto **always** uses the conjunction **ke** (that) to join an indirect statement to the verb, whereas in English we usually leave it out.

2. The suffix **-eg-** in Esperanto indicates greatness in size or intensity: **vento** (wind), **ventego** (high wind, storm); **pluvo** (rain), **pluvego** (downpour); **granda** (large), **grandega** (enormous); **domo** (house), **domego** (mansion); **bone** (well), **bonege** (excellently); **varma** (warm), **varmega** (hot).

3. Notice the words for **there** and **here** in Esperanto: **tie** (there) **ĉi tie** (here). This use of **ĉi** to express the idea of nearness in comparison to some other object or person is a general rule in Esperanto: **tiu** (that certain one), **ĉi tiu** (this certain one); **tio** (that thing), **ĉi tio** (this thing); **tia** (that kind of), **ĉi tia** (this kind of). The **ĉi** may also follow the pronoun or adjective. The meaning remains the same: **tiu ĉi, tio ĉi, tie ĉi,** etc.

4. Note again that Esperanto uses only the verb, with no mythical **it** in the expressions: **Pluvos.** (It will rain.) **Pluvas.** (It is raining.) **Ventegos.** (It will storm.)

5. The verb **porti** is used with reference to **wearing clothes.** It also means **to carry** something. This is true in a number of other languages, and you can see the logic of the two uses. If you wear something you carry it, don't you?

GENERAL NOTE

Throughout your study of Esperanto you should keep in mind that the precise meaning of your English phrase must be translated, not the literal words alone. Better still, try to think directly in Esperanto. Apply the words and phrases you already know to a given situation. Soon you will find yourself **thinking** and speaking or writing Esperanto directly. That is your aim!

CONVERSATION

F-ino Parker and S-ino Melo are engaged in an important topic of conversation: the weather!

Note: In Esperanto, the article **la** is often used with the possessive to express the English forms **mine, yours, ours,** etc.: **la mia, la via, la nia.**

F-ino P: Mi esperas, ke la vetero estos bona hodiaŭ, ĉar S-ro Petit **diris,** ke li venos al via hejmo hodiaŭ—por viziti nin.

S-ino M: Ĉu por viziti **nin?** Mi opinias, ke li preferas viziti **vin!**

F-ino P: Li diris, ke ni faros ekskurson en la kamparon. Mi tre ŝatas la kamparon, sed ne kiam pluvas. Tiam estas tro kote!

S-ino M: Ĉu multe pluvas en via lando, fraŭlino?

F-ino P: En la printempo multe pluvas, sed kutime la somero kaj la aŭtuno estas sufiĉe sekaj.

S-ino M: En mia lando multe pluvas ... en la printempo, en la somero, kaj en la aŭtuno. Fakte, en la aŭtuno pluvegas!

F-ino P: S-ro Petit opinias, ke la vintro estas la plej bela sezono. . . . Nu, li diris, ke li venos je la deka. Kie li estas? Kial li ne jam alvenis?

S-ino M: Ho, la sinjoroj diras multon! . . . Fraŭlino, mi opinias, ke pluvos hodiaŭ. Tial vi devas kunporti pluvombrelon. Mi donos al vi la mian.

F-ino P: Ho, ne, sinjorino! Mi estas certa, ke mi ne malsekiĝos. Mi portos pluvmantelon. Tio sufiĉos!

S-ino M: Nu . . . bone . . . sed kiam fulmotondros, kaj pluvegos, kaj ventegos, vi certe bedaŭros, ke vi ne kunportis kaŭĉukajn ŝuojn, pluvombrelon, kaj. . . .

F-ino P: Rigardu, sinjorino! Jen estas S-ro Petit! Ho, rigardu! Li portas dikan pluvmantelon, grandajn kaŭĉukajn ŝuojn, kaj eĉ pluvombrelon! Sajne li opinias, ke pluv-eg-eg-egos!

NOW, YOU MAKE THE CONVERSATION

You and a friend discuss the various seasons of the year: which season you like best and why, when does it rain most, when is it driest, wettest, coldest, cloudiest. Which month is the best, the loveliest, what month you like best and why. What you usually do in summer, what kind of clothes you wear, whether you travel or stay home, whether you like to travel, where you want to travel, etc.

NEW WORDS FROM OLD IDEAS

Discover the meaning of the following words made from roots, suffixes, prefixes, and prepositions which you have already learned: **vendejo, reĝa, infana, eksteraĵo, triangula, belulino, maljunulino, havaĵo, alkutimiĝi, malrapidas, jesas, malsatulo, troas, dolĉega, dolĉulino, neas, verdstelulo, klubejo, tagiĝas.**

From words and roots already known to you, translate the following English words into Esperanto: **queen, meeting-place, homeland, brothers and sisters, monthly, opinion, set of teeth, a hatter, to plead, a gardener, to put on, a shoemaker, spotless (clean), well-being, a fact, disagreeable, a promenade (place), to be displeasing (to).**

TRANSLATION

Translate and give the Esperanto version orally

1. What kind of weather do you have in summer?
2. Do I need a raincoat today?
3. My rubber shoes, which are very muddy, are in the hotel.
4. I will give you my umbrella and raincoat.
5. Does the bad weather displease you?
6. It is very disagreeable in the country when it rains.
7. Very interesting! What did she say she would do after dinner?
8. How much rain do you have in winter?
9. Which (relates to number) month of the year is March?
10. How many days are there in a week? In one month? In one year?

LESSON XI (DEK-UNUA LECIONO)

FINDING A PLACE TO LAY YOUR HEAD

loĝi (to dwell, to reside, to live)
pensiono (boarding house, pension)
ĉambro (room)
lui (to rent)
Mi deziras lui ĉambron. (I want to rent a room.)

Mi havas kelkajn ĉambrojn. (I have several rooms.)
etaĝo (a floor, a story of a house)
teretaĝo (ground floor)
banĉambro (bathroom)
sen (without)

Unu kun banĉambro sur la dua etaĝo, alia sen banĉambro sur la teretaĝo. (One with bath on the second floor, another without bath on the ground floor.)

prezo (price)

Kio estas la prezo? (What is the price?)

dolaro, franko, ŝilingo (dollar, franc, shilling)

ĉiutage (everyday, daily)

po (at the rate of—preposition)

Sen banĉambro, ĉiutage po du dolaroj. (Without bath, two dollars a day.)

Kun banĉambro po tri dolaroj. (With bath, three dollars.)

Ĉu mi ankaŭ povas manĝi ĉi tie? (May I also eat here?)

tiuokaze (in that case)

Tiuokaze, kostas kvar dolarojn. (In that case, it costs four dollars.)

Ĉu mi povas vidi la ĉambron? (May I see the room?)

supre (above)

ŝtupo (a step, a stair)

ŝtuparo (stairway, flight of stairs)

supreniri (to go up, ascend)

Ili supreniras la ŝtuparon. (They go up the stairs.)

malfermi (to open)

pordo (door)

mastrino (landlady)

La mastrino malfermas pordon. (The landlady opens a door.)

fenestro (window)

La ĉambro havas du fenestrojn. (The room has two windows.)

luma (light)

Ĝi estas sufiĉe luma. (It is quite light.)

elektra (electric)

lampo (lamp)

super (over)

Estas elektra lampo super la lito. (There is an electric lamp over the bed.)

apud (beside, by)

brako (arm)

seĝo (chair)

Kaj ankaŭ apud la brakseĝo. (And also by the armchair.)

komodo (chest of drawers, commode)

skribi (to write)

skribtablo (desk, writing table)

ĉarma (charming)

Ĝi estas tre ĉarma. (It is very charming.)

tuko (a cloth made up for certain purposes)

lit-tuko (sheet—bed cloth)

kovri (to cover)

kovrilo (a cover, a blanket)

alporti (to bring, to carry to)

servistino (maid servant)

ekstra (extra)

La servistino alportos littukojn kaj ekstran kovrilon. (The maid will bring sheets and an extra blanket.)

pakaĵoj (baggage)

La portisto portos viajn pakaĵojn ĉi tien. (The porter will bring your baggage here.)

purigi (to clean)

koridoro (corridor, hallway)

Li nun purigas la koridoron. (He is now cleaning the corridor.)

lifto (elevator, lift)

Ĉu la lifto funkcias? (Does the elevator work?)

aŭtomate (automatically)

Ne aŭtomate. La portisto devas funkciigi ĝin. (Not automatically. The porter has to operate it.)

ŝlosilo (key)

Ĉu vi havas ŝlosilon por mi? (Do you have a key for me?)

oficejo (office)

Certe! Malsupre en la oficejo. (Certainly! Downstairs in the office.)

NOTES ON GRAMMAR

1. The word **ĉiu** is used as the general or distributive pronoun *everyone*, and also as the pronominal adjective **each**. **Ĉiutage**, then, means *everyday, daily*. The plural form of **ĉiu** is **ĉiuj** (all), which you learned in the sixth lesson. In Esperanto we can say "you all" and not be speaking dialect! **Mi dankas vin ĉiujn** (I thank you all). **Ni ĉiuj estas bonaj Esperantistoj** (We all are good Esperantists.)

2. The preposition **po** means **at the rate of**, and is generally used before expressions of number, where in English we would use **apiece, each**: **Ĉiutage po du dolaroj.** (At the rate of two dollars a day.) **Mi vendis la ombrelojn po tri dolaroj.** (I sold the umbrellas at three dollars apiece.) **Ili ricevis po du kovriloj.** (They received two blankets each.)

3. The word **supreniras** is an interesting one in Esperanto: **supre** (above, up) plus the **-n** indicating **direction towards** makes **supren** (upwards), and finally **iras** (goes). An adverb of place such as **supre, antaŭe** is given the **-n** ending when used with a verb expressing motion towards: **iras supren, iras antaŭen** (goes forward); or one word may be used: **supreniras, antaŭeniras, hejmeniras** (goes homeward).

4. The suffix **-ig-** is one of the most important in Esperanto. It means **causing to be, making, bringing about** whatever is expressed by the root. It may be used to form many new verbs from the various parts of speech. From adjectives: **purigi** (to clean), **pretigi** (to make ready), **beligi** (to beautify), **bonigi** (to make something good), **plibonigi** (to improve something), **rapidigi** (to hasten something). From nouns: **grupo** (a group), **grupigi** (to form into a group); **amaso** (heap, pile), **amasigi** (to amass, to accumulate); **limo** (boundary, limit), **limigi** (to set limits to, restrict). From prepositions and numbers: **kunigi** (to connect), **forigi** (to do away with), **enigi** (to put in, insert), **unuigi** (to unite, make one), **duobligi** (to double), **kvaronigi** (to quarter). You will also find such combinations as: **enlitigi** (to put to bed), **enpoŝigi** (to put into a pocket), **surtabligi** (to put on the table), etc.

5. As you have no doubt noticed in Esperanto, some verbs always express an act of the subject that affects something or some person (transitive verb). Thus the object that is affected will need the **-n** ending: **Mi fermis la pordon. Ŝi vendis la cigaron.** Other verbs, however, express a state or action limited only to the actor in the case (intransitive verb): **La pluvo ĉesis. La lifto funkcias. Li sidas.** In English some of these verbs are both transitive and intransitive. For example: **I closed the door** and **The door closed; I stopped the elevator** and **The elevator stopped.** However, in Esperanto, there are a number of verbs which you should note as

being only transitive, such as **fermas, vendas, deziras, ŝanĝas, timas,** and another group which are only intransitive, such as **funkcias, ĉesas, iras, restas.** The second important use of the suffix -ig- is in forming transitive verbs from intransitive verbs, as you perhaps noticed in the sentence: **La lifto ne funkcias aŭtomate; la portisto devas funkciigi ĝin.** Also we would say: **La pluvo ĉesis. La vento ĉesigis la pluvon.**

6. Now, conversely, suppose a verb in Esperanto is only transitive, how do we make it intransitive? Remember that the suffix -iĝ- in lesson seven had the meaning to become, so it is used to form verbs that show an action limited to the subject only, thus intransitive. We add the suffix -iĝ- to transitive verbs to form the intransitive: **La pordo fermiĝas. Kutimoj ŝanĝiĝas.** (Customs change.) **La suno leviĝis.** (The sun rose.) If you learn meaningful phrases in your study, you will automatically learn the correct forms of these verbs.

CONVERSATION

S-ro Adams and S-ro Petit discuss lodgings.

S-ro P.: Kie vi loĝas, S-ro Adams? Ĉu en la "Hotelo Granda"?

S-ro A.: Ho, ne! Estas tro multekoste tie! Mi loĝas en malgranda pensiono.

S-ro P.: En kiu strato?

S-ro A.: En la "Avenuo Esperanto."

S-ro P.: "Avenuo Esperanto"? Kie estas tiu interesa avenuo? Ŝajne, ĝi estas nova, ĉu ne?

S-ro A.: Jes, ĝi estas tre nova. Nur hieraŭ vespere, kiam mi deziris lokon por loĝi, mi vidis malgrandan, ĉarman pensionon. Mi eniris kaj petis ĉambron, kaj la mastrino diris, ke ŝi havas unu malgrandan ĉambron, sed nur sur la plej supra etaĝo. "Do, bone!" mi diris, kaj sekvis ŝin. Ni supren-iris almenaŭ cent ŝtupojn. Ŝi malfermis verdan pordon, kaj tie estis tre ĉarma, tre pura, tre interesa ĉambro. Mi luis ĝin, kaj donis la sumon de kelkaj frankoj al la mastrino. Post tio, mi rapide malsupreniris la ŝtuparon, kaj malsupre sur la strato, mi skribis sur la angulon de la pensiono: "Ĉi tiu strato estas nun la "Avenuo Esperanto," ĉar ĝi multe plaĉas al mi!" Tio estas la historio de tiu loko, mia nuna hejmo!

S-ro P.: Ho, mi komprenas! Tre interese! Sed, sinjoro . . . ĉu vi renkontis Sinjoron Melo hieraŭ vespere?

S-ro A.: Jes, en la klubo. Mi tre ŝatas lin.

S-ro P.: Nu . . . antaŭ kelkaj jaroj, kiam li ne havis loĝejon, li iris al fervojo-oficejo kaj luis vagonon por loĝi en ĝi. Ili donis al li tre bonan, luksan vagonon. Li metis ĝin ekster la urbon, apud Jagon, kaj komforte

loĝis tie. Unufoje, mi vizitis lian hejmon. Estis printempo, kaj pluvis.
Kiam mi alvenis—jen—mi vidis, ke nia sinjoro sidis ekster la vagono,
sub la nigra ĉielo, en granda, komforta brakseĝo. Li portis pluvmantelon,
estis tute malseka, kaj fumis (smoked) cigaron! "Nu . . . kio estas?"
mi diris, "Kial vi sidas tie ĉi? Kial ne sidi en via komforta hejmo?"
"Ho," li diris, "mi ne povas. Tiu malbona fervojo-oficejo vendis al mi
vagonon, kiu diras super la pordo—'NE FUMU ĈI TIE'!"

QUIZ—CHECK AND FILL IN

Look back over the Esperanto lessons and check whether the following
verbs are transitive or intransitive in Esperanto:

ŝanĝas	ŝajnas	vidas	havas
kolektas	bezonas	ĉesas	deziras
fermas	ŝatas	iras	interesas
ĝojas	portas	alvenas	donas
vendas	renkontas	veturas	faras
funkcias	promenas	restas	kunvenas
kostas	levas	preferas	permesas

Now, fill in the blanks to give the correct form of the verb, using
the suffixes -ig- or -iĝ- where necessary, or merely joining verb ending to
root, in instances where neither -ig- nor -iĝ- should be used:

Hodiaŭ la vetero plibon—as. La pluvo ĉes—is. Sed la pluvo malsan—
is la fraŭlinon. Ŝi tim—as la malsanon, sed ŝi bezon—as multan monon
por ir—i al bela lago. Ŝi ĝoj—is kiam ŝi renkont—is Sinjoron Adams. Ili
renkont—is en la Esperanto-Klubo. Ili tre interes—as pri Esperanto, kaj
far—as multon por ĝi. La Esperantistoj kunven—as en la hejmo de
S-ro Petit. Kelkaj el la Esperantistoj maljun—as, kaj kiam la lifto ne
funkci—as, ili dev—as supreniri la ŝtuparon. Ili tre malŝat—as tion, kaj
prefer—as bonan hotelon, kie portisto bone funkci—as la lifton. La
Esperantistoj kutime kolekt—as en granda ĉambro; kelkaj grup—as apud
la fenestro, ĉar la libroj sur la tablo interes—as ilin. Diversaj libroj rapide
vend—as kaj la klubo hav—as monon por far—i novan kunvenon!

LESSON XII (DEK-DUA LECIONO)

TIME OUT FOR CORRESPONDENCE

letero (letter)

Mi devas skribi kelkajn leterojn. (I must write several letters.)

aĉeti (to buy)

koverto (envelope)

papero (paper)

poŝto (mail, the post)

poŝtmarko (postage stamp)

poŝtkarto (postcard)

Kie mi povas aĉeti paperon, kovertojn, poŝtmarkojn kaj poŝtkartojn? (Where can I buy paper, envelopes, stamps and postcards?)

poŝtoficejo (post-office)

Paperon vi aĉetas en la papervendejo. (You buy paper at the stationery store.)

Ĉinujo (China)

Kiom estas la poŝtkosto al Ĉinujo? (What is the postage to China?)

aerpoŝto (airmail)

oni (one, they, people—indefinite)

enpoŝtigi (to mail, put in the mail)

poŝtkesto (mailbox)

Oni enpoŝtigas la leterojn en poŝtkeston. (One mails the letters in a mailbox.)

plumo (pen)

inko (ink)

Ĉu vi havas plumon kaj inkon? (Do you have pen and ink?)

krajono (pencil)

Ne, nur krajonon. (No, only a pencil.)

prunti (to lend, to borrow)

fontplumo (fountain pen)

Mi pruntos al vi mian fontplumon. (I will lend you my fountain pen.)

bonkora (kind, good-hearted)

Vi estas tre bonkora. (You are very kind.)

nenio (nothing)

Ho, estas nenio! (Oh, that's nothing!—gracious response)

plena (full)

Sed ĝi estas malplena; vi devos plenigi ĝin. (But it is empty; you will have to fill it.)

uzi (to use)

blua (blue)

blu-nigra (blue-black)

Uzu nur blu-nigran inkon, mi petas! (Use only blue-black ink, please!)

skrib-maŝino (typewriter—writing machine)

Ĉu vi povas skribi per skribmaŝino? (Can you write with a typewriter?)

sekretario (a secretary—person)

stenografio (stenography)

stenografiisto (stenographer)

feliĉa (happy)

scii (to know, to have knowledge of)

se (if)

Se mi havus sekretarion, kiu scius stenografion, mi estus feliĉa. (If I had a secretary who knew stenography, I would be happy.)

telefono (a telephone)

telegramo (a telegram)

amiko (friend)

sendi (to send)

Aŭ se mi estus riĉa, mi povus telefoni aŭ sendi telegramon al ĉiu amiko. (Or if I were rich, I could telephone or send a telegram to each friend.)

komenci (to begin, to start something)

dato (date)

Vi komencas leteron per dato. (You begin a letter with a date.)

je la 20-a de Julio, la 20-an de Julio (the 20th of July)

maniero (manner, way)

Jen estas diversaj manieroj por la saluto: (Here are various ways for the salutation:)

Estimata s-ro Bruno: (Esteemed Mr. Brown:)

Kara s-ro Bruno, (Dear Mr. Brown, —familiar address)

samideano (fellow Esperantist—one-with-the-same-idea)

Kara amiko, (Dear friend,)

Mia karulino, (My dear one,)

ami (to love)

amato, amatino (loved-one, beloved)

Amato mia, (Loved-one mine,)

pro (for, because of, on account of)

Dankon pro via letero. (Thank you for your letter.)

ricevi (to receive, to get)

respondi (to answer, to respond)

tuj (immediately)

Mi ricevis vian leteron hieraŭ, kaj mi tuj respondas. (I received your letter yesterday, and I answer immediately.)

kaj tiel plu (and so forth, etc.—abbreviation is **ktp.**)

dum (during)

fini (to finish, to bring to an end)

Vi finas la leteron per: (You end the letter with:)

Respekte via, (Respectfully yours,)

Sincere via, (Sincerely yours,)

koro (heart)

Kore, (Cordially, heartily)

Kun kora saluto, Koran saluton, (Cordial greetings,)

Kun multe da amo, (With much love,)

NOTES ON GRAMMAR

1. In an earlier lesson we saw the use of the indefinite preposition **je** with expressions of time and price. However, one of the sixteen rules of Esperanto grammar states that instead of **je** we may use the **-n** ending without a preposition. Thus, in expressions relating to duration of time, a point in time, measures, prices, the **je** can be eliminated: **Je la dudeka de Julio** equals **la dudekan de Julio. Mi iros al Bostono je lundo** equals **Mi iros al Bostono lundon. La lago estas longa je du kilometroj** equals **La lago estas du kilometrojn longa.** (The lake is two kilometers long.)

This use of **-n** has been expanded in Esperanto practice to include its use to replace any preposition: **Mi iras al Parizo** becomes **Mi iras Parizon. Mi promenis dum la tuta tago** becomes **Mi promenis la tutan tagon. En unu bela tago mi renkontis ŝin** equals **Unu belan tagon mi renkontis ŝin.**

Special Note: Of course, when the date, price, measure, etc. is the subject of the sentence, or the same as the subject, and the verb **esti** is used, neither **je** nor **-n** is needed: **Hodiaŭ estas la dudeka de Februaro. Okdek dolaroj estas en la glaso.**

2. Notice the verbs ending in **-us** in the sentence **Se mi havus sekretarion, mi estus feliĉa.** You do not have a secretary, but you base your statement on the supposition that if you had one, you would be happy.

And again in the sentence **Se mi estus riĉa, mi povus telefoni** . . . , presumably you are **not** rich. This **conditional** form of the verb, used in statements that are based on **supposition** or are **contrary to fact**, is formed in Esperanto by the verb ending -us. Note that the second part of the sentence depends on the first part, so that if the first verb is **-us**, the second must necessarily also be **-us**.

Esperanto also uses the -us form of the verb to soften an expression which might otherwise seem to be abrupt, such as: **Mi ĝojus iri.** (I should be happy to go.) **Estus pli bone ne fari tion.** (It would be better not to do that.) An **if**, of course, is usually implied in these instances: . . . if you wish me to, if you don't want to be sorry.

3. The preposition **per** is used to express the **means** by which an act is accomplished: **Mi skribis per plumo. Li kovris sin per kovrilo. Vi komencas leteron per saluto.** You should especially note that the English use of **with** is sometimes translated as **per** in Esperanto, and sometimes as **kun. Kun** indicates accompaniment: **Li promenis kun sia amiko. Li manĝis kun granda plezuro.**

4. It is sometimes necessary, and very convenient, to use a general impersonal expression such as: **One knows, People say, It is said** instead of being specific. **Oni** is the Esperanto pronoun to use in such cases: **Oni diras, ke li estas malriĉa.** (It is said that he is poor.) **Oni metas leteron en poŝtkeston.** (One puts a letter in a mailbox.)

5. The preposition **pro** expresses **cause** or **reason**: **Dankon pro via letero.** (Thanks because of your letter.) **Mi skribis la leteron pro vi.** (I wrote the letter because of you.) **Pro tio, mi ne povas iri kun vi.** (On that account, I cannot go with you.)

CONVERSATION

F-ino Parker is hurrying home when she meets sinjorojn Martel and Adams.

S-ro M.: Bonan tagon, fraŭlino! Kial vi tiel rapide iras?

F-ino P.: Ho, saluton, S-ro Martel kaj S-ro Adams! Mi rapidas hejmen.

S-ro A.: Ĉu vi ne povas promeni en la parko kun ni kelkajn minutojn?

F-ino P.: Mi bedaŭras, sinjoroj, sed mi devas rapidi hejmen por skribi kelkajn leterojn.

S-ro M.: Ĉu vi havas sufiĉe da papero, kovertoj, kaj poŝtmarkoj?

F-ino P.: Jes, mi havas ilin hejme sur la skribtablo, sed mi devas aĉeti aerpoŝtmarkojn. Kie oni povas aĉeti ilin?

S-ro M.: H-m-m . . . Aŭskultu, S-ro Adams! Kie oni povas aĉeti poŝt-markojn? Ĉu vi scias?

S-ro A.: H-m-m . . . jes . . . kie? Ŝajne, ni devas iri kun vi al la poŝtoficejo . . . Ĝi estas proksime al la parko. . . .

F-ino P.: Vi estas tre bonkoraj! (Ili komencas iri al la poŝtoficejo . . .) Ho, ve . . . mi ne ŝatas skribi leterojn. Se mi nur havus sekretarion, kiu farus ĉion tian, mi estus feliĉa!

S-ro A.: Ho . . . mi . . . fraŭlino . . , mi preferus sekretariinon!

F-ino P.: Kompreneble! Do . . . kial vi ne havas sekretariinon, S-ro?

S-ro A.: Ĉar mi ne estas riĉa, fraŭlino! Mi estas riĉa en la koro, sed tio ne sufiĉas por havi sekretariinon! Se mi nur estus riĉa, mi aĉetus aŭtomobilon, kaj mi veturus per ĝi al ĉiuj landoj de tiu ĉi malgranda tero.

F-ino P.: (Post kiam ŝi aĉetis la aerpoŝtmarkojn en la poŝtoficejo) Nun . . . pardonu, sinjoroj, sed mi absolute devas foriri. Koran dankon pro via intereso. Mi vidos vin morgaŭ! Ĝis revido!

NOW, YOU MAKE THE CONVERSATION

You decide to write a letter, you go into a friend's room to ask him if you may borrow his pen. You greet him, ask how he is. He says, fine. You ask how he likes the weather. He says, not too well, there's too much rain for him. You say you like the rain because you can then write letters. He answers that he doesn't like to write letters. He would prefer to have a secretary, or to send a telegram, or to telephone. You ask if he will lend you his fountain pen. He says, yes, but it's empty, that you will have to fill it. You say, O.K., but in that case may you borrow some ink too? He says, well . . . yes . . . if you will lend him some cigarettes.

A PRACTICAL TEST

Study the sample letters in **Part Three.** Then take a postcard or some letter-paper, and start your correspondence with another Esperantist right now! You will find addresses listed in the "American Esperantist" or your national Esperanto journal. Try these suggestions for your letter: Date; Esteemed Sir, Madam, Miss; I saw in the "American Esperantist" that you wish to correspond (korespondi) with American Esperantists. I am a new Esperantist, and I am happy to begin my correspondence with you. I am interested in art, music, philosophy. .. . I live in a small, large city . . . etc. Go on to describe your city a bit, what you do, whether you have a family, etc., etc. Then close with an appropriate expression, and be sure to give your address very plainly. Now, put a special stamp on the envelope, and send your letter to a fellow Esperantist in some other country!

LESSON XIII (DEK-TRIA LECIONO)

PREPARATIONS FOR AN APPOINTMENT (Feminine).

Heleno pretigas sin por rendevuo kun Karlo. Amikino Doroteo estas kun ŝi en la ĉambro.

rendevuo (appointment, 'date', rendezvous)
lavi (to wash)
lavistino (laundress)
re- (again, back, re-)
H.: Ĉu la lavistino resendis mian bluan veston? (Did the laundress send back my blue dress?)
D.: Ne, ŝi diris, ke ŝi resendos ĝin morgaŭ. (No, she said she would send it back tomorrow.)
griza (grey)
jupo (skirt)
H.: Do, mi devos porti la grizan jupon. (So, I will have to wear the grey skirt.)
blanka (white)
ĉemizo (blouse, shirt)
taŭgi (to be suitable, to serve the purpose)
eble (possibly, probably)
Kaj la blanka ĉemizo eble taŭgos. (And the white blouse will probably be suitable.)
frizistino (hairdresser)
buklo (a curl)
haro (a hair)
D.: La frizistino bele bukligis viajn harojn. (The hairdresser beautifully curled your hair.)
fingro (finger)
masaĝi (to massage)

haŭto (skin)
kapo (head)
dolori (to pain, to ache)
H.: Ŝiaj fingroj masaĝis mian haŭton ĝis la tuta kapo doloras! (Her fingers massaged my skin until my whole head aches!)
virino (woman)
suferi (to suffer, to endure)
la beleco (beauty)
pacience (patiently)
ĉio (everything, all things)
D.: La virino suferas ĉion por la beleco! (Womankind suffers everything for beauty!)
helpi (to help, to assist)
pudro (powder)
vizaĝo (face)
kombi (to comb)
kombilo (a comb)
Jen, mi helpos vin: pudro por la vizaĝo, kombilo por kombi la harojn. (Here, I will help you: powder for your face, a comb to comb your hair.)
nervema (nervous)
H.: Ho, dankon! Mi estas tre nervema. (Oh, thanks! I am very nervous.)
vango (cheek)
ruĝeco (redness)
vang-ruĝo (rouge, cheek rouge)

78]

D.: **La vangoj bezonas iom da ruĝeco: jen la vang-ruĝo.** (The cheeks need a little redness: here, the rouge.)
lipo (lip)
lip-ruĝo (lipstick, lip rouge)
Kaj sur la lipoj iom da lipruĝo. (And on the lips some lipstick.)
manpoŝo (handbag, pocketbook)
H.: **Nun, kie estas mia manpoŝo?** (Now, where is my handbag?)

tualet-tablo (dressing table, vanity)
D.: **Mi ne scias. Ĉu ne sur la tualet-tablo?** (I don't know. Isn't it on the dressing table?)
planko (floor)
fali (to fall)
H.: **Ho, jen—ĝi falis sur la plankon.** (Oh, here—it fell on the floor.)
Nu, mi fine estas preta. Adiaŭ kara mia! (Well, I am finally ready. Goodbye, my dear!)

NOTES ON GRAMMAR

1. The prefix **re-** indicates the return of a person or thing to a previous place or state: **reveni** (to return, to come back), **redoni** (to give back), **resendi** (to send back). It also shows repetition of an act: **revidi** (to see again, re-see), **rekomenci** (to begin again, re-commence). It is like the English **re-** in these two respects.

2. Note that the word **tuta** means complete, entire, the whole of anything: **la tuta mondo** (the whole world), **tute** (entirely, completely).

3. Here are three new suffixes for consideration and study:

a. **-ec-** forms words that express abstract ideas of qualities or states shown in the root: **beleco** (beauty), **boneco** (goodness), **juneco** (youth), **amikeco** (friendship). As a separate word **eco** means a quality, a characteristic: **La ecoj de la homo.** (The characteristics of man.)

b. **-il-** indicates the instrument or tool for performing what is expressed by the root: **kombi** (to comb), **kombilo** (a comb); **ŝlosi** (to lock), **ŝlosilo** (a key); **kovri** (to cover), **kovrilo** (a blanket).

c. **-em-** indicates a tendency, inclination or bent towards what is expressed in the root: **nervema** (nervous, tendency to nerves), **dormema** (sleepy), **timema** (timid), **pacema** (peaceful), **ŝanĝema** (changeable).

4. Notice that the article **la** is used before nouns indicating a whole class, substance or quality in a universal sense, such as: **La viro estas pli forta ol la virino.** (Man is stronger than woman.) **La virino suferas ĉion por beleco.** (Womankind suffers everything for beauty.) **La homo estas ŝanĝema.** (The human being is changeable.)

5. The article **la** is often used instead of the possessive **mia, via, sia** in sentences where the possessor is already sufficiently indicated: **Mi kombis la harojn.** (I combed my hair.) **Ĉu vi pudris la vizaĝon?** (Did you powder your face?) **La tuta kapo doloras.** (My whole head aches.) **Mi amas la patron.** (I love my father.) If, however, one wishes to emphasize possession, then the possessive is used.

CONVERSATION

Heleno decides to visit the hairdresser

Frizistino: Bonan matenon, fraŭlino! Ĉu mi povas helpi vin?

Heleno: Jes . . . bonvolu lavi miajn harojn, kaj bukligi ilin bele, ĉar mi devas iri al Esperanto-kunveno hodiaŭ nokte.

Frizistino: Certe, fraŭlino . . . sidu kelkajn minutojn, dum mi pretigas seĝon por vi. Mi petas, fraŭlino, ĉu eble vi deziras masaĝon por la haŭto de la kapo kaj de la vizaĝo? Ĝi helpos multe por freŝigi vin . . . kaj por fari vin pli bela! Kompreneble, vi jam estas bela . . . sed iom pli . . . vi scias . . . ne malhelpos!

Heleno: H-m-m . . . mi ne havas multe da tempo . . . sed ŝajne estas bona ideo. . .

Frizistino: Vi ne bedaŭros ĝin, fraŭlino, ĉar tie ĉi ni havas la plej bonajn servojn. Jen via seĝo!

(Heleno sidiĝas. La frizistino metas grandan tukon sur ŝin kaj komencas masaĝi la kapon kaj la vizaĝon. . . . Dume, ŝi parolas, parolas, parolas senĉese. Fine, Heleno diras:)

Heleno: Sinjorino, tio sufiĉas! Mi petas! Alie, mia tuta kapo doloros. Aj . . . la tuta kapo nun doloras! Mi ne povas sidi ĉi tie dum vi bukligas la harojn. . . . Fakte, mi ne scias . . . kio estas pli malbona, havi mian vizaĝon kia ĝi estis antaŭe, aŭ aŭskulti al vi du horojn! Mi petas . . . donu al mi kombilon. Mi kombos la harojn. Mi devas foriri rapide. . . . Mi havas rendevuon. . . .

Frizistino: Sed, fraŭlino . . . fraŭlino! Vi bezonas pudron, lipruĝon, kaj. . . .

Heleno: Ne . . . mi bezonas nenion! Vi diris, ke post la masaĝo mi estos multe pli bela. Do. . . .

Frizistino: Sed, fraŭlino . . . mi ne finis. . . .

Heleno: Ne finis . . . ? Dio helpu min! . . . Mi ne deziras esti pli bela. Mi sufiĉe plaĉas al mia Karlo! Adiaŭ!

NEW WORDS FROM OLD IDEAS

Using the suffix -ec- added to words already learned in previous lessons, translate the following English words into Esperanto:

goodness	certainty	sweetness	warmth
duality	bigness	purity	rubbery
thickness	richness	gladness	earliness
brightness	freshness	rapidity	paternity
motherhood	friendship	nearness	hostility

See if you understand the meaning of the following words formed with the suffix -em-. Get into the habit of making up your own words in Esperanto from the raw material of roots, suffixes, and endings.

parolema	farema	esperema	manĝemulo
dankema	vojaĝema	sidema	kolektema
biciklema	purigema	pluvema	trinkema
dancemulo	ventema	komprenema	servema

TRANSLATION

Translate the following sentences into Esperanto. This is in the nature of a review.

1. Patience is bitter, but its fruit is sweet.
2. Possibly, I shall wear my green blouse.
3. She gave it to her parents.
4. Hope is the poor man's bread.
5. I want to buy some rouge and lipstick.
6. What kind of powder do you like?
7. In an airplane one can travel very fast.
8. This is a big country, but we can travel from one end to the other in a few days.
9. One day I met an old lady in the street.
10. We traveled for an entire day.
11. Womankind seems to be talkative.
12. We all know the goodness of that man.
13. Please give me six combs and two toothbrushes.
14. Will you lend me your watch?
15. Is your dressing table white or grey?

LESSON XIV (DEK-KVARA LECIONO)

PREPARATION FOR AN APPOINTMENT (Masculine)

En la hejmo de Karlo kaj lia amiko Roberto.

amanto (a lover, one who loves)

R.: Kien vi iras, mia juna amanto? Where are you going, my young lover?)

aranĝi (to arrange)

teatro (theatre)

K.: Mi aranĝis rendevuon kun Heleno; ni iros al la teatro. (I arranged a 'date' with Helen; we are going to the theatre.)

razi (to shave)

R.: Vi devos razi vin, ĉu ne? (You will have to shave, won't you?)

razilo (razor)

K.: Kompreneble! Kie estas la razilo? (Of course! Where is the razor?)

raz-klingo (razor-blade)

demando (a question)

Ĉu mi havas razklingon? Tio estas la demando! (Do I have a razor-blade? That is the question!)

tajloro (tailor)

Ĉu la tajloro resendis mian bluan pantalonon? (Did the tailor send back my blue pants?)

kravato (necktie)

Ĉu vi pruntedonos al mi vian bluan kravaton? (Will you lend me your blue necktie?)

Kaj eble puran ĉemizon? (And perhaps a clean shirt?)

kolo (neck)

R.: Via kolo estas pli granda ol la mia. (Your neck is bigger than mine.)

kolumo (collar)

ĝusta (exact, correct)

mezuro (measure, size)

La kolumo ne havas la ĝustan mezuron. (The collar is not the correct size.)

K.: Kian mezuron ĝi havas? (What size is it?)

colo (inch)

centimetro (centimeter)

R.: Dek-kvin colojn. Tridek-ok centimetrojn. (Fifteen inches. Thirty-eight centimeters.)

K.: Ĝuste bone! (Exactly right!)

forgesi (to forget)

parfum-akvo (cologne water, eau de cologne)

nazo (nose)

naz-tuko (handkerchief)

R.: Ne forgesu meti iom da parfumakvo sur la naztukon! (Don't forget to put some eau de cologne on your handkerchief!)

broso (brush)

K.: Nun, kie estas la broso? (Now, where is the brush?)

okulo (eye)

brili (to shine)

brilanta (shining)

R.: Rekte antaŭ viaj brilantaj okuloj! (Right before your shining eyes!)

laste (lastly)

poluri (to polish)

K.: Kaj laste mi poluros la ŝuojn. (And lastly I shall shine my shoes.)

piedo (foot)

dancanta (dancing)

R.: Ho, jes, brilantaj ŝuoj por dancantaj piedoj! (Oh, yes, shining shoes for dancing feet!)

amatino (beloved—feminine)
Kaj ne forgesu florojn por la amatino! (And don't forget flowers for the beloved!)
silenti (to be silent, to be quiet)
ĝeni (to bother, to disturb)
K.: Silentu, vi ĝenulo, vi. . . ! (Be quiet, you nuisance, you. . . !)

kuri (to run)
tamen (nevertheless, however)
R.: Tamen, se vi deziras esti amata, aŭskultu al mi! (Nevertheless, if you wish to be loved, listen to me!)
Dume Karlo forkuris. (Meanwhile, Karl has run away.)

NOTES ON GRAMMAR

1. The word **eble** (possibly) is formed from the Esperanto suffix **-ebl-** meaning **able to be**, that can be whatever is indicated in the root: **videbla** (visible), **manĝebla** (edible, eatable) **kompreneble** (understandably, of course), **ŝanĝebla** (changeable, that can be changed), **neŝanĝebla** (unalterable, immutable). Note that **-ebl-** often corresponds to English **able** or **ible**.

2. In the word **kolumo** (collar), the **-um-** part is a general suffix. It serves to form words where the relationship to the root-word is rather indefinite. Most of the **-um-** words should be learned by heart. Here are a few of the most frequently used: **manumo** (cuff), **aerumi** (to aerate), **plenumi** (to fulfill), **proksimume** (approximately), **gustumi** (to taste something), **amindumi** (to court, make love to), **malvarmumo** (a cold), **mastrumi** (to keep house).

3. Notice the word **pruntedonos** in the sentence **Ĉu vi pruntedonos al mi vian bluan kravaton?** In practice, Esperantists usually say **pruntedoni** (to give in loan, to lend) and **pruntepreni** (to take in loan, to borrow), instead of just **prunti**, in order to make the action perfectly clear.

4. In the words **amanto, dancanta, brilanta**, the **-ant-** part is a suffix which indicates an action or condition that is going on **at the present time, at the moment** (present active participle). It corresponds to **-ing** in English. With the **-o** ending the meaning is **a person** who is doing whatever is expressed by the root: **amanto** (one who is loving, a lover), **lernanto** (a learner), **aŭskultanto** (listener). The **-a** ending makes the word an adjective, describing the action of someone or something: **brilantaj okuloj** (shining eyes), **dancantaj piedoj** (dancing feet), **falanta akvo** (falling water).

5. The suffix **-at-**, in contrast to **-ant-**, indicates that the person or thing is being affected by the action of the root (present passive participle). The **-o** ending again indicates a person: **amato, amatino** (one who is loved), **konato** (one known, an acquaintance), **instruato** (one being instructed, a

pupil). As an adjective: **la amata knabo** (the beloved boy), **skribata letero** (the letter being written), **permesataj faroj** (permitted deeds). **Special note:** Did you chance to notice that the key to the **present** participles is the vowel -a-? It thus corresponds to the simple **present** tense of the Esperanto verb: **skribAs, skribAnta, skribAta.**

CONVERSATION

Karlo eniras la ĉambron, kie li loĝas kune kun la amiko, Roberto.

Karlo: Kie vi estas, Roberto? Aŭskultu! Ĉu la lavistino resendis la vestajojn?

Roberto: Ne ĝis nun. Kial?

Karlo: Mi bezonas novan ĉemizon!

Roberto: Mi pruntedonos al vi unu el la miaj.

Karlo: Vi estas tre bonkora, amiko . . . sed . . . kiom ĝi kostos?

Roberto: Ne kostos monon, kompreneble . . . sed kostos interŝanĝon! Mi pruntedonos al vi mian bluan ĉemizon, se vi pruntedonos al mi vian ruĝan kravaton.

Karlo: Nu . . . ĉu jes? Kien vi iros?

Roberto: Mi kaj fraŭlino Anjo iros por danci en la parkdancejo.

Karlo: Interese! Estas tie, kie oni ludas tiun sving-muzikon, ĉu ne? Mi ŝatus iri ankaŭ.

Roberto: Vi scias, amiko mia, la malnovan dirajon: "Inter geamantoj tri estas tro multe!"

Karlo: Do . . . mi telefonos al Heleno . . . kaj ni estos kvar!

Roberto: Vi havas respondon al ĉiu demando, ĉu ne? Nu . . . bone . . . sed se vi iros kun ni, vi devas razi vin.

Karlo: Kompreneble! Kiam mi parolas pri rendevuo, ĉio estas aranĝata bele, bone, frue, ĉarme, rapide kaj feliĉe!

Roberto: Ĉesu! Ĉesu, parolemulo! Kaj donu al mi la kravaton kaj naztukon.

Karlo: Kun plezuro, sinjoro. Jen . . . la razilo bone funkcias . . . kaj la kapo bone funkcias. Mi devas poluri la ŝuojn. . . . Sur la naztukon mi metos iom da parfumakvo . . . kaj mi aĉetos florojn por la amatino!

Roberto: H-m-m . . . kaj kion vi uzas kiel monon?

Karlo: Ha! Tio estas facila demando, amiko mia. Mi prunteprenos la monon de vi!

RESPONDU AL LA DEMANDO

1. Kial Karlo demandis pri la lavistino?
2. Kien iros Roberto?

3. Kian kravaton Karlo pruntedonos al Roberto?
4. Kial Karlo deziris iri al la dancejo?
5. Ĉu vi ŝatas sving-muzikon? Kial?
6. Kiel Karlo aranĝas rendevuon?

NOW, YOU MAKE THE CONVERSATION
S-ro A, getting ready to go out, calls to his roommate, S-ro B.

A: Do you know where my pants are?
B: No, I don't know. Probably in the chest of drawers.
A: No, they aren't. Oh, here they are, on the chair. Now, where is a clean shirt?
B: The laundry hasn't sent it back.
A: But I must have a clean shirt!
B: Well, you will have to wash a shirt. I don't have it to lend to you.
A: I shall wear the old green shirt, and cover it with my jacket. Do you like to see shining shoes, my friend?
B: Well . . . yes . . . Why do you ask?
A: Will you shine my shoes for me while I shave?
B: Absolutely not! I am not your servant!
A: Very well. But I shall probably be late for my 'date'. Did you see my brush?
B: I think it fell on the floor behind the table.
A: What a fine place for it! But . . . there is exactly where it is!
B: (As A starts to leave:) Did you take a clean handkerchief? And don't forget to send flowers to your beloved!
A: That is a good idea! I'll telephone to the florist. Well . . . I am all ready. I'll be back late. So long!

MALGRANDA ŜERCO (a little joke)

Malgranda knabo iras en vendejon kaj diras: "Mi deziras kolumon por mia patro."
Vendisto: "Unu kiel la mia?"
Knabo: "Ne, puran!"

KONSILO POR EDZO (advice for a husband)

Nova Edzo: Mia edzino preferas trinki kafon matene, sed mi preferas teon.
Malnova Edzo: Ne ĝenu vin, amiko! Post kelka tempo vi alkutimiĝos al la kafo!

LESSON XV (DEK-KVINA LECIONO)

LA UNIVERSALA ESPERANTO-KONGRESO

Each year, the Universal Esperanto Association holds a Congress in some part of the world, with attendance up to five thousand delegates from over fifty different nations.

salono (salon, hall)
La granda salono estas plena je homoj. (The large hall is full of people.)
standardo (flag, standard of a country or group)
flirti (to flutter, to float)
amaso (a mass, heap, pile)
hom-amaso (crowd)
La verda standardo flirtas super la homamaso. (The green standard flutters above the crowd.)
podio (platform, podium)
reprezenti (to represent)
registaro (government)
nacio (nation)
Sur la podio sidas reprezentantoj por la registaroj de tridek nacioj. (On the platform sit representatives for the governments of thirty nations.)
loka (local)
komitato (committee)
La prezidanto de la Loka Kongresa Komitato (LKK) malfermas la kunvenon: (The president of the Local Congress Committee opens the meeting:)
Bonvenon! (Welcome!)
bonvenigi (to welcome, to make welcome)
Gesinjoroj, estimataj reprezentantoj, mi bonvenigas vin! (Ladies and Gentlemen, Esteemed Representatives, I welcome you!)
honoro (honor)
gasto (guest)

Ni havas la honoron gastigi vin en nia urbo. (We have the honor to entertain you in our city.)
vivi (to live, to be alive)
pruvo (proof)
inter (among)
popolo (people, inhabitants of one country)
vere (really, truly)
Nia kongreso estas vivanta pruvo, ke la internacia, interpopola interlingvo vere funkcias. (Our congress is living proof that the international, inter-people interlanguage really works.)
kapti (to catch, to capture, to take)
Ni deziras, ke vi kaptu la okazon por amikiĝi kun samideanoj. (We desire that you grasp the occasion to become friends with fellow-Esperantists.)
elekti (to elect, to choose, to select)
Ni nun elektos la Kongres-Prezidanton. (We will now elect the Congress President.)
laŭ (according to, in accordance with)
konsilo (advice, counsel)
proponi (to propose)
ĉefa (chief, main)
kandidato (candidate)
Laŭ konsilo de la komitato, S-ro Marko estas proponata kiel la ĉefa kandidato. (In accordance with the advice of the committee, Mr. Mark is proposed as the chief candidate.)

koni (to know, to be acquainted with)

S-ro Marko estas bone konata al vi ĉiuj. (Mr. Mark is well known to you all.)

Se ne estas alia propono . . . (If there is no other proposal . . .)

voĉdono (vote by voice—voice-giving)

Ni elektos laŭ voĉdono. (We shall elect by voice-vote.)

subteni (to support)

Tiuj, kiuj subtenas S-ron Marko, respondu per "jes" . . . (Those, who support Mr. Mark, answer with "yes" . . .)

Kontraŭe? (To the contrary?)

Neniu! (No one!)

akcepti (to accept)

Do, S-ro Marko, akceptu la prezidantecon! (Therefore, Mr. Mark, accept the presidency!)

parolado (a speech)

Sekvas parolado de la Kongres-Prezidanto. (A speech by the Congress President follows.)

estro (leader, head)

estraranoj (officials of an organization)

Sekvas salutado per la estraranoj de la Universala Esperanto-Asocio. (Greetings by the officials of the Universal Esperanto Association follow.)

NOTES ON GRAMMAR

1. Note that the -u form of the Esperanto verb is also used in indirect phrases that express wish, entreaty or command, introduced by the connecting word **ke** (that): **Ni deziras, ke vi kaptu la okazon. . . . Mi konsilas, ke vi parolu malrapide. Mi petas, ke vi sendu la leteron. Estas necese, ke ĉiu aŭskultu.** You can see the reason for this usage when you consider that if the wish, entreaty or order were said directly, the -u form would be used as a matter of course: **Kaptu la okazon. Sendu la leteron. Parolu malrapide. Ĉiu aŭskultu!**

2. The suffix -ad- indicates that an action or condition **continues for some time**, and is not just momentary: **parolo** (a word), **parolado** (a speech); **saluto** (a greeting), **salutado** (continued greetings); **viziti** (to visit), **vizitadi** (to frequent). Nouns with -ad- are often equivalent to -ing words in English denoting arts or practices: **danco** (a dance), **dancado** (dancing); **kanto** (a song), **kantado** (singing) **fumi** (to smoke), **fumado** (smoking, habit of smoking).

3. The word **estro** is formed from the suffix -estr- meaning **leader, ruler, head** of something. Many words are formed from this suffix: **urbestro** (mayor), **ŝipestro** (captain of a ship), **lernejestro** (principal of a school).

4. The suffix -an- indicates an **inhabitant** or a **member**: **policano** (a member of the police, a policeman), **urbano** (a city dweller), **kamparano** (a country-fellow), **Bostonano** (a Bostonian), **Luterano** (a Lutheran),

Usonano (an inhabitant of the United States). **Ano** alone means a member: **Mi estas ano de la Esperanto-klubo**.

5. Special note: From the two suffixes above plus the suffix **-ar-** you notice that the word **estraranoj** is formed: **estr-** (leader), **-ar-** (group of), **-an-** (member), **estraranoj** (members of the group of leaders). You will find many words in Esperanto constructed from a number of suffixes or with a root and a number of suffixes. So when you meet up with new words, try dissecting them. Usually, you will find it best to start at the end of the word and work backwards. This agglutinate (gluing together) quality of Esperanto makes it especially well liked by the oriental peoples, whose language habit is also the combining of syllables into ideas and sentences. Just for fun, figure out this word. (We don't think you will meet it in your reading however!): **malriĉegulinarejego**. (mal-riĉ-eg-ul-in-ar-ej-eg-o).

6. In forming compound words in Esperanto, the ending **-o** may be used to connect the two roots, if that makes the resulting word sound better or easier to pronounce: **lernolibro** sounds better than **lernlibro**; **librovendisto** better than **librvendisto**; **fervojostacio** or **fervojstacio**; **fontoplumo** or **fontplumo**.

7. You will note that the form **-ata** is used with the present tense of the verb **esti** to form a compound verb which expresses an act or condition as affecting the subject of the verb (passive voice) at the present time: **S-ro Marko estas proponata**. (Mr. Mark is proposed.) **La letero estas skribata**. (The letter is being written.) Esperanto has a system of present, past, and future participles which may be combined with the present, past, or future forms of the verb **esti** to form a series of compound verbs of very precise meaning, used when exactness is needed. An analysis of these compound tenses will be found on pages immediately following this lesson.

8. The word **neniu** meaning **no one** is a part of a series of negative words in Esperanto beginning with **nen-**. These words follow the same system as the question words, which begin with **k-**. The endings of all the words in the system (the correlatives) indicate the meanings, and the initial letters identify the type of word:

Question	Demonstrative	Negative	General
kiu (who)	tiu (that one)	neniu (no one)	ĉiu (everyone)
kio (what)	tio (that)	nenio (nothing)	ĉio (everything)
kia (what kind)	tia (that kind)	nenia (no kind)	ĉia (every kind)
kie (where)	tie (there)	nenie (nowhere)	ĉie (everywhere)

The following diagram gives the complete system for your reference, but don't bother to learn it all at once. Take any path and follow arrows to find the meaning of any certain combination. For example, take the indefinite, which has no beginning letter: iu (any person), io (anything), ie (any place), etc.

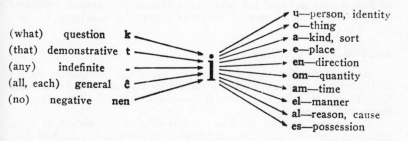

(what)	question	k
(that)	demonstrative	t
(any)	indefinite	-
(all, each)	general	ĉ
(no)	negative	nen

i

u—person, identity
o—thing
a—kind, sort
e—place
en—direction
om—quantity
am—time
el—manner
al—reason, cause
es—possession

NEW WORDS FROM OLD IDEAS

Look over the previous word lists, and find at least 15 roots to which the suffix -an may be added to form a new word. Also find at least 10 roots to which estro might be added to form a compound word.

WRITE A LETTER

Imagine that you have just attended one of the Universal Esperanto Congresses. You write a letter to an Esperanto friend about it. Tell about the opening session, who spoke, did you like the speech. How many government representatives were there. Did your country have a representative. Could you understand all the speeches. Was it interesting to see and hear so many different peoples speaking together and all talking Esperanto. Tell about the excursions you made, the various sights, and then tell about the final dance—called "La Internacia Kostum-Balo." How were the people dressed. How were you dressed. With whom did you prefer to dance most. Make it up as you go along. Write as much as you can. Put in everything you've learned so far!

COMPOUND TENSES OF THE VERB IN ESPERANTO

The **compound tenses** of the verb in Esperanto make it possible to be very precise in meaning. Ordinarily, however, the simple tense forms are sufficiently precise, and are most used. Compound verbs are formed by using one of the tenses of the verb **esti**, plus a participle. For example: the auxiliary verb **estas** combined with the participle **manĝanta** make a compound verb **estas manĝanta** (is eating), which is very precise about the time and state of the action—someone is eating, right now, at this moment. The simple tense form **manĝas** (eats, or is eating) is less precise, in that it may or may not mean an action at this precise moment—dependent upon the context of the entire sentence or statement.

ACTIVE PARTICIPLES

Active participles show the state of the action undertaken by the subject of the sentence. They are formed by adding the suffixes: **-anta** (present—action going on), **-inta** (past—action finished), **-onta** (future—action to be undertaken).

Suppose we describe the dining habits of a certain person. It is his custom to dine always at 6:00 p.m. We observe him at 5:00 p.m., 6:00 p.m., and 7:00 p.m. Then the next day we tell someone what he did yesterday. And then we predict what he will do tomorrow. We wish to be very precise. Here is a chart which describes the dining habits of **la sinjoro**, and shows the use of the active participles in Esperanto:

The Subject	Time of Our Observation	State of His Action

We observe him at these hours, and describe the state of action:

hodiaŭ, je la 5-a, la sinjoro	estas	manĝonta
hodiaŭ, je la 6-a, la sinjoro	estas	manĝanta
hodiaŭ, je la 7-a, la sinjoro	estas	manĝinta

We tell what we observed yesterday, and describe the state of action:

hieraŭ, je la 5-a, la sinjoro	estis	manĝonta
hieraŭ, je la 6-a, la sinjoro	estis	manĝanta
hieraŭ, je la 7-a, la sinjoro	estis	manĝinta

We predict what we will observe tomorrow, and describe the action:

morgaŭ, je la 5-a, la sinjoro	estos	manĝonta
morgaŭ, je la 6-a, la sinjoro	estos	manĝanta
morgaŭ, je la 7-a, la sinjoro	estos	manĝinta

Note: Don't try to translate these tenses into complicated English forms. Just think directly of the Esperanto meaning and you can't go wrong! Remember that **estas** (present), **estis** (past), **estos** (future), simply express the point in time from which we view some state of action.

PASSIVE PARTICIPLES

Passive participles show the state of the action that affects the subject of the sentence. They are formed by adding the suffixes: -ata (present—is being affected), -ita (past—was affected), -ota (future—will be affected).

Suppose we describe the same dinner, but this time we'll concentrate on what happens to the meat **la sinjoro** eats. He happens to be inordinately fond of meat! Here is a chart showing the use of passive participles:

The Subject	Time of Our Observation	State of Action, Affects Subject

We observe the meat at these hours, and describe the state of action:

hodiaŭ, je la 5-a, la viando	estas	manĝota
hodiaŭ, je la 6-a, la viando	estas	manĝata
hodiaŭ, je la 7-a, la viando	estas	manĝita

We tell what we observed yesterday, and describe the state of action:

hieraŭ, je la 5-a, la viando	estis	manĝota
hieraŭ, je la 6-a, la viando	estis	manĝata
hieraŭ, je la 7-a, la viando	estis	manĝita

We predict what we will observe tomorrow, and describe the action:

morgaŭ, je la 5-a, la viando	estos	manĝota
morgaŭ, je la 6-a, la viando	estos	manĝata
morgaŭ, je la 7-a, la viando	estos	manĝita

ADJECTIVE PARTICIPLES

Adjective participles are practical and useful when they serve to shorten expressions, and make for more fluency. For example:

La knabo, kiu staras tie, ploras. = La knabo, staranta tie, ploras. La viro, kiu venis hieraŭ, estas mia frato. = La viro, veninta hieraŭ, estas mia frato. La aŭtomobilo, kiu veturos al Parizo, estas je la hotelo. = La aŭtomobilo, veturonta al Parizo, estas je la hotelo.

ADVERBIAL PARTICIPLES

Adverbial participles are very frequently used in Esperanto. They indicate the relationship between the participle and the chief verb, and always refer to the subject. They shorten many expressions:

Dum mi laboras, mi kantas. = Laborante, mi kantas. Dum ŝi kisis, ŝi fermis la okulojn. = Kisante, ŝi fermis la okulojn. Post kiam mi ricevis vian leteron, mi respondas. = Ricevinte vian leteron, mi respondas. Antaŭ ol manĝi, li trinkis glason da biero. = Manĝonte, li trinkis glason da biero.

COMPLETE GRAMMAR OF ESPERANTO

The Sixteen Fundamental Rules

1. There is no indefinite article; there is only a definite article **la**, alike for all sexes, cases and numbers.

2. All **nouns** end in **o**. To form the plural **j** is added. There are only two cases: nominative and accusative; the latter is obtained from the nominative by simply adding **n**.

3. All **adjectives** end in **a**. Case and number as for nouns. The **comparative** is made by means of the word **pli**, with the conjunction **ol**; the **superlative** by **plej**.

4. The fundamental **numerals** (not declined) are: **unu, du, tri, kvar, kvin, ses, sep, ok, naŭ, dek, cent, mil**. Tens and hundreds are formed by simple junction of the numerals. To mark the ordinal, **a** is added; the multiple, **obl**; the fractional, **on**; the collective, **op**.

5. The personal **pronouns** are: **mi, vi, li, ŝi, ĝi, si, ni, vi, ili, oni**. Possessives are formed by adding **a**. Declension as for nouns.

6. The **verb** undergoes no change with regard to person or number. Forms of the verb: present time takes the termination **-as**; past, **-is**; future, **-os**; conditional, **-us**; imperative, **-u**; infinitive, **-i**. Active participles, **-ant, -int, -ont**. Passive participles, **-at, -it, -ot**.

7. The **adverb** ends in **e**; comparison as for adjectives.

8. All **prepositions** govern the nominative.

9. Every word is **pronounced** as it is **spelled.**

10. The **accent** is always on the next-to-the-last syllable.

11. **Compound words** are formed by simple junction of the words.

12. When another **negative** word is present the word **ne** is left out.

13. To show **direction towards**, words take the termination of the accusative.

14. Each **preposition** has a definite meaning; but if the direct sense does not indicate which it should be, we use the preposition **je**.

15. **International words** undergo no change in Esperanto, beyond conforming to its orthography

16. The **final vowel** of the noun and the article may sometimes be dropped and be replaced by an apostrophe.

List of Prefixes and Suffixes

(See the Esperanto dictionary for definitions and examples.)

bo-	-aĉ	-eg	-ig	-ist
dis-	-ad	-ej	-iĝ	-obl
ek-	-aĵ	-em	-il	-on
eks-	-an	-er	-in	-op
ge-	-ar	-estr	-ind	-uj
mal-	-ebl	-et	-ing	-ul
mis-	-ec	-id	-ism	-um
re-				

THE MODERN
ESPERANTO READER

****

RIDU KAJ RESTU SANA

Anekdoto pri Profesoro kaj Studento

La telefono de la lernejo sonoris. La profesoro iris al la telefono.

Profesoro: Jen, Profesoro Martelo!

Telefonanto: Mi deziras informi vin, ke Karlo ne povas viziti la lernejon hodiaŭ, ĉar li estas malsana.

Profesoro: Tion mi tre bedaŭras; mi deziras bonan resaniĝon!—Kiu estas ĉe la telefono?

Telefonanto: Mia patro!

Akcidento

Vi aspektas terure, Jozefo. Ĉu vi havis akcidenton?

Jes, teruran akcidenton, kaj nur ĉar la kelnero ne bone komprenis Esperanton.

Ĉar la kelnero ne bone komprenis Esperanton? Kiel do?

Hieraŭ mi iris kun Fraŭlino Anjo al restoracio por vespermanĝi. Anjo trovis muŝon en la supo. Ŝi vokis la kelneron kaj kriis kolere: "Forigu la insekton!" Kaj li prenis min kaj ĵetis min malsupren du ŝtuparojn. . . .

Ĉu Vere?

Svisa kamparano, kiu parolis nur france, vojaĝis al Britujo; amiko informiĝis:

Sed, amiko, tie en Britujo . . . ĉu vi povis paroli al la britoj?

Mi? KomprenEble! Mi povis bone paroli al ili . . . sed la britoj ne povis respondi al mi. . . !

Ĉe la Doktoro

Kuracisto: Sinjoro, via kazo estas tre interesa. Ĝi riĉigos la medicinan sciencon.

Paciento: Ve, kaj mi pensis, ke ĝi kostos al mi nur kvin aŭ dek dolarojn!

Virto

Se mi vidus homon, kiu batas azenon, kaj mi ĉesigus lin, kiun virton mi praktikus?

Fratamon!

"SUZI"

GEORGE S. RAYMOND

En nia domo ni havas ban-kuvon. Ĝi estas granda, blanka kaj kelkfoje glita! Ankaŭ ni havas katinon, kiu estas la patrino de du belaj katidoj. Ankaŭ ni havas infanojn.

Hieraŭ vespere okazis, ke unu el la infanoj enlitiĝis kaj lasis la ban-kuvon duonplena de akvo; kaj la katino, tre ruza besto, kaŝis sin kiam venis la tempo por iri al ŝia lito, kaj, kvankam ĉiuj vokis ŝin, neniu povis trovi ŝin. Tial ŝi povis dormi en la domo anstataŭ en la ĉevalejo, kie ŝi devus dormi.

Tio estus sufiĉe bona, sed je la mateno, tre frue, Sinjorino Katino soifis kaj kaŝvagis ĉirkaŭe por serĉi ion por trinki. Ne trovante lakton sur la tablo, nek akvon ie en la kuirejo, ŝi suprensaltis kaj ektrovis la akvon en la ban-kuvo.

Tiun matenon, kiel ĉiumatene, mi leviĝis frue; tial mi vidis tion kion ŝi faris. Tre malsaĝe ŝi penis stari sur la rando kaj trinki el la ban-kuvo. Siaj akraj ungoj, utilaj por grimpi arbojn aŭ kapti musojn, ne konvenis por alkroĉiĝi al tia glata ebeno. Kompreneble, ŝi enfalis, la kompatinda kreito, kaj mi, pardonu min Dio, mi ridis!

Sed mi vere kompatis ŝin, kaj mi permesis, ke ŝi sidu en nia plej bona seĝo dum ŝi sekigis sian felon, ĉar mi tre multe ŝatas ŝin. Ŝi estas gracia, kaj ŝia nomo estas "Suzi." Unufoje, mi konis tre belan fraŭlinon nomitan "Suzi"!

NOVAJ ĈAPELOJ

DORIS TAPPAN CONNOR

Personaro: Karlo (la edzo, mezaĝa, en simpla vesto); Lilio (la edzino, mezaĝa, frivola).

Necesaj objektoj: Ĉapelujo, en kiu estas virinaj ĉapeloj, unu kovrita per violetoj, la alia per margaritoj.

Scenejo: Verando, aŭ ĉambro de domo. Ĉeestas sole Karlo, kiu sidas kaj legas gazeton, kaj parolas al si mem.

Karlo. Kiajn ĉapelojn la virinoj portas! Kaj la kosto—terure! Ho, jes, virinoj ne havas komprenon pri la elspezo de mono—aŭ pri matematiko. Lilio telefonis al mi, ke ŝi intencas iri al la urbo por aĉeti ion, sed—bedaŭrinde—mi timas, ke ankaŭ ŝi ne komprenas la matematikon. (Li vidas, ke iu venas). Ho, jen ŝi venas! Dio mia! Kion ŝi portas?

Lilio (envenas. Si portas ĉapelujon kaj ekscite komencas paroli).
Karlo—mi absolute ne povis rezisti! Mi serĉis ĉapelon. Kiel vi scias, mi havas absolute neniun ĉapelon, decan kaj bonan. Mi serĉis ĉapelon—sed mi trovis du—tre belajn. Tamen, mi ne povis decidi inter ili. Nun, mi kunportis ambaŭ, kaj mi deziras vian opinion!

Karlo. Kiom ili kostas, kara?

Lilio. Ne gravas nun—ne demandu, kara—sed momenton! Mi iras por kombi la harojn. Atendu—nur momenton! (Si eliras).

Karlo. (Dume li prenas la ujon, malfermas ĝin, kaj komencas rigardi la prezojn.) Nu, ĉapelo kun margaritoj—du dolarojn! Jen, alia—kun violetoj —dek dolarojn! (Li surmetas la ĉapelon kovritan per violetoj kaj komencas danci. Li imitas virinan voĉon) Bonan tagon, fraŭlino, ĉu ne estas bela tago . . . (subite li rimarkas, ke la edzino revenas, kaj li rapide remetas la ĉapelon en la ujon). Jen ŝi venas!

Lilio (envenas). Nun—ni decidu. Mi montros ilin al vi. Ambaŭ estas kovritaj per floroj, sed kiun mi pli ŝatas, mi ne scias. . . .

Karlo (subspire). Margaritoj, du dolarojn! Violetoj, dek dolarojn!

Lilio (komencas surmeti ĉapelon). Kion vi diras, Karlo? Ĉu vi ŝatas ĉi tiun—kun la margaritoj? (Surmetas la ĉapelon, faras gestojn, k.t.p.). Aŭ, jen, rigardu tiun—kovritan per violetoj?

Karlo. Kial vi demandas al mi, kara? Sendube vi jam decidis kiun vi pli ŝatas. Certe ne dependas de mi.

Lilio. Jes, Karlo—mi deziras vian honestan opinion. Kiun vi pli ŝatas?

Karlo. Nu, provu la margaritojn. (Si surmetas ĝin). Nun, la violetojn . . . nun la margaritojn denove . . . nun, la violetojn, unufoje. . .

Lilio (fine montras ĉagrenon). Ne! tio sufiĉas! Sur . . . de sur . . . sur . . . mi estas laca. Kiun vi pli ŝatas?

Karlo. Nu, se vi deziras mian honestan opinion absolute . . . mi preferas . . . la margaritojn!

Lilio. Ho, ĉu vere? Ĉu ĝi estas la pli taŭga, la pli bela?

Karlo. M-m-m-m-m, nun ni rigardu la koston! (Li rigardas la kvitancon). Nur du dolarojn! Estas bone!

Lilio (kun surprizo). Ho, ne—ne estas! (Si rigardas la du kvitancojn). Kia afero! Ili intermiksis la du kvitancojn! Jen, rigardu—ĝi diras: ĉapelo kun violetoj, du dolarojn . . . kaj la margaritoj kostas dek dolarojn! (Si ree surmetas la margaritojn). Jes, vi havas bonan guston. Mi ankaŭ preferas la margaritojn!

(La edzo preskaŭ svenas, kaj kapo en manoj, eliras).

SUR LA INSULO KAPRI'
(On the Isle of Capri)

Sur la Insulo Kapri' mi esploris
Kaj en la ombro de arb' sidis ŝi,
Ho, kiel bele la floroj odoris
Dum somer' en Insulo Kapri'.
Plej dolĉa ŝi kiel roz' en mateno
Ne destinita de sorto por mi,
Mi forveturis, sed malgraŭ la peno
Tenas koron Insulo Kapri'.

Tien iris mi vojaĝe
Al Itala suna flam',
Tamen petis mi kuraĝe:
"Diru nur vorteton pri am' ".
"Vi ne plu restu!" ŝi saĝe konsilis
Kaj sian manon etendis al mi,
Edzina ringo de ŝi ore brilis!
Do, adiaŭ! Insulo Kapri'.

LEGENDO DE LA KOLIBRO

DORIS TAPPAN CONNOR

La kolibro estas la birdo de Ameriko. En ĉiu lando de la Nova Mondo estas specoj de tiu mirinda birdeto. En Brazilo oni nomas ĝin la **Beija-Flor** (beja-flor), aŭ Esperante la flor-kisanto. En Brazilo estas pli ol ducent-okdek specoj de la flor-kisanto. Multaj indianaj gentoj tre adoras la kolibron. Ĝi estis eĉ la Dio-Birdo de unu gento. Mi rakontos al vi nun la legendon pri la origino de tiu mirinda birdeto:

Potí signifas en la Gvarania lingvo *floro*. (La **Guaraní** estas indiana gento en Brazilo kaj Paragvajo.) En la pratempo, tiu nomo estis ankaŭ la nomo de tre bela indiana fraŭlino, kies lipoj estis dolĉaj kiel la nektaro de la floroj en la arbaro. Potí amis junulon kies nomo estis **Guanumbi**. Li apartenis al malamika gento de indianoj. Inter la amerikaj indianoj—kiel inter la indianoj de aliaj landoj en la mondo—oni ne permesas amon inter personoj de malamikaj gentoj. Do, Potí kaj Guanumbi povis renkonti unu la alian nur en sekreta loko.

Je krepusko, kiam la suno estis preskaŭ preta por dormi, la geamantoj renkontiĝis en la arbaro, apud gaja rivereto. Ili povis esti kune nur dum kelkaj minutoj, ĉar se ili restus pli longe la gento de Potí suspektus ion. Amiko de Potí—malfidela amiko, malamiko eĉ—malbela, envia—elkovris la sekreton de la junulino, kaj rapidis por raporti al la ĉefo de la gento. Sekvis, ke Potí kaj Guanumbi ne plu povis renkontiĝi en la arbaro.

La Luno vidis la malĝojon de la indiana junulo, kaj diris al li unu nokton: "Hieraŭ mi vidis la fraŭlinon Potí. Ŝi multe ploris, ĉar ŝi devis edziniĝi kun indiano de sia propra gento. Fine ŝi turnis sin al **Tupá**, la Spirito de la Bono, kaj plore petis, ke la Spirito permesu ke ŝi mortu, aŭ ke la Spirito faru ion—ion, ĉar ŝi ne amas la edzon. Tupá aŭdis la preĝon de Potí; la Spirito ne permesis, ke ŝi mortu, sed transformis ŝin en floron. Mia amiko, la Vento, diris tion al mi."

"Diru al mi, Luno, kia floro mia amatino nun estas?" petis Guanumbi.

"Ha, mia junulo, tion mi ne scias. La Vento ankaŭ ne scias."

"Tupá, Tupá," lamentis Guanumbi, "mi scias, ke en la petaloj de Potí mi rekonos la dolĉecon de ŝiaj kisoj. Mi **devas** trovi ŝin. Helpu por ke mi trovu ŝin, Vi, kiu povas fari ĉion."

Antaŭ la leviĝo de la Luno, la korpo de Guanumbi komencis malgrandiĝi, velkis ĝis li estis eta, delikata, mult-kolora birdeto, kiu forflugis tre rapide. Estis la florkisanto, tiu mirinda, amerika birdeto.

Depost tiu nokto la malĝoja amanto, en tiu bela metamorfozo, dum la tuta tago kisas espere kaj senspire la lipojn de la floroj, kaj serĉas por unu—nur **unu.** Sed (oni diras) ĝis nun li ne trovis sian amatinon.

LA MIRINDA VESPERTO

La vesperto estas nokta besteto, kiu ĉiam flugas en la mallumo. Ĉu ĝi do ne riskas koliziі kun arboj kaj konstruaĵoj? La vesperto tute ne povas vidi objektojn antaŭ si. Certe ĝi devas uzi iun instinktan metodon por eviti danĝeron. Kaj vere, eksperimentoj antaŭnelonge pruvis, ke tiu stranga, eta besto senĉese ellasas akrajn kriojn—kiuj tute ne estas aŭdeblaj por la homa orelo—kaj ĝi analizas la eĥojn, kiuj resonas de iu objekto. Tiu instinkta analizado ebligas al ili tuj scii kie staras objektoj, kaj tiamaniere ili kapablas flugi en la plej densa mallumo sen akcidento!

La suprajn faktojn raportis Doktoroj Donald Griffin kaj Roberto Galambos de la Medicina Lernejo de Rochester, Usono. Kiam la du sciencistoj imagis al si, ke eble la vespertoj ellasas supersonajn kriojn, ili faris diversajn eksperimentojn pere de speciala ilo, kiu ebligas, ke oni aŭdu supersonajn vibradojn. Ili trovis, ke dum libera flugado la vespertoj eligas ĉirkaŭ 30 kriojn ĉiusekunde, sed se estas antaŭ ili ia objekto, ili duobligas la nombron da krioj. La Doktoroj per tuko ligfermis la buŝon de kelkaj vespertoj kaj poste liberigis ilin al flugo. Sed la kompatindaj vespertoj tute ne sciis kien flugi. Ili nur ŝvebis en la aero. Kiam la Doktoroj ŝtopis la orelojn de la vespertoj, estis same danĝere por la bestetoj, ĉar en tia okazo ili koliziіs kun ĉirkaŭaj objektoj.

La vesperto, do, uzas tiun saman principon je kiu la radar-aparato estas bazita. Vere, mirіndaĵo! Oni faris ja tian bruegon pri la eltrovo de la "RADAR"-aparato! Kaj tamen la vesperto, tiu malamata sed utila besteto, kiun ni foje vidas rapidege flugi en la mallumo de la nokto, jam ekde la kreo de la universo kunportis en sia malbela kapeto . . . "RADAR"-aparaton!

—El "Steleto Rosaria," Argentino

TRIANGULO DE LA MORTO

W. SOLZBACHER

La freneza ideo venis al ni, ke ni povus preni tiun aeroplanon kaj forflugi al libera lando. Mi neniam pilotis aeroplanon; Beno kaj Georgo estis same senspertaj. Kiel en febra sonĝo niaj manoj serĉis butonon, kiu funkciigus la motoron. La motoro restis morta. Hodiaŭ mi scias, ke neniu estus forlasinta tiun aeroplanon, se ĝi estus estinta en bona ordo. Sed en tiu momento ni ne estis normalaj homoj. Ni trovis la aeroplanon en kampo, proksime al Lombartzijde, survoje al Dunkirko (Dunkerque), en tiu 28a de Majo de 1940, kiam la belga armeo kapitulis kaj la trupoj de Hitler rapide marŝis okcidenten. Kugloj kaj grenadoj fajfantaj super niaj kapoj memorigis nin, ke ni estis inter la batalfrontoj, en tiu regiono, kiu estis por kelkaj horoj "nenies lando." Mi estis unu el tiuj malsataj, lacaj, ĉifonvestitaj, sendefendaj aĉuloj, kiuj malespere atendis iun miraklon por saviĝi el la infero.

Neniu miraklo okazis pri la aeroplano. Seniluziigite ni klopodis atingi la Ijzer-riveron. Britaj kaj francaj trupoj estis je la alia bordo, kaj unu ponto nedetruita ŝajnis promesi savon. La distanco al Dunkirko estis malpli ol 12 mejloj. Mi havis amikojn tie. Kiel ofte, survoje al Londono aŭ revenante de tie al Luksemburgo aŭ Parizo, mi estis tie, inter Esperantistoj! Mi estis farinta paroladon en la bela domo de la Komerca Ĉambro, por la Dunkirka Esperanto-Societo. La prezidanto estis haveninĝeniero. Ni do iru al Dunkirko! Sed estis neeble atingi la ponton. Kugloj fajfis ĉirkaŭ niaj oreloj. Mi metis poŝtukon, kiu iam estis blanka, sur bastonon kaj diris al miaj kunuloj, ke ili iru kun mi alte sur la dunoj, tiel ke la trupoj vidu, ke ni venas kun amikaj intencoj. Sed la ratatat de maŝinpafilo elrevigis nin. Neeble! Kion fari? Ni komencis la vojon returne.

Ni havis neniun klaran ideon pri la milita situacio kaj ne sciis, ke en Dunkirko ni estus estintaj en muskaptilo. Eĉ ne ĉiuj soldatoj povis enŝipiĝi por iri al Anglujo. Mia Esperantista amiko, la haveninĝeniero, estis unu el la malmultaj nesoldatoj, kiuj sukcesis forveturi. Unu jaron poste mi revidis lin en Marseille, kaj ni interŝanĝis raportojn pri niaj aventuroj. . . .

Vespero venis. Ni estis lacaj. Ni ne timis bombojn kaj grenadojn. 18 tagoj da milito estis farintaj nin fatalistaj pri tiuj danĝeroj, de kiuj oni ne povas forkuri. Sed ni timis la maŝinpafilojn de la malalte flugantaj aeroplanoj, kiuj serĉadis iujn vivajn atakobjektojn. Kaŝu vin! Ĵetu vin teren! Defendo kontraŭ ili ne estas hazardo, sed arto—arto sennerviga kaj laciga.

Niaj nazoj flaris ion bonan. Ĉu alia trompo kiel la aeroplano? Ne, tio estis vera odoro de supo, de viando, de io nepriskribeble bona por malplena stomako. Miraklo! Jen tuta soldatkuirejo, ega kaldrono kun supo entenanta viandon, terpomojn, rizon kaj fabojn. Kun raŭka krio ni atakis ĝin, prenante pecojn da viando en niajn manojn, trinkante el aluminia soldat-pelvo la supon, furioze maĉante fabojn kaj terpomojn kiel senanimaj bestoj malsategaj. La artileria fajro, kiu komencis plifortiĝi, kaj la bomboj, kiuj falis multnombre sur la regionon de la ponto, lasis nin indiferentaj. Francaj trupoj, kiuj estis rapideme retiriĝintaj trans la Ijzer-riveron, regalis nin per manĝo, kiun mi neniam forgesos.

En Middelkerke, vilaĝo de fiŝkaptistoj kaj, en "bonaj tempoj," de tur-istoj, ni vidis kandellumon en kafejo. Virino kun du infanoj estis en la kuirejo. "Ĉu vi havas ion por manĝi aŭ trinki?" demandis Beno. Ni ne estis vere malsataj, sed kion oni povis demandi por komenci konversacion? "Ni havas panon," diris la mastrino, "kaj kelkajn botelojn da ruĝa vino."

Ni trinkis la vinon, penante forgesi la travivajojn de la tago. "Ĉu vi vidis la germanojn?" demandis timeme la mastrino. "Oni diras, ke ili estas en Bruĝo?" "Ne multajn, nur unu grupon da motorbiciklistoj!" "Kaj ĉu vi vidis la ŝipojn?" "Kiajn ŝipojn?" "Britaj militŝipoj estas tute proksimaj," diris la virino. "Ili certe bombardos . . . " La marŝ-marŝ de trupkolono aŭdiĝis de tute proksime. Silente la mastrino elblovis la kandelon. Tra la mallumo, stranga fajro brilis el la vino. Kiam la bruo de la prusaj botoj malproksimiĝis, Johano, kiu venis al nia grupeto dum la manĝado el la soldatkuirejo, levis sian glason kaj diris: "Vivu la morto!" Mi respondis: "Vivu la vivo!" La vorto estis la malo, la penso estis la sama.

La mastrino donis al ni la ŝlosilon de apuda domo, kies enloĝantoj estis forlasintaj la belgan marbordon. Ni dormis en litoj, bonaj, molaj litoj, sed la dormo ne daŭris longe. La britaj militŝipoj komencis bombardi la germanajn trupojn, kiuj antaŭeniris en la regiono en kiu la belga armeo kapitulis. Ni do estis en vera triangulo de la morto. La triangulo estis formata de la Norda Maro, el kie pafis la britaj militŝipoj, la Ijzer-rivero, malantaŭ kiu la francoj kaj angloj uzis sian artilerion por protekti la enŝipigon de siaj trupoj, kaj la germanoj venantaj de Bruĝo. En la tri-angulo jam estis kelkaj germanaj patroloj, sed ankoraŭ ne solidaj trup-masoj.

Mi ne diros, ke mi estis sentima en tiu nokto, sed dank' al Dio nia grupeto restis viva kaj sana. Johano havis razilon—mia propra razilo kuŝis sur la fundo de la maro, en bombdetruita ŝipo en la haveno de Ostendo. Ni razis kaj lavis nin kaj fariĝis iom pli homsimilaĵ. Por vivi aŭ por morti? Ni ne scias. Sed la fakto ke la "bumbum" de la kanonoj malpliiĝis, donis esperon.

En la mateno ni daŭrigis nian piedvojaĝon, forlasante la marbordon. Ni baldaŭ estis inter tiuj centmiloj da belgoj, kiuj reiris al siaj domoj, aŭ al la ruinoj de tiuj domoj. Ni vidis la germanan armeon, kiu moviĝis al la marbordo kaj la Ijzer-rivero. Unu divizio post la alia. La infanterio estis konfiskinta biciklojn (en Belgujo preskaŭ ĉiu posedas biciklon).

Trupoj, aŭtomobiloj, kanonoj plenigis la ŝoseon. Ĉiu bombo jetita sur ĝin en tiuj horoj estus detruinta amason da militmaterialo. Sed eĉ ne unu brita aŭ franca aeroplano aperis. Oni rakontis strangajn historiojn pri mistera magneta forto, per kiu la germanoj detruis aeroplanojn kaj tankojn. La triumfo de la Nazi-tiranoj ŝajnis senfina.

La bela urbo Bruĝo, feliĉe ne detruita per bomboj, estis plena de germanaj trupoj. La vivo ankoraŭ ne estis tute adaptita al la novaj cirkonstancoj. "Vidu, jen via nomo!" Georgo alvokis min. En montrofenestro de librovendejo troviĝis, en bone videbla loko, la nederlanda eldono de unu el miaj libroj, forte kontraŭ-hitlera! Eble ankoraŭ iu aĉetos ĝin antaŭ ol la Gestapo venos. . . .

Post malmulte da tempo ni estis gastoj en Esperantista familio. La patro, la patrino kaj kvar gefiloj estis Esperantistoj. La plej aĝa filo, Paŭlo, unu el miaj bonaj amikoj, estis aktiva en la Flandra Ligo Esperantista, kaj mi estis farinta paroladon en ĝia Bruĝa grupo, laŭ lia invito. La patro kaj la patrino, politike iom diferencaj de la gefiloj, estis membroj de la Reĝa Belga Ligo Esperantista kaj de ĝia tre granda Bruĝa grupo. Nun, en la uragano de la milito kaj en urbo jus invadita de malamika armeo, estis granda ĝojo por ni, havi amikan lokon, kie oni povis ricevi inteligentajn informojn anstataŭ la fantaziaj onidiroj, kiujn oni aŭdis ĉie. Ni interparolis Esperante kaj kelkfoje, pro miaj kunuloj, france, kaj ricevis multajn bonajn konsilojn. Paŭlo helpis nin trovi restejon por la nokto. Ni dormis sur pajlo en katolika lernejo, inter centoj da rifuĝintoj, kaj kompetenta flegistino prizorgis Johanon, kies piedoj aspektis kiel senformaj sangaj buloj. En la mateno ni havis bonan matenmanĝon ĉe la gastema familio Esperantista. Poste ni daŭrigis nian piedvojaĝon en la direkto al Bruselo kaj al nekonata estonteco. . . .

Kelkajn monatojn poste, kiam mi malespere serĉis eblecon eliri el Belgujo, mi ricevis poŝtkarton skribitan en Esperanto de Marie-Rose, filino de la Bruĝa familio. Ŝi diris: "Ni ofte pensas pri vi. Ni esperas, ke vi restos viva kaj sana kaj efektivigos viajn planojn." Du semajnojn poste mi estis ekster la belga landlimo.

"SUR LA KAMPO—" 1945

SOLDATO D. B. RICHARDSON

Sur la kampo neĝo brilas
Blanke sub la pala lun';
Kie tage ni batalis,
  Kelkaj venkis, kelkaj falis,
Reĝas nokta paco nun.

Bombardado malproksima
Ekruĝiĝas en ĉiel';
Kvazaŭ sango de l' mortintoj
  Kaj la ardo de l'venkintoj
Intermiksas en paŝtel'.

Tie staras mi la gardon,
Dum kunuloj en tranĉe'
Dormas pace sur la neĝo;
 De mi supren iras preĝo
Ke la dorm' rompiĝu ne.

Io movas; malamiko?
Haltu, formoj, kiuj ajn!
Kiaj ajoj tiel iras,
 Marŝas kaj nenion diras,
Ho, silenta noktotrajn'?

La pasantaj ombroj estas
Nur fantomoj de l' memor';
Scenoj el la infaneco,
 Revoj de la pasinteco,
Plej proksimaj al la kor'.

Venas pensoj pri la hejmo,
Trans la blua salondar';
Pri la patro kaj patrino,
 Kaj la kara amatino,
Kaj fidela amikar'.

Mi revenos, ho, fantomoj!
Baldaŭ kune estos ni;
Nun, dum ombrojn mi rigardas,
 Ne mi vin, sed vi min gardas;
Kaj trankvila restas mi.

LANDO DE LIBERECO

(Selection from the address of Dr. L. L. Zamenhof, the author of Esperanto, at the sixth annual international Esperanto congress, Washington, D.C., August, 1910.)

Lando de libereco, lando de estonteco, mi vin salutas! Lando pri kiu revis kaj nun ankoraŭ revas multaj suferantoj kaj senkulpaj persekutatoj, mi vin salutas. Regno de homoj, kiu apartenas ne al tiu aŭ alia gento aŭ eklezio, sed al ĉiuj siaj honestaj filoj, mi klinas min antaŭ vi, kaj mi estas feliĉa, ke la sorto permesis al mi vin vidi kaj spiri almenaŭ dum kelka tempo vian liberan, de neniu monopoligitan aeron.

Saluton al vi, Usono, plej potenca reprezentanto de la nova mondo. Ni, filoj de la malnova kaj maljuna kontinento, venis al vi kiel gastoj; sed ne vidama turismo enŝipigis nin, ne la espero de ia komerca akiro pelis nin al via bordo; ni venis al vi por alporti al vi novan senton kaj novan ideon, ni venis por alporti novan kuraĝon al tiuj niaj samideanoj kaj samidealanoj, kiuj ĝis nun laboris inter vi, kaj kies vortoj pri ia nova popolo eble ŝajnis al vi tro fabelaj. Peco de tiu miksdevena kaj tamen lingve kaj kore unuigita popolo nun staras antaŭ vi reale kaj vivante. Rigardu nin, aŭskultu nin, kaj konvinkiĝu ke ni ne estas fabelo. Ni estas diversgentanoj, kaj tamen ni sentas nin kiel samgentanoj, ĉar ni komprenas nin kiel samgentanoj, havante nenian bezonon humiligi aŭ fremdlingve balbutigi unu la alian. Ni esperas ke danke al nia laborado pli aŭ malpli frue la tuta mondo similiĝos al ni kaj fariĝos unu granda homa gento, konsistanta el diversaj familioj, interne apartlingvaj kaj apartmoraj, sed ekstere samlingvaj kaj sammoraj. Al tiu nia laborado, kiu celas krei iom post iom unuigitan, sekve fortigitan kaj spirite altigitan homaron, ni nun invitas vin, filoj de Usono. Kaj ni esperas, ke nia voko ne restos vana, sed ĝi baldaŭ ehe resonos en ĉiuj anguloj de via lando kaj tra via tuta kontinento.

NOVA KANTO

A. DOMBROWSKI

Ho! eksonu nova kanto
Pri la lingvo Esperanto
Pri ligil' internacia,
Revo nia, amo nia!
Kreitaj' la plej mirinda,
Vere estas ĝi laŭdinda
De verkistoj, de poetoj,
En poemoj kaj odetoj,
Pli ol tondro de bataloj,
Pli ol dolĉaj najtingaloj,
Pli ol belaj aktorinoj,
Pli ol fajfoj de maŝinoj,
Pli ol oro la plej brila,
Pli ol gloro senutila,
Pli ol ĉiu, pli ol ĉio,
Krom la amo kaj la Dio.
Dum venonta la centjaro,
Sciu esperantistaro,
En Eŭropo, Ameriko,
En Azio kaj Afriko,
Kie ajn vi veturados
Esperanton vi trovados,
Sur la strato, en vagono,
En hotelo, en salono

Kaj eĉ en privata domo;
Ĝin parolos ĉiu homo;
Laboristo, profesoro,
Kaj juĝisto, kaj doktoro,
Kaj hebreo, kaj kristano,
Kaj litovo kaj japano,—
Kaj pereos la plendado:
"Mi vin ne komprenas, frato."
Por ke venu tiu horo—
Kune fratoj, al laboro!
Jen per kanto, jen per vorto,
Jen agante ĝis la morto,
Servu ni al la afero,
La plej bela sur la tero,
Gardu ĝin de la forgeso
Per parolo en la preso;
Iru kiel apostoloj
Ĝin prediki por popoloj,
Kaj eksonu nia voko
Sur la ter' en ĉiu loko,
En vilaĝoj, en urbetoj,
En lernejoj, en gazetoj,
Kaj servantajn al la vero
Nin fortigu la Espero.

(a) PRIVATA LETERO

Mabel Miller
135 Main Street   12 Februaro 1947
New York 49, N. Y.
Usono

S-ro Ivan Grigorov
Torgovska Ul. N-ro 37
Sofia, Bulgarujo

Kara samideano:

Mi legis en "Amerika Esperantisto," ke vi deziras korespondi kun junulo aŭ junulino en Usono. Mi estas 21-jara fraŭlino kaj laboras en komerca oficejo en New York. Miaj geamikoj diras pri mi, ke mi estas bela, inteligenta kaj bonhumora. Mi ne scias, ĉu ili estas pravaj. Mi ofte legis pri via lando kaj ĝojus korespondi kun vi regule kaj amuze. Vi sendube scias, ke New York estas la plej granda urbo en la mondo. La urbo mem havas 7,730,000 enloĝantojn, la urba regiono (kun antaŭurboj) proksimume 12 milionojn. Mi volonte respondos al viaj demandoj pri mia urbo kaj aliaj usonaj aferoj.

Mi sendas al vi mian foton kaj plezure ricevus vian. Mi interesiĝas pri multaj aferoj, ekzemple fotografado, kino, naĝado kaj sunbanado, kaj ankaŭ pri vivo en aliaj landoj. En la kinofilmoj mi ŝatas speciale tiujn, en kiuj aperas Van Johnson aŭ Lauren Bacall. Ĉu oni povas vidi Hollywood-filmojn en via lando? Ĉu oni faras filmojn ankaŭ en Bulgarujo?

Mi ankaŭ interesiĝas pri Esperanto. Mi intencas korespondi kun gejunuloj en diversaj landoj. Eble iam mi povos ŝpari sufiĉe da mono por fari longan vojaĝon kaj viziti kelkajn el miaj gekorespondantoj, eble eĉ vin en Bulgarujo!

Mi legis la libron "Bulgara Lando kaj Popolo" de Ivan Krestanov. Ĉu ekzistas ankoraŭ aliaj libroj pri via lando en Esperanto? Ĉu estas vere, ke la Esperanto-movado estas tre vigla en Bulgarujo? En Usono dum longa tempo ĝi ne estis tre forta, sed nun intereso pri ĝi fariĝas multe pli granda.

Mi esperas baldaŭ ricevi vian afablan respondon. En mia dua letero mi esperas doni al vi respondojn al multaj demandoj, kiujn vi eble sendos al mi. Sendube ni baldaŭ estos bonaj geamikoj.

Kun multaj salutoj,

sincere via,
Mabel Miller

(b) PROFESIA LETERO

D-ro John Smith
Washington College
Grand City, Indiana
Usono

9 Aprilo 1947

Brazila Instituto de Geografio kaj Statistiko
Rio de Janeiro, Brazilo

Estimata Sinjoro Direktoro:

Mi estas profesoro de historio kaj geografio kaj permesas al mi peti vian helpon pri afero, kiu multe interesas min. En miaj lecionoj de geografio mi ofte instruas pri Brazilo. En unu klaso ni studis antaŭ nelonge libron pri la Amazona Rivero, kiun eldonis la Asocio por Eksterlanda Politiko (Foreign Policy Association) sub la titolo "The Amazon: A New Frontier?" Eble vi konas la verketon, kies aŭtoro estas Earl Parker Hanson. La libro ankaŭ priskribas la grandajn ekonomiajn eblecojn de la Amazona Teritorio, kiu eble iam estos unu el la plej riĉaj regionoj en la mondo. Mi dezirus scii, ĉu via Instituto posedas aŭ publikigis materialon pri novaj esploroj, studoj kaj spertoj en la Amazona regiono, speciale de la ekonomia vidpunkto: pri la kulturado de kaŭĉuko, rizo, nuksoj, kakao, fibroj, manioko, kinino, pri la minado de mineraloj, ktp.

Mi speciale ĝojus, se tia materialo ekzistus en Esperanto aŭ kun resumoj en Esperanto. Fotografajoj, statistikoj, freŝdataj raportoj de oficialaj institucioj aŭ privataj personoj estus speciale bonvenaj. Vi ja komprenos, ke mi deziras doni al la studantoj la plej bonajn kaj novajn informojn pri ĉio. Mi ĉiam klopodas en miaj kursoj helpi la bonajn rilatojn inter Brazilo kaj Usono kaj inter ĉiuj nacioj de la Amerika kontinento.

Dezirante al via laboro grandan sukceson kaj atendante vian afablan respondon, mi estas

respektoplene kaj sincere via,
John Smith

(c) KOMERCA LETERO

New World Watch Co.

909 California Drive

Boston 69, Massachusetts

Usono

9 Junio 1947

Horlogers Réunis, S.A.

189, Rue de la Vallée

Le Locle (Neuchâtel)

Svislando

Estimataj Sinjoroj:

Nia firmo importas altkvalitajn poŝhorloĝojn kaj brakhorloĝojn kaj havas grandan klientaron en la Bostona regiono. S-ro MacFarlane, kiun vi konas, parolis al ni pri via firmo, dirante, ke la mekanikajo de viaj horloĝoj estas tre preciza kaj ke vi povus liveri horloĝojn je sufiĉe malalta prezo, se ni aĉetus grandajn kvantojn regule kaj pagus tuj post ricevo de la varo.

Bonvolu sendi al ni aerpoŝte detalan oferton kun livero- kaj pago-kondiĉoj por kompletaj horloĝoj kaj ankaŭ por mekanikajoj solaj.

Esperante, ke via respondo permesos al ni starigi inter vi kaj ni komercajn rilatojn agrablajn kaj por ambaŭ partoj profitdonajn, ni salutas vin kun estimo.

New World Watch Co.

Andrew J. O'Donnell, Direktoro

GUIDEBOOK FOR THE
PRACTICAL ESPERANTIST

****

USE ESPERANTO—NOW!

A KNOWLEDGE of Esperanto is in many ways like a telephone connection. It enables you to speak directly to hundreds of thousands of people. To make the fullest possible use of what one might call the "Green Network,"* it is, however, necessary to have a directory. This guide-book is planned to be just that. It aims at enabling anyone who has learned Esperanto to make the most of his knowledge without waiting for the Interlanguage to be used universally.

All items of information given here, in particular figures and addresses, are as up-to-date and accurate as possible. Changes are, of course, taking place continuously. In general, addresses are given only when there is a reasonable expectation of permanency.

To keep informed about all developing practical uses of the World Interlanguage, it is desirable to join some local Esperanto club as well as a national and an international Esperanto organization. Among the many Esperanto journals, the **American Esperantist** is particularly helpful for beginners.

In addition to the practical benefits derived from active membership in an Esperanto organization, it makes you part of an important worldwide cultural movement and gives you the satisfaction of helping to bring about the solution of the age-old problem of international understanding.

INTERNATIONAL PEN-FRIENDSHIPS

Hundreds of thousands of letters written in Esperanto are regularly crossing the border lines, many of them between persons who have never met. Some deal with scientific, philosophical, technological, or other highly specialized topics. Others are written "just for fun." Many talk of friendship and love. A number of international Esperantist marriages are testimony to the fact that this may lead to extreme consequences! An enor-

---

* *Esperantists throughout the world wear a green star emblem to show that they speak the Interlanguage.*

mous number of Esperanto letters deal with the collecting and trading of postage stamps, others are devoted to the collecting of coins, books, folk songs, movie star photos, or what have you. Religious and political ideas are discussed and criticized by those who wish to do so. The object of a great many correspondence partnerships is simply to learn more about other countries and nations, about how people live, what they think, what they like and dislike. This is also an excellent way of getting the most out of foreign travel which one may plan for the future. Visiting old pen pals in their own homes has been a thrilling experience for a great many people who used Esperanto extensively for correspondence with foreign countries. Businessmen, journalists, scholars, clergymen, labor leaders, etc., have found new opportunities and sources of information through correspondence in Esperanto.

Anyone may start an interesting correspondence partnership after having become reasonably familiar with the grammar and vocabulary of Esperanto. Even before this stage is reached, the venture may be begun if some experienced Esperantist is available to help and advise you. Write in a simple and lively style. Keep your letters interesting and put some effort into your writing. Tell about yourself, your work or your studies, your special interests or hobbies, the city, state, and country you live in. Send your correspondent, though not necessarily in your first letter, your photograph, a few picture postcards of your town, or some illustrated folder published by the local Chamber of Commerce. Send copies of your favorite Esperanto journal and other Esperanto material.

A few simple rules, most of them obvious rules of politeness, should be strictly adhered to. When answering a **Deziras Korespondi** ad, be sure to respect special wishes expressed in it. If someone wants to correspond about philosophy and history, do not ask him to trade stamps with you. If he advertises for correspondence with a Hollywood star or a General Motors executive, do not write him if you are a grocery clerk. If correspondence with young people is sought, do not say that you "feel young" although you are seventy-five.

Letters should be answered as promptly as possible. If you expect to be sometimes so busy that long delays will be inevitable, tell your correspondent in advance. If you find your partner dull, or otherwise unsatisfactory, or if you believe that you cannot find the time to keep up the correspondence, it is perfectly permissible for you to discontinue it— but not without informing your correspondent of this in a polite note.

A little gift at Christmas, New Year, or your correspondent's birthday is entirely appropriate. An Esperanto book or a subscription to an Esperanto journal would be excellent suggestions.

When placing a correspondence ad in an Esperanto journal, be as specific as possible. If you receive more replies than you can handle, choose those correspondents to whom you believe you will be able to write regularly. To the others you owe at least a short note of regret.

Most Esperanto journals print correspondence ads. For placing such ads, the **American Esperantist** (New York), **Esperanto** (Rotterdam), **Norda Prismo** (Stockholm), and **Heroldo de Esperanto** (Scheveningen, Netherlands) would be good choices. For correspondence on specialized topics, the different professional, religious, political, or other Esperanto journals are recommended. Correspondents may also be obtained through the **Koresponda Servo Mondskala**, Daniel Luez, Laon (Aisne), France.

International correspondence by means of Esperanto gives you a key to the entire world. It enables you, at almost no cost, to enlarge your horizon, to learn about foreign countries and peoples, to gather important information on your special field of interest, to prepare future trips abroad, and to make a modest, but very real, contribution to the cause of international understanding and cooperation.

STAMP COLLECTING AND ESPERANTO

For the philatelist, Esperanto is an invaluable instrument for establishing direct contacts with an unlimited number of countries. Many correspondence ads in Esperanto journals express a wish for exchanging stamps, poŝtmarkoj, often abbreviated **PM.** When replying to such an ad, you may find it advisable to send some stamps—but not too many—with your first letter. It is not always clear whether the advertiser is a beginner or an advanced philatelist and what, exactly, he is able to offer. In addition to some common stamps of your country, it is wise to send also some stamps which are new or uncommon enough to be of interest to an advanced collector. In the covering letter be as specific as possible as to what you are interested in and on what basis you exchange.

Be considerate in all your dealings. Avoid long delays in answering letters. There is always time to send a postcard. It is not necessary to send everything by registered mail. When really valuable stamps are enclosed in a letter or when your correspondent's country is one of those where postal relations are not entirely reliable, the protection afforded by registration, and possibly insurance, is well worth the cost.

The following Esperanto organizations specialize in philately:

Internacia Asocio de Poŝtmark-Kolektantoj, International Stamp Collectors' Association, Ingemar Nordin, Skolvägen 8, Arjäng, Sweden; publishes the **Internacia Poŝtmarka Revuo.**

La Filatelisto, Ligilo inter la Esperantistaj Filatelistoj, J. Coste, 60 boulevard d'Argenson, Neuilly-sur-Seine, France.

A helpful booklet for philatelists is the **Filatela Terminaro,** by Herbert M. Scott, 3rd édition published by the Universal Esperanto Association in 1945. It gives the philatelic terms in Esperanto with translations in English, French, and German, and definitions in Esperanto.

Philatelists will also be interested in the stamps with Esperanto text as well as in other official postal uses of Esperanto. Twenty-six stamps of Austria, Brazil, Bulgaria, Hungary, Poland, the Soviet Union, and Yugoslavia, carry text in Esperanto. There are 400 different postal cards and envelopes issued by seven postal authorities (Brazil, Soviet Union, Netherlands, Hungary, Czechoslovakia, Danzig, and Liechtenstein) with text in Esperanto, and more than eighty different postmarks in Esperanto from nineteen countries (including France, Belgium, Switzerland, Austria, Germany, Japan, Soviet Union, Brazil).

BUSINESS CORRESPONDENCE IN ESPERANTO

A large number of business firms, tourist agencies, railroad administrations, shipping and air lines, etc., use Esperanto in their correspondence and have Esperantist employees on their staffs. It may be assumed that such is the case for all those who use Esperanto for their publicity. Even firms which have not made permanent arrangements for correspondence in Esperanto, will know how and where to have necessary translations made. The League of Nations Report on Esperanto (1922) said: "A merchant in a little town of Sweden, receiving a letter in Esperanto from Brazil or China, is more certain to get it translated on the spot than in Portuguese or Chinese." The same League of Nations Report explained the usefulness of Esperanto in advertising: "A circular or pamphlet in Esperanto can circulate throughout the world at little expense, without translating into twenty or thirty different languages."

Firms and organizations of international reputation which have used Esperanto for a variety of purposes include: TWA (Trans World Airlines, USA), KLM (Royal Dutch Airline), SAS (Scandinavian Airlines System), Air-France, Swissair, BEA-BOAC (British European Airways—British Overseas Airways Corporation), German Federal Railroads, Austrian Railroads, Swedish Railroads, Danish Railroads, Bern-Loetschberg-Simplon Railroad in Switzerland, trade fairs and exhibitions in many parts of the world, Philips Electrical Company in the Netherlands, Gevaert Photo Corporation in Belgium, Banco Nacional de Minas Gerais in Brazil, Chemische Fabrik in Crailsheim, Germany, manufacturers of building materials such as Ytong in Sweden and Asbestona in the Netherlands, Tuypens Laboratories in Belgium, important drug manufacturers in Japan, etc.

It may be taken for granted that any firm of importance will be able to handle correspondence in Esperanto. Letters written in the Interlanguage should be marked "Esperanto" in the upper left hand corner. All letters should, of course, be bona fide business letters. No business letters in Esperanto should be written from English-speaking to other English-speaking countries. Esperanto aims at facilitating international correspondence, not at making it more complicated.

THE USE OF ESPERANTO "KEYS"

Even when writing to persons who do not know the Interlanguage yet, it is possible to make oneself understood through Esperanto, by adding a "Key" in the language of the receiver. An Esperanto "Key" is a miniature booklet containing the grammar and basic vocabulary in a practical form, so as to enable anyone to read and understand an Esperanto text by looking up the words and word elements in the alphabetical list. A "Key" weighs usually only a fifth of an ounce and can be included in a letter without requiring extra postage.

Suppose you have to write to someone in Albania, Iran, or Iceland, who does not understand English and may or may not know Esperanto. You write your letter in Esperanto and enclose a "Key" in Albanian, Persian, or Icelandic. Keys cost only a few cents, and a collection in about 20 different languages can be bought for approximately two dollars. Esperanto "Keys" exist in thirty-nine languages: Afrikaans, Albanian, Arabic, Basque, Bulgarian, Catalan, Croatian, Czech, Danish, English, Estonian, Finnish, Flemish, French, German, Greek, Hungarian, Icelandic, Iranian (Persian), Italian, Japanese, Lettish, Lithuanian, Malay, Netherlands, Norwegian, Polish, Portuguese, Romanch, Rumanian, Russian, Serbian, Slovak, Slovenian, Spanish, Swedish, Ukrainian, Welsh, Yiddish.

Small Esperanto textbooks in other formats, which can be used for the same purpose, exist in another thirteen languages: Armenian, Asturian, Chinese, Friulian, Georgian, Hebrew, Hindustani, Ladino (Sephardic), Latin, Tagalog, Tartar, Turkish, Visayan. This makes a total of fifty-two languages.

ESPERANTO "DELEGATES"

Several Esperanto organizations, of which the Universal Esperanto Association (**Universala Esperanto-Asocio**) is the most important, have worldwide networks of representatives who function as "consuls" whose services are at the disposal of members from other countries for any information, advice or help they may need. Their names and addresses appear in the Year Book **(Jarlibro).** In the Universal Esperanto Association (UEA) these "consuls" are known as Delegates **(Delegitoj).**

Suppose you need some information from Copenhagen, Cologne, Montevideo, Reykjavik, or Jerusalem. You write in Esperanto to the Delegates in those cities. Their services are free but you have to repay their expenses. This means that you have to enclose an "International Reply Coupon" (available at your post office) for postage. If your request is of such a character that further expense will be involved, you should add a few extra reply coupons. You have to prove that you are a member of UEA. This is done by enclosing in your letter a "service coupon" **(servokupono)** from a booklet which you receive on paying your dues to the international organization. Members of many national Esperanto organizations are automatically members of UEA and receive a booklet containing twenty "service coupons" (more can be obtained on request). The Year Book **(Jarlibro)** containing the addresses of the Delegates is supplied on payment of an extra $1.90. It appears at present in two parts, one in April, so as to be up-to-date for any summer trips members may plan, the second in October, containing additions and changes.

Matters about which information may properly be requested from the Delegates include: business and industry, communications and transportation, labor, salaries, chances of finding a job, tourist information, education, youth, student, and women's affairs, etc. Confidential information about the solvency of a firm or the moral character of a person is excluded. If such information is desired, the Delegate may, however, put the inquirer in touch with some local agency specializing in confidential research of this kind.

If the service requested is of a complicated nature and would require a great deal of time and effort on the part of the Delegate, he may decline to deal with the matter in more than a summary way, and it will be proper to arrange for his or someone else's services for the more complicated work on a paid basis. If, for instance, the Delegate is a lawyer, and his advice is sought on some intricate legal problem, it would obviously be unfair to expect this to be given free of charge.

Under the regulations, the Delegate is also permitted to refuse services which he considers as "contrary to his honor or conscience." This would possibly apply, for instance, in the case of inquiries touching religious or political matters or dealing with the liquor trade, lotteries, etc.

In larger cities, there are Vice Delegates to assist the Delegates or substitute for them in case of absence, illness, etc. There are also Special Delegates **(Fakaj Delegitoj)** for Commerce, Industry, Labor Problems, Education, Women's Problems, Philately, Athletics, Scouting, Cooperatives, Medical Problems, Religious Affairs. They give their services on the same basis as the Delegates, in their own specialized field.

Esperantists who have done a great deal of traveling abroad are full of praise for the helpfulness of the Delegates in foreign countries. Delegates have met the foreign Esperantist at the railroad station, have handled his hotel reservations, invited him into their homes, introduced him to local Esperantists and to persons who could be of help in some particular field, have shown him around their city or town, served as his interpreters, etc. These are, of course, services rendered "above and beyond the call of duty." Esperanto Delegates are not obliged to meet traveling Esperantists at the station or airport and to serve as their interpreters and errand boys. They are, however, expected to help traveling Esperantists to the extent of their ability, to give information and advice in personal interviews or over the telephone, to introduce the traveler, at his request, to the officers of the local Esperanto Club, etc. Whenever possible, travelers should inform the Delegate at least forty-eight hours in advance of their coming.

ESPERANTO AND FOREIGN TRAVEL

Whether you travel for business or pleasure, Esperanto can help you in many ways. The services of the Delegates, described in the preceding chapter, will make your trip more efficient and more pleasant. Through Esperanto you will be able to meet people whose acquaintance may prove to be extremely profitable or enjoyable. Other possibilities include attendance at Esperanto Congresses and visits to persons with whom you have been ·in correspondence. Let us consider a number of practical examples.

Suppose you are now saving money to make a trip to Europe in two years' time. You plan to go on your own and to visit in particular Norway, France, and Switzerland, while passing quickly through a number of other countries. You will wish to read some books about the countries you are going to visit, in English as well as in Esperanto. You will write for free tourist literature, in English and Esperanto. Correspondence with a number of Esperantists in those countries will give you useful ideas for your trip. You may also like to subscribe to Esperanto journals published in those countries. When the time comes to plan your trip in detail, you may want to include in your itinerary attendance at some international or national Esperanto Congress. On this occasion you will undoubtedly make many interesting and useful acquaintances. You may also want to visit with your correspondents. Some of them are likely to invite you into their homes. You may find hotels where the manager and staff speak Esperanto. You will see and learn a great deal more than you could by following the beaten track of conducted tours.

Or take the case of a business trip which you have to make to South America, the Far East, or Europe, on behalf of a company manufacturing photographic equipment and cameras. Your firm supplies you with a list of its customers and with instructions how to handle them, and tells you where you are expected to make new contacts. You make up a tentative itinerary and write the Esperanto Delegates in the principal cities, explaining the purpose of your trip and requesting a list of firms which it would be useful for you to visit. You also inquire from each Delegate whether he or some other local Esperantist would be in a position to introduce you to the executives of some of these firms. You also contact the Special Delegates for Photography in the cities and countries which you plan to visit. Thus you will undoubtedly make a number of important contacts—which eventually may make all the difference between success and failure of your trip.

ESPERANTO CONGRESSES AND CONFERENCES

Universal Congresses of Esperanto have been held every year since 1905 with the only interruptions from 1916 to 1919 and from 1940 to 1946. Attendance has been between 1,000 and 5,000. There were 4,963 Esperantists in attendance at Nuremberg, 1923, 3,400 at Vienna, 1924, close to 2,500 in Copenhagen, 1956, Marseille, 1957, and Mainz, 1958.

A Universal Congress of Esperanto consists not only of large assemblies with formal speeches and of business meetings dealing with the organizational life and the promotional activities of the Esperanto movement but also of a great variety of educational, social, and tourist events. There is always an International Summer University, at which scholars from different countries lecture in Esperanto on timely topics. There are sectional meetings for teachers, lawyers, physicians, businessmen, journalists, trade unionists, people interested in the Cooperative movement, stamp collectors, radio amateurs, etc. There are religious services for Catholics, Protestants, Jews, etc., with sermons in Esperanto. There are excursions to places of scenic, historic, or artistic interest. There are a number of variety shows in Esperanto and at least one major theatrical performance. For the young people—and some of the older ones—the climax is an International Ball.

In addition to these neutral Congresses, the Workers' Esperanto Movement (SAT), the Catholic Esperanto League (IKUE), the International Christian Esperanto League (KELI), the International Esperanto League of Railroad Employees (IFEF), the Esperanto World Youth Organization

(TEJO), the Scout Esperanto League (SEL), etc., organize their own international Congresses and gatherings. Before and after the Universal Congress, neighboring countries often hold what is called an **Antaŭkongreso** ("Pre-Congress") or a **Postkongreso** ("After Congress"). When the Congress happens to be in Brussels, for instance, these additional Congresses are likely to be held at Paris, London, Cologne, and Basel, for the benefit of those who happen to have some extra time to spend on their way to and from the Universal Congress.

The different national Esperanto organizations also hold annual Congresses at which usually a number of foreign guests are present. The Esperanto Association of North America has been holding its Congresses ever since 1908, with the only interruption, for obvious reasons, from 1943 to 1945.

ESPERANTO BOOKS

Original and translated literature in Esperanto is already more comprehensive and varied than the literature of many national tongues. Those whose mother tongue is English have, of course, access to the world's most important literary and technical publications through English translations; for them the advantages of Esperanto in this particular field are, therefore, not as great as for Lithuanians, Finns, Hungarians, Portuguese, or even Spaniards and Italians. It has been noted, however, that in some cases the Esperanto translations are better and more congenial to the original than existing English translations. It has also happened repeatedly that Esperanto translations of topical books were published **before** the English translations. Such was the case, for instance, for Count Folke Bernadotte's **The Curtain Falls**, published in 1945. The Esperanto edition hit the market immediately after the Swedish original while translations in English and a dozen other languages were delayed.

A number of book stores and department stores carry Esperanto books. If greater choice is desired, it is advisable to get in touch with some Esperanto book service, for instance one of the following:

Esperanto Association of North America, 114 West 16th Street, New York 11, N. Y.

British Esperanto Association, 140 Holland Park, London W 11, England.

Internacia Instituto de Esperanto, Riouwstraat 172, The Hague, Netherlands.

Liga Brasileira de Esperanto, Praça da Republica, 54, Rio de Janeiro, Brazil.

Book Service, Australian Esperanto Association, Mrs. S. Milligan, 274
Mount Albert Road, Surey Hills, Victoria, Australia.

Many public libraries have Esperanto books; some of them, for
instance New York, Boston, Los Angeles, and Cleveland, have fairly
large numbers. The largest Esperanto libraries are those of the Paris
Chamber of Commerce, the Universal Esperanto Association in Geneva,
the British Esperanto Association in London, and the International
Esperanto Museum in Vienna.

AN INTRODUCTION TO THE ESPERANTO PRESS

About 135 Esperanto journals are published at present. About sixty
of these appear exclusively in Esperanto, while the others also print
articles and news items in national tongues. In the case of the **American
Esperantist, British Esperantist, New Zealand Esperantist** and **The
Australian Esperantist,** this language is English.

For a variety of reasons both the birth rate and the death rate in the
Esperanto press have been high. New journals and bulletins are started
every month, but not all of them grow up beyond the stage of infancy.

Often a distinction is made between the **Por-Esperanta Gazetaro** (the
"for Esperanto" press), dedicated to the promotion of the Interlanguage,
and the **Per-Esperanta Gazetaro** ("through Esperanto" press), which
uses Esperanto for the dissemination of information and the discussion
of opinions on scientific, cultural, religious, political, or other topics. In
some cases, however, the line is not easy to draw.

As changes in the Esperanto press are frequent, no list can claim to
be complete and up-to-date for more than a short time. Undue insistence
on "completeness" would also lead to the inclusion of a number of amateur-
ish and irregularly appearing periodicals which are of little interest to a
wider public.

One daily newspaper in Esperanto, started in Bulgaria in 1934, and a
number of weekly papers did not survive. One weekly paper, however, the
Heroldo de Esperanto, became a first-class, interesting, thoroughly international, and highly attractive journal. For some time (1925-26), it was
published twice a week. Founded in 1920, it was published regularly until
May, 1940, when the Nazi invasion of the Netherlands made the continuation impossible. It had then published 1,049 issues. After the war, it resumed
publication in April, 1946. It is now published semi-monthly.

Esperanto journals in different professional, technical, cultural, religious, and political fields are listed in the **Classified Directory,** later in this
book.

The best Esperanto journals of a general nature are:

The American Esperantist, 114 W. 16th St., New York 11, N. Y., edited in English and Esperanto bimonthly. Internationally recognized as one of the liveliest and most interesting Esperanto journals. $3 a year, $5 including EANA membership.

Heroldo de Esperanto, Harstenhoekweg 223, Scheveningen, Netherlands, in Esperanto, semi-monthly, $4.00 a year.

La Praktiko, Universala Ligo, Riouwstraat 172, The Hague. Netherlands, in Esperanto, monthly, $2.50, including UL membership.

Esperanto, Universala Esperanto-Asocio, Eendrachtsweg 7, Rotterdam-C, Netherlands, monthly, Esperanto, $3.75 a year incl. membership.

The British Esperantist, British Esperanto Association, 140 Holland Park Avenue, London W 11, England, monthly, in English and Esperanto, 20 shillings ($2.80) a year, including BEA membership.

Norda Prismo, Barnhusgatan 8, Stockholm, Sweden, "kultura, socia, literatura revuo", bimonthly, 10 Swedish kroner ($2.00) a year. It has published special issues on Iceland, Norway, Finland, Germany, etc.

ESPERANTO CLUBS AND ORGANIZATIONS

Membership in an Esperanto Club gives you an opportunity for perfecting your fluency in the Interlanguage and for becoming acquainted with different Esperanto activities. Clubs usually organize classes, conversation circles, lectures, social evenings, etc., and carry out promotional activities for Esperanto.

In some cities Esperanto Clubs are listed in the telephone book under "Esperanto." If there is no Club in your city or town, you may wish to take the initiative in starting one. You may know a number of Esperantists in the neighborhood, and you may be able to get in touch with others through the national Esperanto organization or through a letter to the local newspaper.

Perhaps you will wish to start out very informally, for instance with an **Esperanto-Rondo** ("Esperanto circle"), meeting weekly, monthly, or bi-monthly at some hotel, club, or a private home. After bringing together a small group of capable and enthusiastic Esperantists, you may wish to go a step further and set up a Club with all the trimmings (President, Vice Presidents, Secretary, Treasurer, Finance Committee, Membership Committee, Education Committee, Promotion Committee, etc.)

The national organization for the United States and Canada is the **Esperanto Association of North America** (EANA), 114 West 16th Street, New York 11, N. Y.

The development of the Esperanto language and vocabulary is supervised by the Esperanto Academy **(Akademio de Esperanto)**, which has its headquarters at the following address: Wassenaarseweg 11c, The Hague, Netherlands. The Esperanto Academy has special Sections for Grammar, General Vocabulary, Technical Vocabularies, and Literature. Members include Dr. William Solzbacher, Washington, D. C., and Mr. Joseph R. Scherer, Los Angeles, California.

There are more than sixty international Esperanto organizations for special interest groups, political, religious, or cultural endeavors, as well as for teachers, scientists, lawyers, businessmen, etc. The most important of these are listed in the "Classified Directory."

A LIST OF SELECTED BOOKS

Step by Step in Esperanto, Montâgu C. Butler, London, Esperanto Publishing Company, 7th edition, 280 pp. An excellent textbook for those who wish to learn Esperanto leisurely and thoroughly.

Universala Esperanto-Metodo, D-ro Wm. S. Benson, Newark 1932, Benson School of Esperanto, 560 pp. Direct picture-method of instruction and definition, 11,000 pictures. Textbook, reader, dictionary.

Fundamento de Esperanto, D-ro L. L. Zamenhof, Paris, Esperantista Centra Librejo. Many editions. The "five-language" edition (French, English, German, Polish, Russian) contains the grammar in these languages, Zamenhof's own "Ekzercaro," and the basic word list with translations in the five languages. 196 pp.

Practical Grammar of the International Language, (Esperanto), Ivy Kellerman Reed, 5th edition 1945, Washington, D. C., 142 pp., a thorough but short textbook.

Say It In Esperanto, by George Alan Connor and Doris Tappan Connor. Advice given by Dr. William Solzbacher of the Akademio de Esperanto. New York 1958, Dover Publications Inc., 160 pp. A practical phrase book.

Fundamenta Krestomatio, D-ro L. L. Zamenhof, Paris, Esperantista Centra Librejo, many editions, 472 pp. Interesting reading matter, translations and originals from all over the world, in classical Esperanto style. Selected and revised by Dr. Zamenhof.

The "Edinburgh" Esperanto Pocket Dictionary, Esperanto-English and English-Esperanto, London, Thomas Nelson & Sons, Ltd., many editions, 288 pp. Excellent and very popular.

Esperanto-English Dictionary, Edward A. Millidge, London, Esperanto Publishing Company, 489 pp.

The Standard English-Esperanto Dictionary, Fulcher & Long, London, Esperanto Publishing Company, 346 pp.

Originala Verkaro, D-ro L. L. Zamenhof, Leipzig 1930, Hirt & Sohn, 664 pp. An almost complete collection of everything Zamenhof published, including letters and articles, but excluding his translations.

The Life of Zamenhof, Edmond Privat, London 1931, George Allen & Unwin, 124 pp.

Historio de la Lingvo Esperanto, Edmond Privat, The Hague, Internacia Esperanto-Instituto, 273 pp.

Bibliografio de Internacia Lingvo, P. E. Stojan, Geneva 1929, Universala Esperanto-Asocio, 560 pp., an almost complete bibliography of everything published in and on Esperanto and on the language problem in general, up to 1929. Extremely interesting comments by the author, a Russian linguist.

Enciklopedio de Esperanto, Bleier-Kökény-Sirjaev, 2 volumes, Budapest 1933, Literatura Mondo, 1,000 pp., richly illustrated, information on everything concerning the Esperanto movement.

La Sankta Biblio en Esperanto, the complete Bible in Esperanto, Old Testament translated by Dr. Zamenhof, New Testament by Committee of British scholars, London, British and Foreign Bible Society, 996 pp.

The Language Problem, Its History and Solution, E. D. Durrant, London 1943, Esperanto Publishing Company, 168 pp., excellent history of the language problem and the Esperanto movement.

Cosmopolitan Conversation, The Language Problems of International Conferences, Herbert N. Shenton, New York 1933, Columbia University Press, 804 pp. This book presents the results of considerable, though incomplete, research. It contains many facts about the use of Esperanto at international conferences.

League of Nations Secretariat, Esperanto as an International Auxiliary Language, adopted by the Third Assembly of the League of Nations, Geneva 1922, League of Nations Secretariat, 57 pp., one of the most important documents on Esperanto.

The World's Chief Languages, Mario A. Pei, New York, S. F. Vanni, 4th edition 1955, 664 pp. Complete practical textbooks of 8 languages, including Esperanto, and introductions into all the major languages of the world. Extremely valuable, the standard handbook of the practical linguist.

A Guide to the Languages of Europe, Archibald Lyall, London 1932, Sidgwick & Jackson, 316 pp. Practical phrase book and dictionary in 25 languages, including Esperanto.

ADULT EDUCATION & PEOPLES COLLEGES

Eŭropa Asocio de Popoluniversitatoj (European Association of Peoples Colleges), Pierre Petit, Prezidanto, 26 rue Rochebrune, Rosny-sous-Bois (France), uses Esperanto, which was the principal translation language of its conferences at UNESCO Headquarters in Paris (1957) and in Florence, Italy (1958). Part of its magazine, **La Eŭropa Popoluniversitato,** is in Esperanto.

Coordinated Esperanto Classes, Dr. Tina Peter-Ruetschi, Volkshochschule Zürich, Zurich, Switzerland, promotes cooperation among peoples colleges and adult schools, especially in England, France, Germany, Italy, Denmark, Sweden, Norway, Finland, Belgium, the Netherlands, Austria, and Switzerland, by coordinating their Esperanto classes and organizing direct contacts among their students through travel, correspondence, and the exchange of educational materials.

The Esperanto Association of New Jersey, Henry Kruse, 107 Center Avenue, Chatham, N. J., affiliated with the Esperanto Association of North America and the Adult Education Association of New Jersey, has organized Esperanto classes in more than twenty adult schools and is in a position to give advice on how it is done and how best results can be achieved.

Adult education centers in many countries, including the United States, Brazil, Japan, and almost all of Europe, have been teaching and using Esperanto for many years.

AGRICULTURE & GARDENING

Scienca kaj Profesia Faka Organizo de Agronomoj Esperantistaj, Sterjo S. Kukusev, MTS 1, Belozem, Dep. Plovdiv 2, Bulgaria, publishes **La Kulturita Planto.**

Amikoj de Kaktoj, Bruno R. Zeiner, 26 Canon Street, Barry, Glamorganshire, Wales, Britain, is a quarterly bulletin for cactus growers.

Articles and summaries in Esperanto are published or have been published in the **Reports of the Swedish Government Institute for Horticultural Research,** at Alnarp, the **Annual Reports of the Plant Pathological Laboratory J. E. Ohlsens Enke,** in Copenhagen, the **Netherlands Journal of Agricultural Science,** the publications **(Radova)** of the **Department of Agriculture and Forestry of the University of Sarajevo,** Yugoslavia, and several Japanese publications including the **Technical Bulletin of Kagawa Agricultural College,** the Bulletin of the Faculty of Agriculture of Yamaguti University, the Bulletin of the College of Agriculture of Nihon University, and the Protokolo de la Rikoltaĵscienca Societo.

Some of the best books in Esperanto on horticulture are **La Vivo de la Plantoj,** by Dr. Paul Neergaard, with illustrations by Mads Stage, published in La Laguna, on the Canary Islands, in 1957, and **Atakoj kontraŭ Ĝardenplantoj,** an illustrated book on garden pests by the same author, published in England in 1954. **Arboj de la Arbaro kaj Kampo,** by F. Booth, published in England, is also recommended.

ARCHEOLOGY

Esperanto has been used at a number of international archeological student work camps in Denmark, under the direction of the National Museum of Copenhagen. These work camps, operated with a subsidy from the Danish government, used Esperanto as the daily means of communication among the participants from different countries. They cooperated on such projects as the digging out of the ancient Viking fortress of Aggersborg and of an Early Iron Age village on the island of Bornholm.

Publications using Esperanto include the **Bulletin de la Société de Géographie et d'Archéologie de la Province d'Oran,** in Algeria, and **the Journal of the Stone Age Research Association,** in Japan.

ARCHITECTURE & TOWN PLANNING

Universala Terminologio de la Arkitekturo, by Francisco Azorín, 2,000 illustrations, 217 pages, published in Madrid, Spain, in 1932, provides translations of Esperanto terms in Spanish, Portuguese, Italian, French, English, and German, sometimes also in Swedish, Russian, and Polish.

Konstruteknika Terminaro—Byggnateknisk Ordlista, by K. J. Moberg, 100 pages, published in Malmö, Sweden, in 1958, gives Esperanto terms for the building trades.

ART

Artfaka Profesia Esperanto-Organizo, Josip Vrančić, Umj. Galerija, Dubrovnik, Yugoslavia, is an organization of painters, sculptors, art critics, art historians, museum administrators, etc.

Art books in Esperanto are numerous. Published in the Netherlands, Norway, Finland, Hungary, Brazil, France, Germany, and England, they include **Pri l' Moderna Arto,** with 74 pictures, by S. Grenkamp-Kornfeld and Dr. Jan Brzekowski, **La Pentroarto en la Malnova Hungarujo,** with 102 pictures, by Genthon Istvan, and **Rembrandt, la Magiisto,** with 100 pictures, by H. Muller, also a book on the Vigeland sculptures in Oslo, by Kjaer. Of the literary magazines in Esperanto, **Norda Prismo** in Sweden, **Suda Stelo** in Yugoslavia, and **Prometeo** in Japan pay much attention to art.

ASTRONOMY

Astronomers, astronomical observatories, and astronomical societies in Finland, Spain, Germany, Yugoslavia, Japan, and other countries have used Esperanto for the publication of reports, articles, and summaries. The volume **Sciencaj Studoj**, Copenhagen 1958, includes articles on astronomical subjects (originals, not translations) by Professor Y. Vaisala, Director of the Astronomical-Optical Institute of the University of Helsinki and a Member of the Finnish Academy, Dr. Paul Hustaanheino, of the Astronomical Observatory in Helsinki, and Professor Boža Popović, of the Astronomical Observatory of Belgrade.

Journals which have published Esperanto summaries include **Tähtitaivas** in Finland, the **Publications of the Astronomical Society of Japan**, and the **Sendai Astronomical Reports** in Japan.

Dr. Wilhelm Förster, Director of the Astronomical Observatory of Potsdam, founder of the German Astronomical Society and at one time President of the University of Berlin and President of the International Committee on Weights and Measures, served as President of the International Association for Esperanto in Science in 1912-13.

Two asteroids (minor planets) discovered a few years ago by a Spanish astronomer, were named by him "Esperanto" and "Zamenhof".

AVIATION & AIR TRANSPORT

E. D. Durrant's **Aeronaŭtika Terminaro** was published in England in 1941. An older and more voluminous book is the 156-page **Lexique Aéronautique en Six Langues**, by R. d'Arman, published by the Librairie Aéronautique in Paris, France, in 1914. It explains aeronautical terms in French and translates them into English, German, Italian, Spanish, and Esperanto.

The Third International Aviation Congress, held at Brussels, had before it a proposal in favor of Esperanto supported by the Aero-Clubs of France and Spain, and adopted a resolution recognizing "the important services which the use of the international language Esperanto would render to aeronautics."

Airlines which have published promotional materials in Esperanto or have otherwise used the language include TWA, KLM, SAS, Air-France, BEA-BOAC, and Swissair.

BAHA'I MOVEMENT

This religious group, founded in Iran by Mirza Ali Mohammad ("The Bab") and Mirza Hossein Ali ("Baha'u'llah") and later spread to many parts of the world under the leadership of Abdul Baha and Shoghi Effendi, advocates the introduction of a universal language. Many of its leaders and followers have used and promoted Esperanto, and a great deal of Baha'i literature has appeared in the Interlanguage. Some of it is available from the Baha'i Publishing Company, Wilmette, Illinois.

BANK EMPLOYEES

Bank-Faka Esperanto-Asocio, Thomas Carstensen, Postfach 30, (24b) Ahrensbök, German Federal Republic.

BEEKEEPING

Ministère de l'Agriculture, Direction des Services Agricoles, Place Questel, Nîmes (Gard), France, is the address for information about an annual Summer School for Beekeeping at Saint-Christol near Alès (Gard). It is sponsored and financed by the French government (Department of Agriculture) and provides assistance to foreign participants through the services of an Esperanto-speaking Frenchman.

La Revue Française d'Apiculture, 38 boulevard de Sébastopol, Paris 4, organ of the French Beekeeping Association, uses Esperanto in its promotion.

A book on beekeeping by H. C. Andersen, **Pri Bredado de Abeloj,** is helpful.

BLIND

Ligo Internacia de Blindaj Esperantistoj (LIBE), Oskari Lertivaara, Aleksis Kivenkata 22, Helsinki, Finland; representative for the United States: Henry Kruse, 107 Center Avenue, Chatham, N. J. This organization publishes the magazine **Esperanta Ligilo.** There are half a dozen other Esperanto periodicals in Braille.

A great deal of Esperanto literature has been published in Braille script or in the form of "talking books". The National Library for the Blind in Great Britain lists 920 volumes of Esperanto reading matter in Braille in its catalogue. These books are loaned free of charge to the blind in Britain and abroad. St. Hendrik's Institute for the Blind in Grave, Netherlands, has recorded on tape a number of full-length Esperanto books and has also produced a great deal of Esperanto material in Braille. It is made available to blind people all over the world.

The Hadley School for the Blind, Winnetka, Illinois, runs Esperanto correspondence courses.

Many institutions for the blind have taught Esperanto for many years. The Third Pan American Congress of the Blind, held at Montevideo, Uruguay, in 1958, adopted unanimously a resolution recommending the organization of Esperanto classes in all institutions for the blind in the Western Hemisphere.

BUDDHISTS

Budhana Ligo Esperantista, S. Persson, Grev. Turegt. 18/III, ö. g., Stockholm, Sweden, publishes the quarterly bulletin **La Budha Lumo.**

Budhana Esperanto-Instituto, Njanasatta Thero, Bandarawela, Ceylon. Items include **La Koro de Budhismo** ("The Heart of Buddhism").

World Institute of Buddhist Culture, Mandalay, Burma. Publications include **Ekrigardo al Budhismo** ("A Glimpse of Buddhism"), by Dr. R. L. Soni, also available from Clarach, Abbey Drive, Gronant, Prestatyn, North Wales, Britain.

A great deal of Buddhist literature, also on various Buddhist sects such as Zen Buddhism, has been published in Japan.

CAMPING & TRAILER LIVING

Internacia Kontakt-Centro de Esperantistaj Kampuloj, P. Jacquesson, 35 Avenue Aristide Briand, Bourges (Cher), France.

Camping Club International de France, 62 avenue Parmentier, Paris 11, France, uses Esperanto.

CATHOLICS

Internacia Katolika Unuiĝo Esperantista (IKUE), F-ino Truus Durenkamp, Dordrecht, Netherlands; representative for the United States: Mrs. William McGrogan, 2109 Parkwood Drive, N.W., Warren, Ohio; representative for Canada: Jean Forgeau, 784 Beaubien Est, Montreal, P.Q. IKUE has received the blessing of several Popes, from Pius X to John XXIII, has organized numerous World Congresses (the first in Paris, 1910, the 28th scheduled to be held in Munich in 1960), and has a network of "consuls" to assist members traveling abroad or needing information.

The 1959 IKUE Year Book lists representatives in 21 countries, 7 affiliated national organizations, and 192 consuls in 24 countries. National organizations and representatives publish news letters or periodicals in the United States **(La Kruco)**, Argentina, Japan, France, Germany, Italy, Spain, and the Netherlands.

Birdo, Wormerveerstraat 5, Den Haag, Netherlands, is the magazine of the Youth Section of IKUE.

Internacia Katolika Informejo (IKI), Rev. H. Rosen, Huize St. Gerlach, Akersteenweg 260, Heer (Limburg), Netherlands. IKI gives information on the Catholic Church to non-Catholics.

Memorlibro de la Tria Esperantista Eŭkaristia Mondkunveno, Rev. D-ro J. B. Kao, O.F.M., Convento de S. Antonio, Largo de Carioca, Rio de Janeiro, Brazil, is a 216-page volume, richly illustrated, on the Esperanto sessions at the 36th International Eucharistic Congress in Rio de Janeiro (1955). Esperanto was also used at the Eucharistic Congresses of Budapest (1938) and Barcelona (1952) and will be used at the Eucharistic Congress in Munich (1960).

Catholic literature in Esperanto includes the gospels (a Catholic edition of the entire Bible is in preparation), the **Imitation of Christ** by Thomas a Kempis, the **Spiritual Exercises** of St. Ignatius Loyola, the **Fioretti** of St. Francis of Assisi, the **Pious Verses** of St. Alphonsus Liguori, Giovanni Papini's **Story of Christ,** Cardinal Wiseman's **Fabiola,** the catechism, about 15 prayer and hymn books, and publications on theology, apologetics, Church history, and worldwide mission activities.

CHESS

Esperantista Ŝaka Ligo Internacia, Jean Duthilleul, 35 rue de Bayeux, Caen, Calvados, France, organizes international chess tournaments by means of Esperanto.

CHEMISTRY (see also SCIENCE)

English-Esperanto Chemical Dictionary, by Dr. D. R. Duncan, published in 1956 by the British Esperanto Association for the British Scientific Esperantist Association, is recommended.

CHILDREN AND PARENTS

Geonkloj Esperantistaj, J. H. Sullivan, 3 Berwick Avenue, Urmston, Manchester, England. Members of this group help children who are learning Esperanto by means of letters, advice, occasional gifts, etc.

Denaskaj Esperantistoj, F-ino Sirkku Koivu, Untamontie 4 D 23, Helsinki, Finland. There are increasing numbers of children, some of them in the United States and Canada, who have been speaking Esperanto from early childhood.

Infanoj de la Mondo, Hongo 6-13, Tokyo, Japan, is a magazine for and about "the children of the world".

CHRISTIANS (see also CATHOLICS and FRIENDS, SOCIETY OF)

Kristana Esperantista Ligo Internacia (KELI), Dirk de Boer, Druivenstraat 32, Den Haag, Netherlands, publishes the magazine Dia Regno; representative for the United States: Edwin C. Harler, 47 Hardy Road, West Levittown, Pennsylvania; representative for Canada: F. Enskaitis, P.O.B. 78, Rodney, Ontario.

The Fellowship of British Christian Esperantists (Kunularo de Britaj Kristanaj Esperantistoj), Mrs. F. W. White, Secretary, White Lodge, 13 Mareschall Road, Guildford, Surrey, is the British KELI affiliate. It publishes Kristana Alvoko, edited by the Reverend William J. Downes, a Member of the Esperanto Academy, 45 Fernbank Road, Redland, Bristol 6. Similar newsletters or magazines published by KELI affiliates are Esperanto-Oikumene, in Germany, KUNE-Bulteno in the Netherlands, Kristana Bulteno in Switzerland, Kristliga Esperantoförbundets Medlemsblad in Sweden, and Kristana Voĉo in Norway. KELI publishes from time to time Membership Directories.

Internacia Kristana Frataro, Livingstone Jenkins, 29 Cornwall Road, Bexhill-on-Sea, Sussex, England, publishes the quarterly Vojo de la Vivo, with a supplement, La Vera Lumo. The Finnish branch, Kristana Frataro de Finnaj Esperantistoj, Hugo Salokannel, Maunula, Laihia (Vaasan lääni), Finland, has done some publishing of its own.

La Navigantoj, Örebro, Sweden, runs correspondence courses on Christianity and the Bible.

Esperanto-Missionen, Klackavägen, Nora Stad (Västmanland), Sweden, publishes and distributes Christian Esperanto literature.

Interdenominational religious services in Esperanto are held at many Esperanto conferences and are organized regularly in London, Bristol, and Bournemouth, in England, and from time to time in many other cities throughout the world.

The complete Bible in Esperanto was published in 1926 by the British and Foreign Bible Society. There are a number of hymn books, among them Himnaro Esperanta (212 hymns), compiled by Montagu C. Butler, published in England, and Espero Internacia (240 hymns with music), compiled by Ann E. Beatty and published by the Christian Home Orphanage, Council Bluffs, Iowa. The very extensive Christian Esperanto literature includes denominational literature of the Anglicans (Church of England and Protestant Episcopal Church), Presbyterians, Lutherans, Baptists, Methodists, Congregationalists, New Church (Swedenborgians), Quakers (Society of Friends), Swedish Evangelical Mission Covenant, Pentecostal Churches, Seventh-Day Adventists, Jehovah's Witnesses, as well as the Unitarians and Universalists and also, of course, the Roman Catholics and some of the Eastern Orthodox Churches.

COLLECTING (see also article on STAMP COLLECTING)

Esperantista Kolektanto, Raoul Mélo, 6 Place Jules Ferry, St. Etienne (Loire), France. This periodical also publishes a **Tutmonda Esperantista Kolektanta Adresaro.**

Esperantajojn Kolektanta Internacia Klubo (EKIK), Louis Obreczian, P.O. Box 51, Waterman, Pennsylvania, publishes **La Glumark-Kolektanto,** catalogues, address lists of its members, etc.

COMMERCE & INDUSTRY

Esperanto Parolata, published by M. Rétot, 162 boulevard Aristide Briand, Montreuil (Seine), France, is a partial list of business firms using Esperanto.

The Universal Esperanto Association (UEA) listed in its 1958 Year Book 69 specialized "delegates" for commerce from 26 countries, 12 delegates for industry from 8 countries, 18 delegates for banking from 11 countries, 31 delegates for crafts and small business from 16 countries throughout the world.

COOPERATIVES

Cooperative Esperanto League, A. A. Ager, 8, Pelham Road, Beckenham, Kent, England, publishes **The Cooperator Esperantist,** edited by William A. Gething, O.B.E., 15 Campden Road, Cheltenham, Gloucestershire, England.

Ĉielarko is the organ of the Esperanto Section of the Casa de Rochdale, Museo Social Argentino, Avenida Corrientes 1723, Buenos Aires, Argentina.

DUODECIMAL SYSTEM

The Duodecimal Society of America, 20 Carlton Place, Staten Island

4, New York, publishes some of its literature in Esperanto.

ENGINEERING & TECHNOLOGY (see also Aviation, Radio, Science)

Technical vocabularies in the interlanguage Esperanto exist for Electrical Engineering, Mechanical Engineering, Aeronautical Engineering, Radio Engineering, Railroad Engineering, Illumination, the Building Trades, Saws, and Pigments. There is a great deal of original and translated literature.

Periodicals which have published articles or summaries in Esperanto include **Ingegneria Meccanica** in Italy, **Water** and **Verfkroniek** in the Netherlands, the **Journal of the Institution of Water Engineers** in England, and a number of Japanese publications, among them the **Quarterly Reports of the Laboratory of Industrial Technology** in Osaka, the **Journal of the Electrotechnical Society of Waseda University, Ohm** (a journal of electrical engineering), the **Journal of the Osaka Institute of Science and Technology,** the **Proceedings of the World Engineering Congress** in Tokyo (1929), the **Bulletin of the Illumination Society of Japan,** the **Journal of the Society of Brewing,** and the **Reports of the Aeronautical Research Institute.**

FREE MASONRY

Universala Framasona Ligo, Carl Barthel, Wohlerstrasse 14, Frankfurt, Germany (Federal Republic), organizes international Masonic meetings using Esperanto, both at Esperanto Congresses and independently. Esperanto has been used by Masonic organizations in a number of countries. Masonic lodges consisting exclusively of Esperanto-speaking members exist in Paris, France, and Rio de Janeiro, Brazil.

FRIENDS, SOCIETY OF (Quakers)

Kvakera Esperantista Societo, A. J. Saunders, Sydney Lodge, Bath Rd., Ventnor, Isle of Wight, England, publishes **La Kvakera Esperantisto.**

Quaker literature in Esperanto, some of it published by the Friends' Service Council in London, includes biographies of George Fox and William Penn, books by Edward Grubb and Caroline E. Stephen, as well as a number of pamphlets by T. Corder Catchpool, Edward Grubb, William E. Wilson, and Henri Van Etten.

GEOGRAPHY

Internacia Geografia Asocio, Prof. J. E. Jackson, Dept. of Geography, Downing Pl., Cambridge, England; publishes the **Internacia Geografia Revuo,** A. W. Thomson, 315 Bellegrove Road, Welling, Kent, England. There is a great deal of geographical literature in Esperanto.

GRAPHIC ARTS & PRINTING

Internacia Grafika Esperanto-Ligo, A. Frangeul, 42 rue du Pré-Pigeon, Angers (Maine-et-Loire), France, publishes a bulletin.

Several editions of the **United States Government Printing Office Style Manual** contained a fairly detailed "guide to the typography of the more important languages," including Esperanto.

HUMANISM

Brita Esperanto-Humanistaro, G. L. Dickinson, 21, Gribble Road, Liverpool 10, England, publishes a bulletin.

Spiritscienca Instituto de Martinus, Esperanto-Fako, Mariendalsvej 94-96, Copenhagen, Denmark, publishes the magazine **Kosmo** and other literature (5 books up to 1959).

JOURNALISM

Tutmonda Esperantista Ĵurnalista Asocio, Dr. Dino Fabris, Borgo Bassano 5, Cittadella (Padova), Italy. Service for the exchange of articles **(Interŝanĝservo):** G. Norgaard Jepsen, Skövvangen 17, Silkeborg, Denmark. Magazine: **Internacia Ĵurnalisto,** Ivan Keremidĉiev-Esperov, bulv. Hristo Botev 92, Sofia 2, Bulgaria.

JUDAISM & ZIONISM

Esperanto—Lingvo Internacia, edited in Esperanto and Hebrew, is the organ of the **Esperantista Ligo Izraellanda,** N. Drezner, 4 Johanan Hasandlar, Tel Aviv, Israel.

Herzl's **The Jewish State** and other Zionist literature exists in Esperanto. There are numerous translations from Hebrew and Yiddish.

There are several Esperanto textbooks in Hebrew and Yiddish and one in Sephardic Spanish. And an "Esperanto Key" exists in Yiddish.

Jewish religious services have been held at numerous Esperanto Congresses.

LABOR

Sennacieca Asocio Tutmonda (SAT), 67 Avenue Gambetta, Paris 20, France. Journals **Sennaciulo** and **Sennacieca Revuo.** From 1921 to 1959 SAT has held 32 World Congresses usually attended by 600-1000 representatives.

There are numerous national and special-interest Esperanto organizations operating in the labor movement. Most of them advocate various brands of Socialism, a few have pro-Communist leanings. They publish the following magazines or bulletins (among others):

The Worker Esperantist, 27 Argyle Road, Ilford, Essex England.

Samideano, Esperanto tomo no kai, 6-672. Koenzi Suginami-ku, Tokyo, Japan.

SAT-Amikaro, 67 avenue Gambetta, Paris 20, France.

La Esperantista Laboristo, 4 rue Malleterre, Paris 16, France.

La Libera Esperantisto, Reinhard Uhde, Utbremer Ring 154, Bremen. German Federal Republic.

Liberigo de Mizero, H. Cottereau, La Brétaudiere, Vaupillon par La Loupe (Eure-et-Loire), France (promotes the ideas of Edward Bellamy's "Looking Backward").

LANGUAGE LEARNING

The study of French via Esperanto has been practiced successfully at international summer courses held for a number of years, beginning in 1956, at the Château de Grésillon in France, with the moral support of the French Ministry of Education. The Château de Grésillon functions as a cultural center of the French Esperanto movement **(Esperantista Kulturdomo).** Requests for information should be addressed to the Maison Culturelle de l'Esperanto, H. Micard, Epineux-le-Seguin (Mayenne), France.

A textbook of French in Esperanto, **Franca Gramatiko por Esperantistoj,** by P. Boulet, was published in Dijon years ago. Italian and Japanese serialized lessons in Esperanto have appeared in magazines.

The use of Esperanto as a "general language" in schools has been advocated and practiced in a number of countries. Helen S. Eaton's **General Language Course** uses Esperanto as a basis for the following reason:

"It aims to make the pupil look at language objectively. This has seemed extremely difficult to bring about through the medium of the student's own vernacular. One of the advantages felt to be obtained by the use of Esperanto as the language of the text is that it seems to accomplish this purpose more easily."

LAWYERS

Internacia Asocio de Juristoj-Esperantistoj, Jean Duthilleul, 35 rue de Bayeux, Caen (Calvados), France.

LIBRARIES

The most complete Esperanto libraries in the world are those of the British Esperanto Association, the Universal Esperanto Association in Geneva, the International Esperanto Museum in Vienna, and the Chamber of Commerce in Paris.

In the United States many public libraries and university libraries have large Esperanto collections, especially the Library of Congress in Washington, the Public Libraries of New York, Boston, Detroit, and Cleveland, and the Libraries of Harvard University and the University of Illinois.

Klasifo de Esperantaj Temoj, by M. C. Butler, is a good description of the classification system used by the Library of the British Esperanto Association and usable for other Esperanto Libraries.

LITERATURE

Internacia Verkista Asocio, William Auld, Knockfarril, Thornside Road, Johnstone, Renfrewshire, Britain, is an organization of Esperanto writers and is devoted to the promotion of their professional and other interests.

The most important literary magazines in Esperanto are:

La Norda Prismo, Barnhusgatan 8, Stockholm, Sweden.

Nica Literatura Revuo, 5 boulevard Stalingrad, Nice, France.

La Suda Stelo, Miklošičeva 7, Ljubljana, Yugoslavia.

Prometeo, Nakatu-hamadori 2-20, Oyodoku, Osaka, Japan.

MATHEMATICS

Dr. C. M. Bean's **Matematika Terminaro,** published in England in

1954, is one of several mathematical vocabularies in Esperanto. There are numerous mathematical publications in the Interlanguage.

Periodicals publishing articles or summaries in Esperanto have included the **Annali di Matematica Pura ed Applicata** in Italy, **Portugaliae Mathematica** in Portugal, **Compositio Mathematica** in the Netherlands, the **Journal fur die Reine und Angewandte Mathematik** in Germany, the **Bulletin de la Société des Mathematiciens et Physiciens de la R. P. de Serbie** in Yugoslavia, the **Yokohama Mathematical Journal** and **La Funkcialaj Ekvacioj** ("Functional Equations"—the name of this journal is in Esperanto) in Japan.

MEDICAL PROFESSION

Tutmonda Esperantista Kuracista Asocio (TEKA), Dr. V. Jovanović, Maslesina 8, Zemun-Beograd VIII., Yugoslavia.

Medicina Revuo, Profesoro Masao Suzuki, Fiziologia Instituto, Tiba, Japan.

There is a great deal of medical literature in Esperanto. The best dictionary is Dr. M. Briquet's **Esperanta Teknika Medicina Vortaro,** which gives definitions in Esperanto, translations in Latin and, when necessary, in English, French, German, Italian and Spanish. There are also specialized Esperanto terminologies for anatomy, physiology, and pharmacology.

Medical journals which have published articles or summaries in Esperanto include the **Journal de Médecine de Lyon** and **Le Phare Médical de Paris** in France, **Acta Orthopaedica Belgica** in Belgium, **Therapeutica Nova, L'Igiene Moderna,** and **Giornale di Clinica Medica** in Italy, the **Arquivos do Departamento de Assistência a Psicopatas do Estado de São Paulo** in Brazil, and more than a dozen periodicals in Japan, including the **Folia Anatomica Japonica,** the **Acta Anatomica Nipponica,** the **Journal of the Physiological Society of Japan,** the **Journal of Biochemistry,** the **Gunma Journal of Medical Science,** the **Nihon University Medical Journal,** and the **Lepra Journal.**

Bibliografio de Medicina Literaturo Esperanta en Japanujo, a 48-page booklet published in Tokyo in 1956, lists or mentions 1,010 medical publications in Esperanto or with Esperanto summaries.

The Use of Esperanto in Medical Science (American Esperanto Magazine, March 1957) and **Facts about the Scientific Uses of Esperanto in Japan** (AEM, March 1958) are recommended for further information.

METEOROLOGY

A voluminous handbook of meteorology by General Emile Delcambre, published by the French Government's **Office Météorologique National**, contains a 12-language **Lexique Météorologique** in French, English, Spanish, Italian, German, Portuguese, Rumanian, Russian, Polish, Czech, Croatian, and Esperanto. For all languages except Russian and Esperanto, the terminologies were provided by the official meteorological institutions of the countries concerned. The Esperanto terminology was furnished by Maurice Rollet de l'Isle, a former Director of the Central Hydrographic Office of the French Navy.

The Aerological Observatory of Tateno, Japan, published more than 2,500 pages of reports in Esperanto. Articles or summaries in Esperanto also appeared in other publications such as the **Journal of the Meteorological Society of Japan** and the **Bulletin of the Central Meteorological Observatory of Japan.** A bibliography of scientific literature published in Japan in Esperanto lists 58 items from the field of meteorology.

MOSLEMS

There are several Esperanto publications on Islam, for instance, **Islamo Esperantiste Rigardata** by Colin Evans (Qassim Isma'il). Esperanto has been used for Moslem missionary activities. An **Islama Koresponda Rondo,** which used to function with headquarters in London, had not been heard from for some time when this book went to press.

MOTION PICTURES

Hollywood feature films in which Esperanto was used in one way or another include **Road to Singapore** (with Dorothy Lamour, Bob Hope, and Bing Crosby), **Idiot's Delight** (with Norma Shearer and Clark Gable), Charlie Chaplin's **The Great Dictator, Neutral Port** (with Yvonne Arnaud and Will Fyfe), **The Hermit of Samburan** (with Betty Field, Frederic March, and Cedric Hardwick), **Conspiracy,** and others.

Esperanto films, some of them high quality productions in color and sound, have been produced by a number of governments, including those of Australia, New Zealand, and Denmark, to attract tourists.

An **Esperanto Film-Grupo** in Bergen-op-Zoom, Netherlands, has produced a large number of films usable at club meetings.

MUSEUM (see also ART)

Internacia Esperanto-Muzeo, Wien I., Hofburg, Austria, is an autonomous division of the Austrian National Library and is housed in the former Imperial Palace in the center of Vienna. It is supported in part by a government subsidy, in part by contributions from members of the Esperanto movement. It publishes a bulletin, catalogues, and other materials.

NATURE FRIENDS

Turista Asocio La Natur-Amikoj, Esperanto-Fako (TANEF), A. J. Beekmans, Belfaststraat 5, Antwerpen, Belgium; or Max Finkenzeller, Oswaldgasse 16, Wien XII., Austria.

OOMOTO

Oomoto, Esperanto-Revuo, Kameoka, Kyoto-hu, Japan. A Japanese religious organization of Shintoist origin, with great emphasis on universal brotherhood, peace, world federation, etc., Oomoto has been promoting and using Esperanto for many years. Its magazine, **Oomoto,** in addition to religious and inspirational articles, has published articles on Japanese culture, folklore, art, and literature as well as on the Esperanto movement in Japan and abroad and has thereby attracted interest in wider circles.

PEACE MOVEMENT

Universala Ligo, Riouwstraat 172, Den Haag, Netherlands; works for world federation and international understanding, using Esperanto as its official language. It publishes literature in Esperanto, including the illustrated monthly magazine **La Praktiko** and a Yearbook.

Pax Christi, Esperanto-Sekcio, Professor Max Mielert, Wurzerstrasse 18/III, München 22, Germany; or Jaime Juan Forné, Martí 3, Valencia, Spain. This is a Catholic peace organization.

Mondcivitana Respubliko, Esperanto-Fako, 13 Prince of Wales Terrace, Kensington, London, England. This world citizenship organization publishes literature in Esperanto.

Internacio de Militrezistantoj (War Resisters' International), Lansbury House, 88 Park Avenue, Enfield, Middlesex, England, uses Esperanto, together with national tongues, at its conferences and in correspondence. It publishes **Militrezistanto.**

Some users of this book may come across a group known as **Mondpaca Esperantista Movado** (MEM) and its magazine **Paco** published every month in a different country, sometimes behind the iron curtain, usually in the free world. The officers of MEM reside in Czechoslovakia, Austria, and Sweden. There are representatives in 30 countries, including the Soviet Union, Communist China, Communist North Vietnam, the Soviet Zone of Germany, Bulgaria, Czechoslovakia, Hungary, Poland, and Rumania. MEM is connected with the Communist-inspired and Communist-controlled World Peace Council, although it has a few supporters in other circles. In a number of iron curtain countries, where the Esperanto movement was suppressed and persecuted for many years, Esperantists have tried to use MEM as a means of overcoming their isolation and establish contacts with Esperantists in the free world. The result of all this is that the following kinds of people are found in MEM and **Paco:** (1) Communists; (2) fellow travelers, most of them with long records of pro-Communist activities; (3) old and new Esperantists in iron curtain countries, some of whom are Communists, but most of whom are not; (4) a very few others, including some who are too naive to understand who is behind MEM. MEM was founded in 1952.

POLICE

Internacia Polica Ligo, August Weide, Eggerstedtstrasse 41, Hamburg-Altona, Germany (Federal Republic).

RADIO & TELEVISION

In early 1959 shortwave programs in Esperanto were broadcast daily from Rio de Janeiro, four times a week from Bern, three times a week from Rome, twice a week from Sofia, weekly from Vienna, Guatemala City, Caracas, Rio de Janeiro, São Paulo, Juiz de Fora, once a month from Tangier. Regular medium wave radio broadcasts in Esperanto were featured by stations in Austria, Brazil, France, Guatemala, the Netherlands, Spain, Venezuela, and Yugoslavia.

Esperanto television and radio programs broadcast on special occasions and interviews on Esperanto were numerous in many countries around the world, including the United States and Canada. When the 48th North American Esperanto Congress was held at Neuville near Quebec in 1958, four television interviews (over three TV stations) and four radio interviews (each on a different station) were devoted to it, in addition to news coverage on numerous radio and TV shows.

Radio amateurs in many countries, including the United States, have successfully used Esperanto for many years. The First International

Congress of Radio Amateurs, held in Paris in 1925, adopted a proposal of the American Radio Relay League in favor of Esperanto.

RAILROADS

Internacia Federacio Esperantista Fervojista (IFEF), J. Lok, Orteliusstraat 108/III, Amsterdam, Netherlands, publishes **La Internacia Fervojisto.** Sections in several countries, e.g. Austria, Belgium, France, Germany, Italy, and Yugoslavia, publish bulletins of their own.

Railroad administrations in Austria, Denmark, Finland, Germany, Japan, Sweden, Switzerland, etc., have published promotional literature in Esperanto or used the language in time tables and services. The German Federal Railroad, for instance, regularly includes in its semi-annual **Reisefernfahrplan** one page of explanations in Esperanto and several pages of "hints for travelers from abroad."

There are several Esperanto vocabularies of railroad terms, including E. M. Rosher's **Fervoja Terminaro.**

ROTARY CLUBS

Esperanto has been successfully used by Rotary Clubs around the world; for details see **Rotary and Esperanto** in the American Esperanto Magazine of March 1955.

The **Rotaria Esperanto-Amikaro,** at times very active, seemed not to be functioning in a formal manner at the time of going to press. The following are the addresses of some Rotarians most active in the field: Marcel Génermont, architecte, 11 place de la République, Moulins (Allier), France; José Silvano Portes, Av. Olegario Maciel 90, Caratinga (Minas Gerais), Brazil; Norman Williams, 237 Two Trees Lane, Denton, Lancs., England.

SCIENCE

Internacia Scienca Asocio Esperantista, D-ro B. Popović, Zagrebacka 20a, Sarajevo, Yugoslavia; representative for the United States: Joseph H. Gamble, 6 Lexington Avenue, Bethpage, L. I., N. Y.

Scienca Revuo, Uitgeverij J. Muusses, Permerend, Netherlands.

Sciencaj Studoj, a large 241-page book published in 1958 in Copenhagen, is the first volume of a series of compilations of scientific and scholarly research reports written directly in Esperanto (**not** translations). Edited by Dr. Paul Neergaard, a phytopathologist, it contains articles contributed by 37 scientists from 19 countries.

An International Scientific and Technological Translation Service, established by ISAE, provides at nonimal cost Esperanto translations of articles and research reports to scientists who need them, but do not understand the language in which they are published.

Scienca kaj Teknika Terminaro, published in Tokyo in 1956, covers many fields of science and technology, especially theoretical and nuclear physics, chemistry, mathematics, and electrical engineering.

Scientific periodicals which have published articles or summaries in Esperanto include: the **Proceedings** of the Royal Academy of Sciences in the Netherlands, **Physica, Chemisch Weekblad, Vegetatio, Ardea, Hydrobiologia** in the Netherlands; the **Journal of Geophysical Research** in the U. S.; the **Bulletin de la Société Entomologique de Mulhouse** in France; the **Bulletin de la Société des Sciences Naturelles** in Morocco; **Geophysica** in Finland; **Tromsö Museums Arshefter** and **Stavanger Museums Arshefter** in Norway; **Geofisica Pura ed Applicata** in Italy; **Speleolog** in Yugoslavia; and an extremely large number in Japan, among them the **Science Reports of Tohoku University,** the **Memoirs of the Faculty of Science of Kyusyu University,** the **Science Report of Gunma University, Progress of Theoretical Physics,** the **Journal of the Chemical Society of Japan,** the **Botanical Magazine,** the **Zoological Magazine,** the **Journal of Oceanography,** the **Japanese Journal of Genetics,** and the **Annotationes Zoologicae Japonenses.**

SCOUTS

Skolta Esperantista Ligo (SEL), Charles Bardsley, 42 Westbourne Street, Oldham, Lancs., England. Agent for the U. S.: C. Stanley Otto, 20 Harvard Terrace, West Orange, N. J. Magazine: **Skolta Mondo.**

Esperanto was recommended by Lord Baden Powell, founder of Scouting, in **Scouting for Boys** (page 234). It has been used at several World Jamborees of the Boy Scouts as well as at special Esperanto Scout Camps organized by SEL.

SERICULTURE

Esperanto has served to establish closer contact between silkworm growers in Japan and France. The **Revue du Ver à Soie,** published by the Silkworm Research Center in Alès, France, and the **Journal of Sericultural Science,** published by the Silkworm Research Center in Tokyo, have published articles and summaries in .Esperanto.

SHORTHAND

Tutmonda Intersteno-Asocio, C. Daglio, Litta Parodi, Alessandria, Italy, publishes **Multlingva Intersteno.**

Many shorthand systems, including Gregg and Pitman, have been adapted to Esperanto use, and have been used in stenographic contests.

SOCIOLOGY

Internacia Komisiono Esperanto kaj Sociologio, C. J. Keur, Moerweg 76, Den Haag, Netherlands. The Chairman is Dr. William Solzbacher, of Washington, D. C.

The Commission has held meetings at a number of Universal Esperanto Congresses and was officially represented at the World Congresses of Sociology at Liége (1953), Amsterdam (1956), and Stresa (1959).

SPIRITUALISM

Esperanto-Spiritista Asocio, BM/LESS, London WC 1, England, publishes **Vivado.**

Spiritisma Esperanto-Movado, Caixa Postal 507, Belo Horizonte, Minas Gerais, Brazil, publishes **Semado.**

The Brazilian Spiritualist Federation **(Federacão Espirita Brasileira),** Av. Passos 30, Rio de Janeiro, has published a large amount of Spiritualist literature in Esperanto.

STATISTICS

The Brazilian Government Institute of Geography and Statistics **(Instituto Brasileiro de Geografia e Estatistica)** has, by law, adopted Esperanto as its official international auxiliary language and has been using it for many of its publications and for summaries in its reports and magazines.

SUMMER SCHOOLS

There are numerous International Summer Courses using Esperanto as the only language of instruction and discussion. Some deal with cultural subjects, international relations, or some particular country, others have the purpose of making participants more fluent in Esperanto or qualifying them as Esperanto teachers, others are simply leisurely vacations in a friendly atmosphere and in beautiful surroundings, with some cultural and recreational community activities. Locations and programs vary from year to year, but they include regularly summer courses at the Château de Grésillon, Baugé, M-et-L., France, and at the International People's College in Elsinore, Denmark, organized by L. Friis, Ingemannsvej 9, Aabyhöj, Denmark.

TEACHERS & SCHOOLS

Internacia Ligo de Esperantistaj Instruistoj, Miss Violet C. Nixon, 183, Woodlands Park Road, Birmingham 30, England. Affiliated groups in Australia, Austria, Britain, France, Germany, Italy, Japan, the Netherlands, and Sweden.

Internacia Pedagogia Revuo, M. Delagneau, Avrolles-par-Saint-Florentin (Yonne), France.

Grajnoj en Vento, Marcel Erbetta, rue des Pins 66, Bienne 7, Switzerland, organizes "chains" of school classes in different countries, which keep in touch through Esperanto.

Internacia Instituto de Esperanto, Riouwstraat 172, Den Haag, Netherlands, organizes throughout the world classes according to the famed Cseh method, trains Esperanto teachers, publishes teaching materials.

TOURIST AGENCIES & TRAVEL

More than a thousand tourist publications have appeared in Esperanto, ranging from high-class guide books (e.g. Rome, Milan, Denmark, Norway, Japan, several Brazilian cities) to publicity folders and train, ship, and airplane timetables. More than 60 appear every year.

Esperanto phrase books and pocket dictionaries for tourists include the following:

Say It In Esperanto, by George Alan Connor and Doris Tappan Connor. Advice given by Dr. William Solzbacher of the Akademio de Esperanto. Each phrase numbered and indexed. This 160-page booklet in a handy pocket format, is published by Dover Publications Inc. in New York in the series of their "SAY IT" books.

A Guide to the Languages of Europe, by Archibald Lyall, can also be recommended. This book covers 25 languages. The excellent Esperanto section is by Montagu C. Butler.

UNIVERSITY STUDENTS

Studenta Tutmonda Esperantista Ligo, J. C. Wells, Secretary, Trinity College, Cambridge, England, affiliated with ISAE.

La Esperantista Studento, 34 rue de Chabrol, Paris X., France, is the official organ of STELO.

VEGETARIANS

Vegetarano, organo de la **Tutmonda Esperanta Vegetara Asocio,** A. Andriu, Salusses par Montsalès (Aveyron), France.

WOMEN'S ORGANIZATIONS

Esperanta Virina Asocio (EVA), Nakacuhamadoori 2-20, Oojodu-ku, Osaka, Japan, publishes a bulletin and pamphlets.

YOUTH (see also SCOUTS and UNIVERSITY STUDENTS)

Tutmonda Esperantista Junulara Organizo (TEJO), Sekretario Nicola Minnaja, Viale Giulio Cesare 223, Rome, Italy. Sections in many countries. Activities include International Esperanto Ski Vacations in the winter and International Youth Conferences in the spring and summer.

PART

5

ESPERANTO-ENGLISH
DICTIONARY

****

LIST OF ABBREVIATIONS

- separates the root-word from its ending, and represents the repetition of the root or word.

— represents, in Esperanto, the incorporation of the root to form a compound word; in English, the repetition of a word used separately.

accus.—accusative
act.—active
adj.—adjective
adv.—adverb
agr.—agriculture
Amer.—American
anat.—anatomy
bot.—botany
Brit.—British
chem.—chemistry
com.—commerce
conj.—conjunction
cul.—culinary
den.—denoting
elec.—electricity
end.—ending
fin.—finance
geog.—geography
geom.—geometry
gov't.—government
gram.—grammar
indef.—indefinite
instr.—instrument

intr.—intransitive
jour.—journalism
leg.—legal
lit.—literature
mech.—mechanics
med.—medicine
mil.—military
min.—mineral
mus.—music
naut.—nautical
part.—participle
pass.—passive
phys.—physics
pol.—political
pref.—prefix
prep.—preposition
pres.—present
rad.—radio
sc.—science
suff.—suffix
theat.—theatre
tr.—transitive
zool.—zoology

ESPERANTO-ENGLISH

A

-a, (adj. ending)

abel-o, bee; -ujo, hive

abism-o, abyss

abomen-o, abomination, disgust

abon-i, to subscribe to (journal, etc.)

abrikot-o, apricot

abrupt-a, abrupt

absolut-a, absolute

absurd-a, absurd

abund-a, abundant, luxuriant

acid-a, acid, sour

-aĉ-, (suff. den. contempt); hundo, a dog; hundaĉo, a cur

aĉet-i, to buy

-ad-, (suff. den. continuation of action); kanto, a song; kantado, singing

adapt-i, to adapt

adiaŭ, good-bye, farewell

adici-o, addition (math.)

adjektiv-o, adjective

administr-i, to administer; -ado, administration, management

admir-i, to admire

admon-i, to admonish

ador-i, to adore, worship

adres-o, address (letter, place, etc.)

adverb-o, adverb

advokat-o, advocate, lawyer

aer-o, air; -umi, to aerate

aeroplan-o, airplane

afabl-a, affable, kind, gracious

afer-o, affair, matter, thing, business

afiŝ-o, poster, placard

aflikt-i, to afflict, distress

afrank-i, to frank, prepay postage

Afrik-o, Africa

ag-i, to act; -ado, action

agarik-o, mushroom

agend-o, agenda

agent-o, agent

agit-i, to agitate, stir up; -isto, agitator

agl-o, eagle

agoni-o, agony, death-throes

agrabl-a, agreeable, pleasant

agraf-o, clasp, hook (dress, etc.)

aĝ-o, age; plen—ulo, adult

ajl-o, garlic

ajn, -ever, soever; io ajn, anything whatever

-aĵ-, (suff. den. something made from, or having quality of); novaĵo, novelty, news; trinkaĵo, beverage; aĵo, thing (tangible)

akademi-o, academy

akcel-i, to accelerate, quicken

akcent-i, to accentuate, stress

akcept-i, to accept, receive

akci-o, share (fin.)

akcident-o, accident

akciz-o, excise (tax)

akir-i, to acquire, obtain, gain

aklam-i, to acclaim

akompan-i, accompany, go with

akord-o, chord (mus.), accord; -igi, to tune

akr-a, sharp, acrid

akre-o, acre

aks-o, axle, axis

aksel-o, armpit

akt-o, act (theat.); deed, act (leg.)

aktiv-a, active

aktor-o, actor

aktual-a, present, of present interest

akurat-a, punctual

akuz-i, to accuse

akuzativ-o, accusative

akv-o, water

al, to, towards (compare -n); -iĝi, to join
ale-o, alley, garden-path, lane
alfabet-o, alphabet
algebr-o, algebra
ali-a, other, another; -e, otherwise; -loke, elsewhere
alkohol-o, alcohol
almenaŭ, at least, anyhow
almoz-o, alms; -ulo, beggar
alt-a, high; -e; highly, aloft
altar-o, altar
alud-i, to allude to, mention
alumet-o, match
alumini-o, aluminum
am-i, to love; -inda, loveable; -indumi, to make love to, court
amar-a, bitter
amas-o, mass, heap; hom—o, crowd
amator-o, amateur
ambasador-o, ambassador
ambaŭ, both
ambici-o, ambition
ambulanc-o, ambulance
Amerik-o, America; -a, American; -ano, an American
amik-o, friend
Amor-o, Amor, Cupid, God of Love
ampleks-o, amplitude; extent, scope
amuz-i, to amuse, entertain
-an-, (suff. den. member, inhabitant, adherent); klubano, club member; vilaĝano, villager; Parizano, a Parisian
analiz-i, to analyse
ananas-o, pineapple
anas-o, duck; -ido, duckling
anekdot-o, anecdote
angl-o, Englishman; -a, English; -ujo, England
angor-o, agony, anguish
angul-o, angle, corner
anĝel-o, angel; ĉef—o, archangel
anim-o, soul; grand—a, magnanimous; unu—a, unanimous
ankaŭ, also, too
ankoraŭ, still, yet

ankr-o, anchor
anonc-i, to announce, give notice of
anonim-a, anonymous
anser-o, goose, -ido, gosling
anstataŭ, instead of; -i, to take the place of; -anto, substitute
-ant-, (end. of pres. part. act.); aŭskultanto, a listener
antarkt-a, antarctic
antaŭ, before, in front of, ago; -a, previous, former; -en, forward, onward; -nelonge, not long ago, recently
anten-o, antenna, aerial (rad.)
anticip-i, to anticipate, expect
antikv-a, ancient, antique
antilop-o, antelope
antologi-o, anthology
antropolog-o, anthropologist; -io, anthropology
anus-o, anus
aparat-o, apparatus
apart-a, apart, special, separate
aparten-i, to belong to
apelaci-i, to appeal (leg.)
apenaŭ, scarcely, hardly
aper-i, to appear, come into sight
apetit-o, appetite
aplaŭd-i, to applaud
aplik-i, to apply
apog-i, to lean, rest on for support
apostol-o, apostle
apotek-o, drug-store
April-o, April
aprob-i, to approve
apud, beside, close by, near
-ar-, (suff. den. collection of, number of); homaro, mankind; vortaro, dictionary
arakis-o, peanut
arane-o, spider
aranĝ-i, to arrange; -o, arrangement
arb-o, tree
arbitr-a, arbitrary, wilful
ard-i, to glow, be ardent
are-o, area
aren-o, arena

arest-i, to arrest, take into custody
argument-o, argument; -i, to argue
arĝent-o, silver
aristokrat-o, aristocrat
aritmetik-o, arithmetic
ark-o, arc; -aĵo, arch
arkitekt-o, architect; -uro, architecture
arkt-a, arctic
arm-i, to arm; -ilo, weapon
arme-o, army
arom-o, aroma; -a, aromatic
art-o, art; -a, artistic; -efarita, artificial
arteri-o, artery
artik-o, joint
artikol-o, article (newspaper, etc.)
artileri-o, artillery (mil.)
-as, (end. den. pres. tense); parolas, speaks, is speaking
asekur-i, to insure; -o, insurance
asert-i, to assert
asign-i, to assign (leg.)
asoci-o, association
aspekt-i, to appear, look
astr-o, heavenly body, -a, astral
astrolog-o, astrologer; -io, astrology
astronom-o, astronomer; -io, astronomy
-at-, (end. of pres. part. pass.); amato, loved-one
atak-i, to attack
ateism-o, atheism
atend-i, to wait for, await
atent-a, attentive; -i, to be attentive, heed, pay attention
atest-i, to testify, bear witness; -o, certificate
ating-i, to attain, reach
atlet-o, athlete; -a, athletic
atmosfer-o, atmosphere
atom-o, atom; -bombo, atom bomb
aŭ, or, either; aŭ . . . aŭ, either . . . or
aŭd-i, to hear; -antaro, audience
Aŭgust-o, August
aŭskult-i, to listen

aŭtentik-a, authentic
aŭtobiografi-o, autobiography
aŭtobus-o, autobus
aŭtomat-o, automaton; -a, automatic
aŭtomobil-o, automobile; -ejo, garage
aŭtonom-a, autonomous
aŭtor-o, author
aŭtoritat-o, authority
aŭtun-o, autumn, fall
av-o, grandfather
avantaĝ-o, advantage
avar-a, avaricious, miserly, stingy; mal—a, generous
aven-o, oats
aventur-o, adventure
avert-i, to warn, caution
avid-a, avid, eager for, greedy for; -i, to covet, long for
aviz-o, notice, advice (com.)
azen-o, ass, donkey
Azi-o, Asia

B
babil-i, to chat, chatter, babble
bagatel-o, a trifle
bajonet-o, bayonet
bak-i, to bake
bakteri-o, bacteria
bal-o, ball, dance
bala-i, to sweep
balanc-i, to swing; -iĝi, swing, sway
balbut-i, to stammer, stutter
baldaŭ, soon
balen-o, whale
balet-o, ballet
balkon-o, balcony
balon-o, balloon
balot-i, to ballot, vote by ballot
ban-i, to bathe; -kuvo, bath tub
banan-o, banana
band-o, band, gang, crew
bandaĝ-o, bandage
bank-o, bank (fin.)
bankrot-i, to become bankrupt
bapt-i, baptize; -opatro, godfather

bar-i, to bar, block, obstruct; **-ilo,** barrier, fence
barakt-i, to struggle, writhe
barb-o, beard
barbir-o, barber
barel-o, barrel, cask
barometr-o, barometer
basbal-o, baseball
baston-o, stick, baton; **lam—o,** crutch
bat-i, to beat, strike
batal-i, to fight, battle
bateri-o, battery (mil., elec.)
baz-o, base, basis
beb-o, baby
bed-o, bed (flower, etc.)
bedaŭr-i, to be sorry, regret; **-inda,** regrettable, unfortunate
bek-o, beak; **-piki,** to peck
bel-a, beautiful, fine, handsome; **-ega,** magnificent; **-eta,** pretty
belg-o, a Belgian; **-a,** Belgian (adj.); **-ujo,** Belgium
ben-i, to bless; **-ado,** benediction
benk-o, bench
benzin-o, (Amer.) gasoline, (Brit.) petrol
ber-o, berry; **vin—o,** grape
best-o, animal, beast
bet-o, beet
bezon-i, to need, want, require
Bibli-o, Bible
bibliografi-o, bibliography
bibliotek-o, library
bicikl-o, bicycle
bien-o, estate, landed property; **farm—o,** farm
bier-o, beer
bifstek-o, beefsteak
bilanc-o, balance-sheet
bild-o, picture, image
bilet-o, ticket, note
bind-i, to bind (books)
biograf-o, biographer; **-io,** biography
biolog-o, biologist; **-io,** biology
bird-o, bird
biskvit-o, biscuit

bizon-o, bison, buffalo
blank-a, white
blat-o, cockroach
blek-i, to bleat, neigh, bellow, etc. (general word for animal cries)
blind-a, blind
blok-o, block, boulder, lump, chunk; **-ado,** blockade
blond-a, blonde, fair
blov-i, to blow
blu-a, blue
bo-, (pref. den. relation by marriage); **-patro,** father-in-law
boat-o, boat
boben-o, reel, bobbin; coil (rad.)
boj-o, bark (dog's)
boks-i, to box, spar; **-isto,** pugilist
bol-i, to boil
bomb-o, bomb
bombard-i, to bombard, shell
bon-a, good; **-e,** well; **Bone!** Fine!, O.K.; **-ŝanco,** good luck; **-volu,** please; **-venon!** Welcome!
bor-i, to bore, drill
bord-o, shore, bank (river, etc.)
border-i, to border, to hem, edge
bors-o, bourse, stock-exchange
bot-o, boot
botanik-o, botany
botel-o, bottle
bov-o, a head of cattle; ox; **-ino,** cow; **-aĵo,** beef
brajl-o, braille
brak-o, arm
branĉ-o, branch; **-eto,** twig
brand-o, brandy
brasik-o, cabbage; **flor—o,** cauliflower
brav-a, brave, valiant; **-e!,** bravo!
Brazil-o, Brazil; **-ano,** a Brazilian
breĉ-o, breach, opening, gap
brems-o, brake (mech.)
bret-o, shelf
brigad-o, brigade
briĝ-o, bridge (game)
brik-o, brick
bril-i, to shine

brit-o, a Briton; **-a,** British; **-ujo,** Britain
broĉ-o, brooch
brod-i, to embroider
bros-o, brush
broŝur-o, pamphlet
brov-o, eyebrow
bru-i, to be noisy, make noise
brul-i, to burn; **-vundo,** a burn; **ek—igi,** to light, set on fire
brun-a, brown
brust-o, breast, chest
brut-o, brute
bub-o, boy, lad, urchin
bubal-o, buffalo
buĉ-i, to slaughter
budĝet-o, = **buĝeto**
buf-o, toad
buĝet-o, budget (fin.)
buked-o, bouquet
bukl-o, curl, ringlet
bul-o, clod, lump (bread, snow, earth)
bulb-o, bulb
bulk-o, roll (bread)
bulgar-o, a Bulgarian; **-a,** Bulgarian (adj.); **-ujo,** Bulgaria
buljon-o, bouillon, broth
bulten-o, bulletin
bulvard-o, boulevard
burd-o, bumble-bee
burĝ-o, bourgeois, freeman, burgess; **-aro,** bourgeoisie, the middle classes
burĝon-o, bud
buŝ-o, mouth; **-tuko,** napkin, serviette; **-umo,** muzzle
buter-o, butter; **-pano,** buttered bread
butik-o, shop, store
buton-o, button; **-umi,** to button

C

car-o, czar
ced-i, to cede, yield, give in
cel-i, to aim at, strive for; **-o,** aim, goal, object, purpose

celeri-o, celery
cement-o, cement
cend-o, cent
cent, hundred; **jar—o,** century
centimetr-o, centimeter
centr-o, center; **al—igi,** centralize
cenzur-i, to censor, act as censor
cep-o, onion
cerb-o, brain; **-umi,** to puzzle over, rack one's brains
cert-a, certain, sure
cerv-o, stag, deer
ceter-a, the rest, remainder; **-e,** as for the rest, besides
ci, thou
cidr-o, cider
cifer-o, a cipher, figure
cigan-o, gypsy
cigar-o, cigar
cigared-o, cigarette
cign-o, swan
ciklon-o, cyclone
cikoni-o, stork
cilindr-o, cylinder
cim-o, bug
cindr-o, cinder, ash
cirk-o, circus
cirkl-o, circle
cirkonstanc-o, circumstance
cirkuler-o, a circular, circular letter
cit-i, to cite, quote; **-aĵo,** quotation
citron-o, lemon
civil-a, civil (not mil.)
civiliz-i, to civilize; **-o,** civilization
col-o, inch

Ĉ

ĉagren-i, to vex, annoy, grieve
ĉambr-o, room
ĉampan-o, champagne wine
ĉap-o, cap
ĉapel-o, hat
ĉapitr-o, chapter (book)
ĉar, because, for
ĉar-o, chariot, car
ĉarlatan-o, charlatan

ĉarm-a, charming, nice
ĉarnir-o, hinge
ĉarpentr-i, to do carpentry
ĉart-o, charter
ĉas-i, to hunt, chase
ĉast-a, chaste
ĉe, at, near to, beside; -esti, to be present
ĉef-o, chief, head, leader; -urbo, capital city; -manĝo, dinner
ĉek-o, check, cheque (fin.)
ĉemiz-o, shirt
ĉen-o, chain; -ero, a link
ĉeriz-o, cherry
ĉerk-o, coffin
ĉerp-i, to draw (water, etc.); el—aĵo, an excerpt, extract; el—ita, exhausted, used up
ĉes-i, to cease, stop, desist from
ĉeval-o, horse
ĉi (den. nearness); ĉi tie, here; ĉi tiu, this one
ĉia, every kind of
ĉial, for every reason, on every account
ĉiam, always, at all times; -daŭra, everlasting; por—a, eternal
ĉie, everywhere
ĉiel, in every way, in all sorts of ways
ĉiel-o, sky, heaven; -arko, rainbow
ĉies, everyone's, everybody's
ĉif-i, to crumple
ĉifon-o, rag
ĉikan-i, to find fault with, cavil at, quibble
ĉimpanz-o, chimpanzee
ĉin-o, a Chinese; -a, Chinese; -ujo, China
ĉio, everything; -pova, almighty, all-powerful
ĉiom, all, the whole quantity
ĉirkaŭ, around, about; -i, to surround; -aĵo, surroundings; -preni, to embrace
ĉiu, each one, every one; -okaze, anyway, in any case; -tage, daily

ĉiz-i, to chisel, carve
-ĉj-, (suff. den. affectionate use for masculine names); Paĉjo, daddy, papa; Viĉjo, Will, Bill
ĉokolad-o, chocolate
ĉu, whether, (also introduces a question)

D

da, of (expresses quantity); glaso da akvo, a glass of water; funto da kafo, a pound of coffee
daktil-o, date (fruit)
dali-o, dahlia
danc-i, to dance
danĝer-o, danger; sen—a, safe
dank-i, to thank
dat-o, date (time); -umi, to date; -reveno, anniversary; freŝ—a, recent
daŭr-i, to continue, endure, last
de, of, from, by, (shows possession or point of origin); — kiam, -post, since
debet-o, debit, -i, to debit, charge against
dec-i, to be becoming, fitting, proper
Decembr-o, December
decid-i, to decide
dediĉ-i, to dedicate, devote
defend-i, to defend
deficit-o, deficit
degel-i, to thaw
dejor-i, to serve, be on duty
dek, ten
deklam-i, to declaim, recite
deklar-i, to declare
dekliv-o, declivity, slope
dekret-o, decree
dekstr-a, right (hand); -en, to the right
deleg-i, to delegate; -ito, a delegate
delikat-a, delicate, fine, dainty
delir-i, to be delirious
demand-i, to ask, question
demokrat-o, democrat; -eco, democracy

dens-a, dense, thick, close; **-igi**, condense

dent-o, tooth

denunc-i, to denounce

depend-i, to depend

depeŝ-o, a dispatch

depon-i, to deposit

deput-i, to depute, appoint as an agent; **-ito**, a deputy

deriv-i, to derive

des, the (used with **ju**): **ju pli longe, des pli bone**, the longer, the better

desegn-i, to design, draw

desert-o, dessert

despot-o, despot

destin-i, to destine, intend for; **-o**, destiny

detal-o, detail, particular; **-e**, in detail

determin-i, to determine

detru-i, to destroy

dev-i, to have to, must, ought to; **-igi**, to compel, force; **-o**, duty

deviz-o, motto, device

dezert-o, desert

dezir-i, to desire, want, wish

Di-o, God; **-servo**, divine service

diabl-o, devil

diagnoz-o, diagnosis, **-i**, to diagnose (med.)

dialekt-o, dialect

dialog-o, dialogue

diamant-o, diamond

diametr-o, diameter

diant-o, carnation

diboĉ-i, to debauch

diet-o, diet

difekt-i, to defect, damage, injure

diferenc-i, to differ, be different, be unlike; **-igi**, differentiate

difin-i, to define, set aside for

dig-o, dike, embankment, dam

digest-i, to digest (food)

dign-o, dignity

dik-a, thick, stout

dikt-i, to dictate (letter, command)

diktator-o, dictator; **-eco**, dictatorship

diligent-a, diligent

diluv-o, deluge, flood

dimanĉ-o, Sunday

dinamit-o, dynamite

diplom-o, diploma

diplomat-o, diplomat; **-io**, diplomacy

dir-i, to say, tell

direkt-i, to guide, direct, steer; **-ilo**, helm, rudder, steering apparatus

direktor-o, director

dis-, (pref. den. separation, dispersal in different directions); **-igi**, to disperse; **-doni**, to distribute

disciplin-o, discipline

disĉipl-o, disciple

disk-o, disk; **fonograf—o**, phonograph record

diskont-i, to discount

diskret-a, discreet

diskut-i, to discuss, argue about

dispon-i, to dispose of; **-ebla**, available

disput-i, to dispute, challenge (statement, etc.)

distanc-o, distance

disting-i, to distinguish, note differences

distr-i, to distract, divert, entertain; **-aĵo**, diversion, entertainment

diven-i, to guess, surmise, make out

divers-a, diverse, varied

divid-i, to divide

do, therefore, then, so

dogan-o, customs; **-ejo**, customs-house

dok-o, dock (ship)

doktor-o, doctor (title)

dokument-o, document

dolar-o, dollar

dolĉ-a, sweet

dolor-i, to pain, ache; **-igi**, to cause pain, to hurt

dom-o, house

domaĝ-o, pity, shame; **-i**, to begrudge

don-i, to give; **al—i**, to add; **el—i**, to publish, issue

donac-i, to make a present of; **-o**, gift, donation

dorlot-i, to pamper, pet, coddle, spoil

dorm-i, to sleep

dorn-o, thorn

dors-o, back (of body)

dot-o, dowry

dram-o, drama

drap-o, woolen cloth

draŝ-i, to thresh

dres-i, to train (animals)

drink-i, to drink to excess

drog-o, drug

dron-i, to drown

du, two; **-o**, a couple; **-punkto**, colon; **-onpatro**, stepfather

dub-i, to doubt

dum, during, while, as; **-e**, meanwhile

dung-i, to hire, engage (servant, etc.)

duŝo, shower, douche

E

-e, (end. den. adverb); **bone**, well; **kune**, together

eben-a, even, flat; **-aĵo**, a plain, level tract of land

-ebl-, (suff. den. possibility, able to be); **videbla**, visible; **eble**, possibly, perhaps, maybe

ebri-a, intoxicated, drunk

ebur-o, ivory

-ec-, (suff. den. abstract ideas); **libereco**, liberty; **ruĝeco**, redness

eĉ, even (adv.)

edif-i, to edify, improve, build up (morally)

eduk-i, to educate, bring up, rear

edz-o, husband; **-ino**, wife; **-iĝi**, **-iniĝi**, to get married

efektiv-a, real, actual; **-e**, really, as a matter of fact

efik-i, to have an effect, be efficacious

-eg-, (suff. den. highest degree of greatness or intensity); **bonega**, excellent; **varmega**, hot

egal-a, equal

eh-o, echo

-ej-, (suff. den. place characterized by, allotted to); **preĝejo**, church; **hundejo**, kennel; **enirejo**, entrance

ek-, (pref.. den. sudden action); **ekiri**, to start, take off; **ekkrii**, to cry out, scream

ekip-i, to equip

eklezi-o, church-body

ekonomi-o, economy (sc.)

eks-, (pref. den. ex-, former, late); **eksprezidanto**, ex-president; **-iĝi**, to resign; **-edziĝi**, to become divorced

ekscit-i to excite

ekskurs-o, excursion

eksped-i, to expedite, dispatch

eksperiment-o, experiment

eksplod-i, to explode

eksport-i, to export

ekspozici-o, exposition, exhibition

ekspres-a, express, rapid

ekster, outside, without

eksterm-i, to exterminate

ekstr-a, extra

ekstrakt-o, extract

ekstrem-a, extreme

ekvator-o, equator

ekzamen-i, to examine

ekzempl-o, example, instance

ekzempler-o, copy, example (book, etc.)

ekzerc-i, to exercise, train, practice

ekzil-i, to exile

ekzist-i, to exist

el, out of, from, (made) of; **-iĝi**, withdraw; **-iro**, exodus

elast-a, elastic

elefant-o, elephant

elegant-a, elegant, tasteful, handsome

elekt-i, to elect, choose

elektr-o, electricity; **-igi,** electrify
elektron-o, electron
element-o, element, constituent
-em-, (suff. den. tendency, inclination); **l a b o r e m a,** industrious; **atakema,** aggressive.
emajl-o, enamel
embaras-o, embarrassment, difficulty
emblem-o, emblem
emfaz-o, emphasis
eminent-a, eminent
emoci-i, to move, affect, stir; **sen—e,** calmly
en, in; into (with accus.); **-iri,** to enter; **-havo,** contents
enciklopedi-o, encyclopedia
energi-o, energy
enket-o, inquiry, inquest
entrepren-i, to undertake; **-o,** undertaking, enterprise
entuziasm-o, enthusiasm
enu-i, to be weary, be bored, mope; **-iga** wearisome, dull
envi-o, envy
episkop-o, bishop
epizod-o, episode
epok-o, epoch, age
-er-, (suff. den. unit); **monero,** coin; **ĉenero,** link of a chain
erar-i, to err, make a mistake, be wrong;**-a,** mistaken, wrong
ermit-o, hermit
erp-i, to harrow (agr.)
escept-i, to except, exclude; **-o,** exception
esenc-o, essence
eskort-i, to escort
esper-i, to hope; **-anto,** Esperanto
esplor-i, to explore, investigate
esprim-i, to express
est-i, to be; **-aĵo,** a being; **-onteco,** (the) future; **-inta,** past, former
establ-i, to establish
estim-i, to esteem
esting-i, to extinguish, put out
-estr-, (suff. den. leader, head, chief); **lernejestro,** principal of a

school; **ŝipestro,** captain of a ship; **-o,** head, chief; **-i,** to lead, act as leader
eŝafod-o, scaffold
-et-, (suff. den. least degree of greatness or intensity); **dometo,** small house, cottage; **infaneto,** baby; **blueta,** bluish
etaĝo, floor, story
etend-i, to extend, stretch out, spread; **-aĵo,** expanse, stretch (country, etc.)
etern-a, eternal; **La Eternulo,** Jehovah, God
etik-o, ethics
etiket-o, etiquette
Eŭrop-o, Europe; **-a,** European
eventual-a, eventual, possibly occurring; **-e,** if occasion should arise
evit-i, to avoid, evade, shirk
evolu-i, to evolve, develop, expand

F
fab-o, bean
fabel-o, story, tale, fairy-tale; **-a,** fabulous, fictitious
fabl-o, fable, myth, animal story with a moral
fabrik-o, factory; **-i,** to fabricate, make in a factory
facil-a, easy
faden-o, thread (cotton, metal, etc.); **metal—o,** wire; **sen—a telegrafo,** wireless telegraph
fajf-i, to whistle
fajl-i, to file (mech.)
fajr-o, fire
fak-o, section, division, compartment; **-ulo,** a specialist
fakt-o, fact; **-e,** in fact
faktur-o, invoice
fal-i, to fall, drop
falĉ-i, to mow; **-ilo,** scythe
fald-i, to fold
fals-i, to falsify, forge, counterfeit
fam-o, fame, rumor, report
famili-o, family

fand-i, to melt, fuse, smelt, cast
fanfaron-i to boast
fantazi-o, fantasy, fancy, imagination
fantom-o, phantom, ghost
far-i, to make, to do; -iĝi, to become, happen
farm-i, to lease, hold on lease, farm; -bieno, farm
farmaci-o, pharmacy
fart-i, to fare, to be (as to health, etc.)
farun-o, flour
fasko, bundle, bunch, sheaf
fason-o, cut, make, shape (of garments, etc.)
fast-i, to fast
fatal-a, fateful, fated, inevitable, fatal
faŭk-o, jaws (wild beast), gorge, opening
favor-a, favorable, -o, favor
faz-o, phase
fe(in)-o, fairy
febr-o, fever
Februar-o, February
federaci-o, federation
fel-o, hide, skin
feliĉ-a, happy
felieton-o, newspaper or journal serial story
felt-o, felt (material)
femur-o, thigh
fend-i, to split; -o, slit, crevice; -ego, chasm
fenestr-o, window
fer-o, iron (chem.); -vojo, railway
ferdek-o, deck (ship)
feri-o, holiday, vacation
ferm-i, to shut, close
fervor-o, fervor, zeal
fest-o, festival, party, celebration
festen-o, banquet, feast
fi!, fie! shame!; (used as pref. den. shamefulness or moral badness); fikomerco, shady business
fiakr-o, cab, taxi

fianĉ-o, betrothed, fiancé; -ino, fiancée; -iĝi kun, to get engaged to
fiask-o, fiasco
fibr-o, fibre
fid-i, to trust, have faith in; -o, faith; -inda, trustworthy
fidel-a, faithful
fier-a, proud
figur-o, figure, image
fiks-i, to fix, fasten, secure
fil-o, son
filatel-o, philately
fili-o, a branch office, affiliate
film-o, film
filozof-o, philosopher; -io, philosophy
filtr-i, to filter
fin-i, to finish, end; -a, final
financ-o, finance
fingr-o, finger; dik—o, thumb; pied—o, toe
firm-a, firm, solid, stable
firm-o, firm (com.)
fiŝ-o, fish; -kaptisto, fisherman
fizik-o, physics
flag-o, flag, banner
flam-o, flame; -ingo, burner
flan-o, pancake, flat pastry
flanel-o, flannel
flank-o, side, flank; de—iĝi, to deviate, turn away from
flar-i, to smell
flat-i, to flatter
flav-a, yellow
fleg-i, to attend, look after, nurse; -istino, nurse
fleks-i, to bend, flex; genu—i, to bow, bend the knee
flik-i, to patch, mend
flirt-i, to flutter, float, flit over
flor-o, flower; -brasiko, cauliflower
flos-o, raft
flu-i, to flow; -o, current, stream
flug-i, to fly; -ilo, wing
fluid-a, fluid
flustr-i, to whisper
flut-o, flute

foiro, fair, (market)

foj-o, time, occasion, instance; **-e**, once, once upon a time; **kelk—e**, sometimes

fojn-o, hay

foli-o, leaf, sheet

fond-i, to found, establish

fonetik-o, phonetics

fonograf-o, phonograph

font-o, spring, source, fount

fontan-o, fountain

for, away, forth, off, gone, absent; **-iri**, to go away; **-igi**, to do away with, get rid of; **iru for! for de mi!** be off! away! be gone!

forges-i, to forget

forĝ-i, to forge (metal)

fork-o, fork

form-i, to form, shape; **ali—igi**, to transform

formik-o, ant

forn-o, stove, furnace, oven

fort-a, strong; **-o**, force, strength; **per—i**, to violate

fortik-a, sturdy, resistant, solid, firm; **-aĵo**, fortress, fort

fos-i, to dig

fosfor-o, phosphorus

fosili-o, fossil

fost-o, post, stake

foto-aparat-o, camera

fotograf-i, to photograph, take pictures; **-aĵo**, photograph

frag-o, strawberry

frak-o, dress coat, full dress

frakas-i, to shatter, smash

frakci-o, fraction

framason-o, freemason

framb-o, raspberry

franc-o, Frenchman; **-a**, French; **-ujo**, France

frand-i, to be fond of eating sweets and dainties; **-aĵo**, dainty, delicacy, tidbit

franĝ-o, fringe

frap-i, to strike, hit

frat-o, brother

fraŭl-o, bachelor, unmarried man; **-ino**, Miss, single woman, young lady

fraz-o, sentence

fremd-a, strange, foreign; **-ulo**, stranger, foreigner

frenez-a, insane, crazy, in a frenzy; **-ulejo**, lunatic asylum

freŝ-a, fresh; **-data**, recent, new

fripon-o, rogue, knave, scamp

frit-i, to fry

frivol-a, frivolous

friz-i, to curl, frizz, dress the hair

fromaĝ-o, cheese

front-o, front

frost-o, frost; **-i**, to freeze (intr.)

frot-i, to rub (tr.); **-ado**, friction

fru-a, early

frukt-o, fruit; **-igi**, fructify; **-odona**, fruitful

frunt-o, forehead

ftiz-o, phthisis, consumption

fulg-o, soot

fulgor-o, firefly

fulm-o, lightning; **-otondro**, thunderstorm

fum-o, smoke; **-i**, to smoke (pipe, cigar, etc.)

fund-o, bottom

fundament-o, foundation, basis

funebr-o, mourning; **-i**, to mourn

funel-o, funnel

fung-o, fungus, mushroom

funkci-i, to function, work, operate (intr.)

funt-o, pound (weight)

furioz-a, furious, raging

fuŝ-i, to bungle, spoil (tr.)

fut-o, foot (measure)

futbal-o, football (game)

G

gaj-a, gay, merry

gajn-i, to gain, win

gal-o, gall, bile

galeri-o, gallery

galop-o, gallop
galoŝ-o, galosh, over-shoe
gamaŝ-o, gaiter
gant-o, glove
garanti-i, to guarantee, become surety for
garbo, sheaf (of grain, hay, straw)
gard-i, to guard, watch over, keep; sin—ema, cautious, careful
gardeni-o, gardenia
gargar-i, to gargle, rinse (mouth, dishes, clothes)
garn-i, to garnish, trim
gas-o, gas (not gasoline); -a, gaseous, gassy; -lumo, gaslight
gast-o, guest; -ama, hospitable; -igi, entertain; -iganto, host
gaz-o, gauze
gazet-o, gazette, magazine
ge-, (pref. den. both sexes together); gepatroj, parents; gefratoj, brother(s) and sister(s)
gem-o, gem
generaci-o, a generation
general-o, general (mil.)
geni-o, genius; -ulo, a genius, highly endowed person
gent-o, tribe, clan
genu-o, knee; -iĝi, to kneel down; -fleksi, to bend the knee
geograf-o, geographer; -io, geography
geolog-o, geologist; -io, geology
geometri-o, geometry
gerani-o, geranium
german-o, a German; -a, German; -ujo, Germany
gest-o, gesture; -i, gesticulate
gigant-o, giant; -a, gigantic
gimnastik-o, gymnastics
gimnazi-o, high-school
gips-o, gypsum, plaster-of-Paris
giroskop-o, gyroscope
gitar-o, guitar
glaci-o, ice; -aĵo, ice, sherbet; krem—aĵo, ice cream

glad-i, to iron (clothes); -ilo, flat-iron
glan-o, acorn
glas-o, drinking-glass
glat-a, smooth, even; -igi, to smooth
glav-o, sword
glim-o, mica
glit-i, to glide, slide; -ilo, skate
glob-o, globe
glor-i, to glorify (tr.); -o, glory, fame ,
glu-o, glue; -i, to glue, stick (tr.)
glut-i, to swallow
golf-o, gulf, bay
golflud-o, golf (game)
gorĝ-o, throat
goril-o, gorilla
graci-a, graceful
grad-o, degree; -e, gradually
graf-o, earl, count
grajn-o, a grain (of corn, wheat)
gram-o, gram
gramatik-o, grammar
granat-o, pomegranate
grand-a, great, large, big; -eco, greatness, size
grandioz-a, grandiose, magnificent
granit-o, granite
gras-o, grease, fat
grat-i, to scratch (tr.); -vundi, to scratch, hurt by scratching
gratul-i, to congratulate, wish joy to
grav-a, important, serious, grave; -i, to be important
graved-a, pregnant
gravur-i, to engrave (tr.)
grek-o, a Greek; -a, Greek, Grecian
gren-o, grain, (Brit.) corn
gri-o, meal, grits; -aĵo, porridge
grifel-o, slate-pencil, stylus
gril-o, cricket (insect)
grimac-o, grimace
grimp-i, to climb
grinc-i, to grind, make a grating noise
grip-o, grippe, influenza
griz-a, gray

grumbl-i, to grumble, growl (intr.)
grund-o, ground, soil
grup-o, group
gudr-o, tar
gulden-o, gulden (Dutch coin)
gum-o, gum (of tree, etc.), mucilage; **maĉ—o**, chewing gum
gurd-o, barrel-organ, hurdy-gurdy
gust-o, taste; **-i**, to taste (intr.); **-umi**, to taste (tr.)
gut-o, drop, drip
guvern-i, to educate or teach in the home, to act as tutor
gvardi-o, guard (mil.)
gvid-i, to guide, lead; **-ilo**, handle-bar (bicycle, etc.)

Ĝ
ĝarden-o, garden
ĝem-i, to groan, moan
ĝemel-o, twin
ĝen-i, to trouble, bother, inconvenience, disturb
ĝeneral-a, general; **-e**, generally, in general
ĝentil-a, polite, courteous, well-mannered
ĝerm-o, germ, (first stage of anything); **-i**, to germinate
ĝi, it; **-a**, its
ĝib-o, bump, hump; **-ulo**, hunchback
ĝin-o, gin (liquor)
ĝiraf-o, giraffe
ĝis, until, up to, as far as
ĝoj-i, to be glad, rejoice
ĝu-i, to enjoy, delight in, find pleasure in
ĝust-a, right, exact, correct; **-atempe**, at the right time; **al—igi**, to adjust, correct, set right

H
ha! ah!, ha!
hajl-o, hail (frozen rain)
hak-i, to hack, chop

hal-o, hall, large room
haladz-o, fume, evil-smelling or suffocating gas
halt-i, to halt, stop (intr.)
har-o, a hair
hard-i, to harden, temper
haring-o, herring
harmoni-o, harmony
harmonik-o, harmonica (instr.); harmonics
harp-o, harp
haŭt-o, skin; **sen—igi**, to skin
hav-i, to have; **-igi**, to get, obtain; **en—i**, to hold, contain; **en—o**, contents
haven-o, harbor, port
hazard-o, hazard, chance; **-e**, by chance, accidentally
hebre-o, Hebrew
hejm-o, home; **-e**, at home
hejt-i, to heat (tr.)
hel-a, bright, light (color)
heliant-o, sunflower
helic-o, screw (of ship); propeller (ship, airplane)
helik-o, snail
help-i, to help, aid, assist
hepat-o, liver
herb-o, grass, herb; **-ejo**, lawn, meadow
hered-i, to inherit
herez-o, heresy
hero-o, hero
hezit-i, to hesitate (intr.)
hieraŭ, yesterday
higien-o, hygiene
himn-o, hymn
hind-o, Hindu; **-ujo**, India, Hindustan
hipnct-o, hypnosis; **-igi**, to hypnotize
hipopotam-o, hippopotamus
hipotek-o, mortgage
hirt-a, bristly, rough (of hair); **-iĝi**, to bristle, stand on end
hirund-o, swallow (bird)
histori-o, history, story
ho! oh!

hodiaŭ, today

hok-o, hook

hold-o, hold (ship)

hom-o, man, human being; -aro, mankind

honest-a, honest

honor-i, to honor;-inda, honorable; mal—o, dishonor, disgrace

hont-i, to be ashamed

hor-o, hour; -aro, time-table

horde-o, barley

horloĝ-o, clock, watch, time-piece

hospital-o, hospital

hotel-o, hotel

huf-o, hoof

humil-a, humble

humor-o, humor, mood, frame of mind; bon—a, good-tempered

hund-o, dog

I

-i, (end. of infinitive); iri, to go; paroli, to speak

ia, some kind of, any; — ajn, any kind whatever

ial, for some reason

iam, at some time; once upon a time

-id-, (suff. den. young of, child of, descendant); bovido, calf

ide-o, idea

ideal-o, ideal

ident-a, identical

idili-o, idyll

idiom-o, language, idiom

idiot-o, idiot

idiotism-o, idiom (peculiar form common to one language but not to others)

ie, somewhere, anywhere

iel, in some manner, in some way, somehow

ies, someone's, somebody's

-ig-, (suff. den. to make, cause to be); blankigi, to make white, whiten

ignor-i, to ignore, disregard (tr.)

-iĝ-, (suff. den. to become, get); ruĝiĝi, to become red, redden; malsaniĝi, to become ill

-il-, (suff. den. instrument, tool, apparatus); trančilo, knife; kombilo, comb

ili, they; ilia, their; -n, them

ilumin-i, to illuminate

ilustr-i, to illustrate

iluzi-o, illusion

imag-i, to imagine, fancy (tr.)

imit-i, to imitate (tr.)

imperi-o, empire; -estro, emperor; -ismo, imperialism

implik-i, to entangle, ensnare; to involve; to implicate

impon-i, to impress, make a great impression upon; -a, imposing

import-i, to import (com.)

impost-o, tax, duty

impres-o, impression, feeling of the heart or spirit

-in-, (suff. den. feminine); patrino, mother; Sinjorino, Mrs.

incit-i, to incite, irritate, provoke

-ind-, (suff. den. worthy of); laŭdinda, praiseworthy; memorinda, memorable

indian-o, American Indian

indiferent-a, indifferent

indign-i, to be indignant (intr.)

indiĝen-o, native, original inhabitant

indik-i, to indicate (tr.)

individu-o, individual

indulg-i, to be lenient, have mercy

industri-o, industry

infan-o, child

infekt-i, to infect; -o, infection

infer-o, hell

inflam-o, inflammation

influ-i, to influence, to affect

inform-i, to inform, give information

-ing-, (suff. den. holder or stand into which one object is put); kandelingo, candle-holder; glavingo, scabbard

inĝenier-o, an engineer

iniciat-i, to initiate, originate, introduce

ink-o, ink

inklin-a, inclined (to), disposed

inkluziv-a, inclusive

insekt-o, insect

insid-a, insidious

insign-o, insignia, crest, badge

insist-i, to insist

inspekt-i, to inspect; -isto, inspector

inspir-i, to inspire

instal-i, to install (tr.)

instanc-o, authoritative source, instance (leg.)

instig-i, to instigate

instinkt-o, instinct

instituci-o, institution

institut-o, institute

instru-i, to teach, instruct

instrukci-o, instructions, orders

instrument-o, instrument

insul-o, island

insult-i, to insult, abuse

-int-, (end. of active past participle)

inteligent-a, intelligent

intenc-i, to intend, mean to; -o, intention

inter, between; among; -paroli, to converse; -tempe, meanwhile; -ŝanĝi, to exchange

interes-i, to interest (tr); -a, interesting

intern-a, internal, inside, inner

interpret-i, to interpret

intervju-o, interview

intest-o, intestine

intim-a, intimate

intrig-i, to intrigue, plot; -o, intrigue, plot (of play, etc.)

inund-i, to flood, inundate

invadi, to invade

invent-i, to invent

invit-i, to invite

io, something, anything

iom, some, any (quantity), a little; — da mono, a little money; -ete, a little, to some extent

ir-i, to go; en—i, to go in, enter; pied—i, to walk; supren—i, to go up, ascend

ironi-o, irony

-is, (end. den. past tense); Mi iris, I went

-ism-, (suff. den. distinctive doctrine, practice); Kristanismo, Christianity; Socialismo, Socialism

-ist-, (suff. den. one professionally occupied with); dentisto, dentist; instruisto, teacher; portisto, porter

-it-, (end. of passive past participle)

ital-o, an Italian; -a, Italian; -ujo, Italy

iu, someone, somebody

izol-i, to isolate

J

-j, (end. den. plural); tabloj, tables; infanoj, children

ja, indeed, assuredly

jak-o, jacket, coat of suit

jakt-o, yacht

jam, already, yet

Januar-o, January

japan-o, a Japanese; -a, Japanese; -ujo, Japan

jar-o, year; -cento, century; super—o, leap-year

jard-o, yard (3 feet)

je, (prep. without a definite meaning; it can be rendered by various English prepositions); je la dua horo, at two o'clock

jen, behold!, lo!, Here is . . . !, There is . . . !; jene, as follows

jes, yes

Jesu-o, Jesus

jod-o, iodine

ju . . . , des . . . , the . . . , the . . . ; ju pli multe, des pli bone, the more, the better

jud-o, a Jew; -ismo, Judaism

jug-o, yoke

jugland-o, walnut

juĝ-i, to judge; **-ejo,** courthouse
juk-i, to itch (tr.)
Juli-o, July
jun-a, young; **-ulo,** a youth
jung-i, to harness
Juni-o, June
jup-o, skirt; **sub—o,** petticoat
jur-o, law, jurisprudence
just-a, just, fair
juvel-o, jewel

ĵ

ĵaluz-a, jealous
ĵargon-o, jargon
ĵaŭd-o, Thursday
ĵet-i, to throw, cast
ĵongl-i, to juggle, to use sleight of hand
ĵur-i, to swear; **-o,** an oath
ĵurnal-o, journal, newspaper
ĵus, just, just now (past); **Li ĵus iris,** He just went.

K

kaban-o, cabin, hut, cottage
kabl-o, cable; **-ogramo,** cablegram
kaĉ-o, gruel, mush, porridge
kadavr-o, corpse, cadaver
kadr-o, frame; **en—igi,** to put in a frame
kaduk-a, rickety, dilapidated, decrepit
kaf-o, coffee; **-ejo,** café
kaĝ-o, cage
kaj, and; **kaj li kaj ŝi,** both he and she
kaj-o, quay
kajer-o, note-book; separate part of a book
kajut-o, cabin (ship)
kaka-o, cocoa
kakt-o, cactus
kal-o, corn (on foot)
kaldron-o, kettle, caldron
kalendar-o, calendar

kaleŝ-o, carriage
kali-o, potassium
kalk-o, lime
kalkan-o, heel (of foot); **-umo,** heel (of shoe, boot, etc.)
kalkul-i, to count, calculate; **-o,** bill, meal check
kalson-o, pair of drawers (undergarment)
kalumni-i, to slander
kalv-a, bald
kamarad-o, comrade
kambi-o, draft, promissory note
kamel-o, camel
kameleon-o, chameleon
kamen-o, fireplace, hearth; **-tubo,** chimney
kamp-o, field; **-aro,** country; **-arano,** country-fellow, peasant
kampanj-o, campaign
kan-o, cane, reed
Kanad-o, Canada; **-ano,** Canadian
kanajl-o, scoundrel, rascal, cad
kanal-o, canal
kanap-o, sofa, couch
kanari-o, canary
kancer-o, cancer
kandel-o, candle
kandidat-o, candidate
kanjon-o, canyon
kankr-o, crayfish
kanon-o, cannon
kanot-o, canoe
kant-i, to sing
kaos-o, chaos
kap-o, head
kapabl-a, capable, able
kapel-o, chapel
kapital-o, capital (fin.)
kapitan-o, captain (mil.)
kapitul-i, to capitulate, surrender
kaporal-o, corporal (mil.)
kapr-o, goat
kapric-o, caprice, whim
kapt-i, to catch, capture
kar-a, dear; **-ulo, -ulino,** dear one, darling

karaf-o, glass water bottle, decanter

karakter-o, character, nature, trait

karavan-o, caravan, group of travelers

karb-o, coal

karcer-o, cell, jail room

kares-i, to caress

karier-o, career

karn-o, flesh

karot-o, carrot

kart-o, card; **poŝt—o,** postcard; **-ludi,** to play cards

kartoĉ-o, cartridge

karton-o, cardboard

karusel-o, merry-go-round, carousel

kas-o, money-box, till; fund; **-isto,** treasurer, cashier

kaserol-o, saucepan

kask-o, helmet

kastel-o, castle

kaŝ-i, to hide (tr.)

kat-o, cat

katalog-o, catalog

katar-o, catarrh

katedral-o, cathedral

katen-o, fetter, chain, bond

katolik-a, Catholic

katun-o, cotton cloth, printed cotton

kaŭĉuk-o, rubber

kaŭr-i, to cower, crouch

kaŭz-o, cause, reason; **-e de,** because of

kav-o, cave, hole, pit, cavity; **-eto,** dent, dimple

kavalir-o, knight, cavalier

kavern-o, cavern

kaz-o, case (gram.)

kazern-o, barracks

k. c. (kaj ceteraj), and others

ke, that (conj.)

kel-o, cellar

kelk-a, some, a few, several; **-foje,** sometimes

kelner-o, waiter

kemi-o, chemistry

kern-o, kernel, stone, pit (of fruit)

kest-o, chest, box

kia, what kind of; **-maniere,** in what manner, how

kial, for what reason, why; **-o,** reason

kiam, at what time, when

kie, at what place, where

kiel, in what way, how, as, like

kies, whose, of which

kilogram-o, kilogram

kilometr-o, kilometer

kinin-o, quinine

kinofilm-o, movie

kio, what (thing)

kiom, how much, how many

kis-i, to kiss

kiu, who, which, that (relative pronoun)

klap-o, valve

klar-a, clear; **-igi,** to clarify, explain

klas-o, class

klasik-a, classical

klav-o, key (piano, typewriter)

kler-a, educated, well-informed, enlightened

klient-o, client

klimat-o, climate; **al—iĝi,** become acclimated

klin-i, to bend (tr.)

kling-o, blade (knife, etc.)

klopod-i, to undertake, busy oneself with, to take steps

klub-o, club, society

knab-o, boy

knar-i, to creak, make a grating noise

kned-i, to knead

kod-o, code

kofr-o, trunk, coffer

kojn-o, wedge

kojot-o, coyote

kok-o, chicken, cock; **-ino,** hen

kokos-o, coconut

koks-o, hip

kol-o, neck; **-umo,** collar

kolbas-o, sausage

koleg-o, colleague

kolegi-o, college

kolekt-i, to collect, gather (tr.)
koler-i, to be angry
kolibr-o, humming-bird
kolizi-i, to collide
kolomb-o, pigeon, dove
kolon-o, column
kolonel-o, colonel (mil.)
koloni-o, colony; **-igi**, to colonize
kolor-o, color; **-igi**, to color, paint
kolport-i, to peddle, to hawk
kom-o, comma
komb-i, to comb; **-ilo**, a comb
komedi-o, comedy
komenc-i, to begin, start (tr.)
komerc-i, to trade, do business; **-aĵoj**, goods, wares
komfort-a, comfortable
komik-a, funny
komisi-i, to entrust, confide (to); **-o**, commission, certain task
komision-o, a commission, board of authority
komitat-o, committee
komiz-o, clerk
komod-o, chest of drawers
kompani-o, company (com.)
kompar-i, to compare
kompas-o, mariner's compass
kompat-i, to pity, have compassion
kompens-i, to compensate (tr.)
kompil-i, to compile
komplet-a, complete; **-igi**, to complete; **-o**, complete set, suit (of clothes, cards); suite (furniture)
komplez-o, favor, kindness
kompon-i, to compose (music, painting, literature)
kompost-i, to set up type
kompren-i, to understand (tr.); **-eble**, of course
komun-a, common, communal; **-umo**, community, township
komunik-i, to communicate; **-o**, communication, message
kon-i, to know, be acquainted with; **bone konata**, well-known

koncern-i, to concern, have to do with (tr.); **-e**, concerning, as to
koncert-o, concert
konciz-a, concise
kondamn-i, condemn
kondiĉ-o, condition, terms
konduk-i, to lead, conduct, escort; **al—i**, to bring, take to; **-isto**, conductor
kondut-i, to behave, act, conduct oneself; **-o**, behavior
konfederaci-o, confederation
konferenc-o, conference
konfes-i, to confess, admit
konfid-i, to entrust, confide
konfirm-i, to confirm
konfisk-i, to confiscate
konfit-i, to preserve; **-aĵo**, jam, preserve
konfuz-i, to confuse
kongres-o, congress
konjak-o, cognac
konjekt-i, to conjecture, surmise
konklud-i, to infer, conclude (tr.)
konkur-i, to compete; **-ado**, competition
konkurs-o, a contest, match, prize competition
konsci-i, to be conscious of
konscienc-o, conscience (moral)
konsent-i, to consent, agree
konserv-i, to conserve, keep, save
konservativ-a, conservative
konsider-i, to consider (tr.)
konsil-i, to counsel, advise; **-antaro**, a council
konsist-i, to consist (of, **el**)
konsol-i, to console, comfort, soothe
konspir-i, to conspire
konstant-a, constant, steadfast, permanent
konstat-i, to recognize as a fact, certify
konstern-i, to dismay, confound (tr); **-o**, consternation
konstituci-o, constitution (pol.)

konstru-i, to construct; **-ajo,** building

konsul-o, consul

konsult-i, to consult (a doctor, specialist, etc.)

konsum-i, to consume (tr.), use up

kont-o, account (com.)

kontant-a, cash, ready money; **-e,** in cash

kontent-a, content, happy, satisfied; **-igi,** to satisfy

kontinent-o, continent

kontor-o, office, counting-house

kontrakt-o, contract, covenant

kontraŭ, against; opposite; **-e,** on the other hand; **—vole,** under protest, against one's will

kontribu-i, to contribute

kontrol-i, to control, check; to audit (accounts)

konven-i, to suit, be suitable (intr.); to be becoming

konversaci-o, conversation, talk

konvink-i, to convince, persuade

kopi-i, to copy

kor-o, heart

korb-o, basket

kord-o, string (musical instrument)

korekt-i, to correct

korespond-i, to correspond, exchange letters

kork-o, cork

korn-o, horn (of cattle, sheep, etc.)

korp-o, body

korporaci-o, corporation

korpus-o, corps (mil.)

kort-o, court(yard); **-ego,** court (king's, etc.)

kost-i, to cost (tr.)

kostum-o, costume, dress

kot-o, mud

kotiz-o, subscription, quota, dues

kotlet-o, cutlet, chop

koton-o, cotton

kov-i, to brood, sit on eggs; **el—i,** to hatch

kovert-o, envelope

kovr-i, to cover; **-ilo,** a cover, blanket, lid

kraĉ-i, to spit

krad-o, grate; **-rostita,** broiled

krajon-o, pencil

krak-i, to crack, crash

kramp-o, clamp; **-oj,** brackets (type)

kran-o, faucet, spigot

krani-o, skull

kravat-o, necktie, cravat

kre-i, to create

kred-i, to believe; **-o,** belief, faith; **-eble,** probably, likely

kredit-o, credit (com.)

krem-o, cream

krepusk-o, twilight

kresk-i, to grow (intr.); **-aĵo,** plant, growth

krestomati-o, chrestomathy, book of selected literary models

kret-o, chalk

krev-i, to burst (intr.)

kri-i, to shout, call, cry

kribr-i, to sift; **-ilo,** sieve

krim-o, crime; **-ulo,** criminal

kripl-a, crippled; **-igi,** to cripple

Krist-o, Christ; **-ano,** Christian

Kristnask-o, Christmas, Yule

kritik-i, to criticize

kriz-o, crisis; **-a,** critical

kroĉ-i, to hook (tr.); **al—iĝi,** to cling

krokodil-o, crocodile

krom, besides, apart from, except

kron-o, crown

kroz-i, to cruise; **-oŝipo,** cruiser (mil.)

kruc-o, cross; **-umi,** to crucify

kruĉ-o, pitcher, jug

krud-a, crude, raw, rough

kruel-a, cruel

krur-o, leg

krut-a, steep

k. t. p. (kaj tiel plu), and so forth, etc.

kubut-o, elbow

kudr-i, to sew

kugl-o, bullet

kuir-i, to cook; **-ejo,** kitchen
kuk-o, cake
kukum-o, cucumber
kukurb-o, pumpkin, squash, gourd
kul-o, gnat
kuler-o, spoon
kulp-a, guilty, at fault; **-ulo,** culprit; **sen—a,** innocent
kult-o, cult
kultur-i, to cultivate, culture (both the earth and the spirit)
kun, with; **-e,** together; **-igi,** to bring together; **-tiri,** draw along; **-ulo,** companion; **-veni,** to meet together
kunikl-o, rabbit
kupe-o, coupé, compartment (train, etc.)
kupon-o, coupon
kupr-o, copper
kur-i, to run
kurac-i, to doctor, to treat (a disease); **-isto,** doctor, physician
kuraĝ-a, courageous; **-i,** to dare, venture
kurb-a, curved; **-igi,** to curve, to bend
kurioz-a, curious, unusual
kurs-o, course (of lessons)
kurten-o, curtain
kurz-o, rate of exchange
kusen-o, pillow
kuŝ-i, to lie, be in reclining position; **-iĝi,** to lie down; **-igi,** to lay (tr.)
kutim-i, to be accustomed to, used to; **-o,** custom, habit; **al—iĝi,** to get accustomed to
kuv-o, tub, vat
kuz-o, cousin
kvadrat-o, square
kvalit-o, quality
kvankam, though, although
kvant-o, quantity
kvar, four; **-ono,** a quarter
kvartal-o, quarter, district (of town, etc.)
kvazaŭ, as if, like, quasi, so to say

kverel-i, to quarrel, squabble
kverk-o, oak
kviet-a, quiet, calm
kvin, five
kvit-a, quit, clear from debt or obligation
kvitanc-o, receipt (fin.)

L

la, the
labor-i, to work, labor; **-ejo,** laboratory; **mal—ema,** lazy
lac-a, tired; **-igi,** to tire, to weary
laĉo, shoe-lace
lad-o, plate-metal, tin-plate; **viando en lado,** tinned meat
lag-o, lake; **-bordo,** shore of lake
laik-o, layman
lak-o, varnish, lac
lake-o, lackey
laks-o, diarrhea
lakt-o, milk
laktuk-o, lettuce
lam-a, lame; **-bastono,** crutch
lament-i, to lament, bewail
lamp-o, lamp
lan-o, wool
land-o, land, country; **sam—ano,** compatriot; **-limo,** border
lang-o, tongue
lantern-o, lantern
lanug-o, soft fine hair, down, fluff
lard-o, bacon
larĝ-a, wide, broad
larm-o, tear (from eye)
las-i, to allow, to let, to leave (tr.); **for—i,** to leave, forsake
last-a, last
latin-o, Latin
latun-o, brass
laŭ, according to; **-longe,** along; **-plaĉe,** as one pleases
laŭb-o, arbor, bower
laŭd-i, to praise, laud
laŭt-a, loud; **mal—e,** quietly
lav-i, to wash (tr.); **-ujo,** wash-bowl, sink

lecion-o, lesson
led-o, leather
leg-i, to read
legend-o, legend
legitim-i, to prove identity of, legitimize
legom-o, vegetable
leĝ-o, law; laŭ—e, legal
lek-i, to lick
lens-o, lens
lentug-o, freckle
leon-o, lion
leopard-o, leopard
lepr-o, leprosy; -ulo, leper
lern-i, to learn; -ejo, school; -ejestro, principal; -olibro, textbook
lert-a, skillful, clever; mal—a, backward, awkward
leter-o, letter (writing)
leŭtenant-o, lieutenant
lev-i, to lift, to raise; -iĝi, to rise, get up
li, he; -a, his; -n, him
liber-a, free; -igi, to free; -eco, freedom, liberty; mal—ejo, prison
libr-o, book; -tenado, bookkeeping
lice-o, lyceum, high-school
lift-o, elevator, lift
lig-i, to tie, bind; -o, league
lign-o, wood
likvid-i, to liquidate; -isto, receiver
likvor-o, liqueur, cordial
lili-o, lily
lim-o, limits, boundary
limonad-o, lemonade
lin-o, flax; -semo, linseed
lingv-o, language; -isto, linguist; -scienco, linguistics
lini-o, line; -ilo, ruler
lip-o, lip
list-o, list
lit-o, bed
liter-o, letter (of alphabet); -umi, to spell
literatur-o, literature
litov-o, a Lithuanian; -ujo, Lithuania

litr-o, liter
liver-i, to deliver, supply
log-i, to lure; al—i, to allure, attract
loĝ-i, to dwell, reside, live; -anto, inhabitant
lojal-a, loyal
lok-i, place; -i, to put in place
long-a, long; -eco, length
lorn-o, field-glass
lot-i, to draw lots
lu-i, to hire, to rent
lud-i, to play; -o, game; -ilo, toy
luks-a, luxurious
lukt-i, wrestle
lul-i, to lull; -ilo, cradle
lum-i, to give light, shine; -igi, to light
lumb-o, loin
lun-o, moon
lund-o, Monday
lup-o, wolf
lustr-o, chandelier
Luter-o, Luther; -ano, Lutheran

M

maĉ-i, to chew, masticate
magazen-o, department store, warehouse
maiz-o, maize, corn (Amer.)
Maj-o, May
majest-a, majestic; -o, Majesty
major-o, major (mil.)
majstr-o, maestro (in art, music, profession)
makaroni-o, macaroni
makler-i, to do business as a broker; -isto, broker
makul-o, spot, stain
makzel-o, jaw
mal-, (pref. den. exact opposite); malgranda, small; malfacila, difficult; -e, on the contrary; -o, opposite
maleol-o, ankle
malgraŭ, notwithstanding, in spite of
malic-a, malicious, spiteful

mam-o, breast; **-nutri, to** suckle; **-pinto,** nipple, teat

man-o, hand; **-plato,** palm; **-radiko,** wrist

mandat-o, mandate, written authority; **poŝt—o,** money-order

manĝ-i, to eat; **-karto,** bill of fare, menu; **-o,** meal; **-aĵo,** food

manier-o, manner, fashion, way; **tia—e,** in such a way

manik-o, sleeve

maniok-o, manioc, cassava

mank-i, to be lacking (intr); **-o,** lack, want, dearth

mantel-o, mantle, coat, cloak

mar-o, sea; **-isto,** sailor; **-armeo,** navy; **-bordo,** coast, seashore

marĉ-o, marsh, swamp

marĉand-i, to bargain, haggle

mard-o, Tuesday

margarit-o, daisy, marguerite

mark-o, mark; **-i,** to mark (tr.); **fabrik—o,** trade mark; **poŝt—o,** postage stamp

marmor-o, marble

Mars-o, Mars

marŝ-i, to walk, march

Mart-o, March

martel-o, hammer; **-i,** to hammer

mas-o, mass, lump, bulk

masaĝ-o, massage

mason-i, to build with stone or brick

mast-o, mast

mastr-o, master (of home); host; **-umi,** to keep house

maŝ-o, mesh, loop, ring, link

maŝin-o, machine

mat-o, mat

matematik-o, mathematics

maten-o, morning; **-manĝo,** breakfast

materi-o, matter

material-o, material

matrac-o, mattress

matur-a, mature, ripe

mebl-o, piece of furniture; **-i,** to furnish

meĉ-o, wick

medi-o, environment

medicin-o, science of medicine

medikament-o, medicine, drug

mejl-o, mile

mekanik-o, mechanics; **-isto,** mechanic

meleagr-o, turkey

melk-i, to milk

melodi-o, melody

melon-o, melon

mem, -self, -selves; **li mem,** he himself; **-stara,** independent

membr-o, limb; member

memor-i, to remember

menci-i, to mention

mend-i, to order (goods, etc.)

mens-o, mind; **-a,** mental

mensog-i, to lie, to fib, to tell untruths

menton-o, chin

menu-o, menu

merit-i, to merit (tr.), deserve

merkred-o, Wednesday

mes-o, mass (church)

met-i, to put, place; **de—i,** to take off

metal-o, metal

metamorfoz-o, metamorphosis

meti-o, trade, handicraft

metod-o, method

metr-o, meter

mev-o, sea-gull

mez-o, middle; **tag—o,** noon; **posttag—o,** afternoon

mezur-i, to measure (tr.); **-o,** measure, size

mi, I; **-a,** my; **-n,** me

miel-o, honey

mien-o, mien, air, expression

migr-i, to migrate; **el—i,** to emigrate; **en—i,** to immigrate

mikrob-o, microbe

mikrofon-o, microphone

miks-i, to mix (tr.)

mil, thousand

milion-o, million

milit-i, to make war; **-o,** war; **-kap-tito,** prisoner-of-war

min-o, a mine (coal, ore, etc.); **-i,** to mine

minac-i, to threaten

mineral-o, mineral

ministr-o, minister (gov't.); **-aro,** cabinet (gov't.)

minut-o, minute (time)

miop-a, short-sighted

mir-i, to be astonished, to marvel; **-inda,** marvelous, wonderful

mirakl-o, miracle

mis-, (pref. den. wrongly, improperly); **misapliki,** misapply

misi-o, mission, task assigned; **-isto,** missionary

mister-o, mystery; **-a,** mysterious

mizer-o, misery

mod-o, mode, fashion

moder-a, moderate; **-igi,** to moderate

modern-a, modern

modest-a, modest

modif-i, to modify

mok-i, to mock, make fun of

mol-a, soft

molekul-o, molecule

moment-o, moment; **Momenton!** One moment!

mon-o, money; **-ero,** coin; **-ujo,** purse; **-erigi,** to make change; **-igi,** to cash (a check)

monak-o, monk

monark-o, monarch

monat-o, month; **ĉiu—e,** monthly

mond-o, world; **tut—a,** world-wide

monopol-o, monopoly; **-igi,** monopolize

monstr-o, monster

mont-o, mountain; **-eto,** hill

montr-i, to show, **-ilo,** pointer; hand of clock

mor-o, custom, usage

mord-i, to bite; **-eti,** nibble

morgaŭ, tomorrow

mort-i, to die; **-o,** death; **-igi,** to kill; **-inta,** dead

moskit-o, m o s q u i t o; **kontraŭ-moskitoreto,** mosquito-net

moŝt-o, (general title of respect, politeness);**Via Reĝa Moŝto,** Your Majesty; **via moŝto,** Your Honor

motiv-o, motive, reason

motor-o, motor (engine)

mov-i, to move (tr.); **-iĝi,** to move (intr.)

muel-i, to grind (corn, grain, etc.); **-ilo,** mill (machine)

muĝ-i, to howl, roar, bluster (as of wind, waves, etc.)

muk-o, mucus

mul-o, mule

muld-i, to cast in a mold

mult-a, much, many; **-e,** great deal, a lot, much; **-ekosta,** expensive **mal—a,** a little

munici-o, ammunition

mur-o, wall

murd-i, to murder

murmur-i, to murmur

mus-o, mouse

musk-o, moss

muskol-o, muscle

mustard-o, mustard

muŝ-o, house-fly

mut-a, mute, dumb

muze-o, museum

muzik-o, music

N

-n, (end. den. direct object; also direction or motion toward a place; also omission of preposition **je**)

naci-o, nation

naĝ-i, to swim

naiv-a, naive

najbar-o, neighbor

najl-o, nail (metal); **-i,** to nail (tr.)

najtingal-o, nightingale

nap-o, turnip

nask-i, to give birth to; to produce, give rise to; **-iĝi,** to be born

natur-o, nature; **-a,** natural; **-e,** naturally

naŭ, nine

naŭz-i, to nauseate, to sicken, disgust (tr.)

naz-o, nose; **-umo,** pince-nez

ne, no, not, non-; **-i,** to deny; **-certa,** uncertain; **ne plu,** no longer

nebul-o, fog

neces-a, necessary; **-ejo,** toilet, water-closet

negoc-o, business, transaction

negr-o, negro

neĝ-o, snow

nek, neither, nor; **nek . . . nek,** neither . . . nor

nekrolog-o, obituary

nektar-o, nectar

nenia, no kind of

nenial, for no reason, on no account

neniam, at no time, never

nenie, at no place, nowhere

neniel, in no way, nohow

nenies, no one's, nobody's

nenio, nothing, none

neniom, none (quantity)

neniu, nobody, no one

nep-o, grandson

nepr-a, absolutely certain, without fail

nerv-o, nerve; **-a,** nervous

nest-o, nest

net-a, clean, clear, sharp, precise

neŭtral-a, neutral

nev-o, nephew

ni, we; **-a,** our; **-n,** us

nigr-a, black

nivel-o, level (of sea, etc.); **-ilo,** a level

-nj-, (suff. den. endearment, used after first letters of feminine names); **Anjo,** Annie; **Panjo,** mama, mummy

nobel-o, nobleman

nobl-a, noble

nod-o, knot

nokt-o, night; **-omezo,** midnight; **tra—i,** to pass the night

nom-o, name; **-ado,** nomination; **-e,** namely, to wit; **-i,** to name

nombr-o, number (quantity), amount

nord-o, north

norm-o, norm, standard

normal-a, normal

not-i, to make note of; **-o,** note; **-libro,** notebook

notari-o, notary

nov-a, new

novel-o, short story

Novembr-o, November

nu! well!

nuanc-o, nuance

nub-o, cloud

nud-a, nude, naked, bare

nuk-o, nape of neck

nuks-o, nut

nul-o, zero, nought; **-igi,** nullify, cancel

numer-o, number

nun, now; **-a,** present; **-tempe,** at the present time

nur, only, merely

nutr-i, to nourish, feed; **-aĵo,** food

O

-o, (end. den. noun)

obe-i, to obey; **-ema,** obedient

objekt-o, object, thing

-obl-, (suff. den. multiple); **triobla,** triple; **duoble,** doubly

obligaci-o, bond (fin.)

observ-i, to observe, watch

obstin-a, obstinate

ocean-o, ocean

odor-i, to smell, emit an odor

ofend-i, to offend, insult

ofer-i, to sacrifice, offer up

ofert-i, to offer (goods, services)

ofic-o, office, function, post; **-ejo,** office, bureau; **-isto** official oficir-o, officer (mil.)

oft-e, often

ok, eight

okaz-i, to occur, happen, take place; -a, occasional; -o, event, case, occasion, chance

okcident-o, west

Oktobr-o, October

okul-o, eye; -haroj, eyelashes; -umi, to eye, ogle; -vitroj, glasses, spectacles

okup-i, to occupy, take up (space, time); -ata, busy; -o, occupation

ol, than

ole-o, oil

oliv-o, olive (fruit)

ombr-o, shadow, shade

ombrel-o, umbrella; sun—o, parasol; fal—o, parachute

omnibus-o, omnibus

-on-, (suff. den. fractions); duono, one half; triono, one third; tri kvaronoj, three fourths

ond-o, wave; -longeco, wave-length; mallong—a, shortwave (rad.)

oni, one, they, the people (indef.); -diro, saying, rumor

onkl-o, uncle; -ino, aunt

-ont-, (end. of future participle active); ironta, about to go; estonteco, future

-op-, (suff. den. collective numerals); duope, by twos

operaci-i, to operate (med.)

opini-i, to think, have an opinion; -o, opinion

oportun-a, opportune, convenient, handy

or-o, gold; -a, golden; -fiŝo, goldfish

oranĝ-o, orange (fruit); -kolora, orange-colored

ord-o, order; -igi, to set in order, arrange

orden-o, order (religious, fraternal, etc.); insignia of honor

ordinar-a, ordinary; -e, ordinarily, usually

ordon-i, to order, bid, command

orel-o, ear

orf-o, orphan

organ-o, organ (anat); gazette, journal (of a party, society, etc.)

organiz-i, to organize; -o, organization

orgen-o, organ (mus.)

orient-o, east, orient

origin-o, origin

orkestr-o, orchestra

orkide-o, orchid

ornam-i, to adorn, deck, ornament

-os, (end. den. future tense); **Mi iros**, I shall go

osced-i, to yawn

ost-o, bone

ostr-o, oyster

-ot-, (end. of future participle passive); **laboro farota**, work to be done

ov-o, egg; -aĵo, omelet; -ujo, ovary; -oforma, oval

P

pac-o, peace; -a, peaceful

pacienc-o, patience; -a, patient

pacient-o, patient (med.)

pacifism-o, pacifism; -isto, pacifist

paf-i, to shoot; -ilo, gun

pag-i, to pay

paĝ-o, page (of a book)

paĝi-o, page(boy)

pajl-o, straw

pak-i, to pack; -aĵo, package

pal-a, pale

palac-o, palace

palis-o, stake, pale

palm-o, palm (tree)

palp-i, to feel (by touch); -ilo, feeler

palpebr-o, eyelid; -umi, to wink

palt-o, overcoat, greatcoat

pampelm-o, grape-fruit

pan-o, bread; -bulo, loaf

panik-o, panic

pantalon-o, pants, trousers

panter-o, panther; -kato, ocelot
pantofl-o, slipper, easy shoe
pap-o, pope
papag-o, parrot
papav-o, poppy
paper-o, paper
papili-o, butterfly
par-o, pair, couple
paraliz-i, to paralyze (tr.); -o, paralysis
parasut-o, parachute
pardon-i, to pardon, forgive; excuse
parenc-o, relative, kin; -a, related
parfum-o, perfume
park-o, park
parker-e, by memory, by heart
parlament-o, parliament
parol-i, to speak, talk; -ado, a speech, talk
part-o, part; -opreni, to take part
parti-o, party, faction; -ano, partisan; sen—a, impartial
pas-i, to pass (intr.); -igi, to pass, spend (time); -inta, past
pasaĝer-o, passenger
paser-o, sparrow
pasi-o, passion; -a, passionate
Pask-o, Easter
pasport-o, passport
past-o, dough
pasteĉ-o, pie, a pasty
pastr-o, pastor, priest
paŝ-i, to step; -o, a step
paŝt-i, to put out to pasture (tr.); -iĝi, to graze; -isto, shepherd
paŝtel-o, pastel (coloured crayon)
pat-o, frying-pan
patr-o, father; -ino, mother; paĉjo, daddy, papa; panjo, mamma
patrol-o, patrol
paŭz-i, to pause; rest (mus.)
pavim-o, pavement; -i, to pave
pec-o, piece
pedik-o, louse
pejzaĝ-o, landscape
pek-i, to sin
pekl-i, to pickle

pel-i, to chase, drive (before one), to impel
pelt-o, fur
pelv-o, basin; pelvis (anat.)
pen-i, to try, make an effort; -o, effort
penc-o, penny (British)
pend-i, to hang (intr.); -igi, to hang (tr.)
pens-i, to think; -o, a thought; el—i, to invent
pension-o, boarding-house, pension
pent-i, to repent
pentr-i, to paint; -aĵo, a painting, picture
pep-i, to chirp, twitter
per, by (means of); -forti, to assault, violate, force
perd-i, to lose; -ita, lost; -iĝi, to lose one's way
pere-i, to perish; -igi, to wreck, destroy; ŝip—o, ship-wreck
perfekt-a, perfect; -e, perfectly; -igi, to perfect
perfid-i, to betray
perl-o, pearl
permes-i, to permit, allow, grant
persekut-i, to persecute
persik-o, peach
person-o, person
peruk-o, wig
pes-i, to weigh (tr.); -ilo, weighing machine, scale
pest-o, plague, pest
pet-i, to ask, request, beg; **Mi petas**, please
petal-o, petal
petol-i, to frolic about, to play pranks or tricks; -ema, mischievous, tricky, petulant
petrol-o, oil (min.); petroleum, kerosene
pez-i, to weigh (intr.), to be heavy; -a, heavy; -o, weight; -ilo, a weight
pi-a, pious
pian-o, piano

pied-o, foot; -fingro, toe; -pilko, football; -signo, foot-print

pigme-o, pigmy, dwarf

pik-i, to pick, prick, sting; -o, a stab, sting; spade (at cards)

piknik-o, picnic

pilk-o, ball (for playing)

pilol-o, pill

pilot-o, pilot

pin-o, pine-tree

pinĉ-i, to pinch; -ilo, pincers

pingl-o, pin; -efiksi, to pin

pint-o, point, tip, top (of tree, etc.)

pip-o, pipe (for tobacco)

pipr-o, pepper

pir-o, pear

pist-i, to pound, crush; -ilo, pestle

pistol-o, pistol

piŝt-o, piston

piz-o, pea

plac-o, public square

plaĉ-i, to be pleasing, to please

plad-o, platter, dish

plafon-o, ceiling

pland-o, sole (of foot or shoe)

planed-o, planet

plank-o, floor

plant-i, to plant; -o, plant

plat-a, flat

plaŭd-i, to splash

pled-i, to plea (leg.)

plej, most; — bona, best; — multe, most; mal-, least

plekt-i, to braid, twist, plait

plen-a, full; -aĝulo, adult; -igi, to fill; -mano, handful; -umi, to fulfil

plend-i, to complain

plet-o, tray

plezur-o, pleasure

pli, more; — alta, higher; — bona, better; pli . . . ol, more . . . than

plor-i, to weep, to cry

plu, further, more (time and space); ne —, no longer; -e, moreover, furthermore

plum-o, pen; feather

plumb-o, lead (metal)

plur-aj, more than one, several

pluv-i, to rain; -mantelo, raincoat

po, at the rate of; -grande, wholesale

podi-o, platform

poem-o, poem

poet-o, poet

poezi-o, poetry

pokal-o, goblet, cup

polic-o, police; -ano, policeman; -ejo, police station

polis-o, policy (insurance)

politik-o, politics

polur-i, to polish

polus-o, pole (elec., geog.)

polv-o, dust

pom-o, apple; ter—o, potato

ponard-o, dagger

pont-o, bridge

popol-o, a people; -amaso, crowd

por, for, in order to, for the purpose of; — ke, in order that

pord-o, door

pork-o, pig

port-i, to carry; to wear; -isto, porter; al—i, to bring

posed-i, to possess, own, have

post, after, behind; -e, afterwards

posten-o, post, position, station

postul-i, to demand, require

poŝ-o, pocket; -horloĝo, watch

poŝt-o, post, mail; -marko, postage stamp; -a stampo, postmark; -o restanta, general delivery

pot-o, a pot

potenc-o, power; -a, powerful

pov-i, to be able; can; -o, power, might

pozici-o, position

pra-, primeval; (as pref. den. removed relationship) -patro, forefather; -tempo, primitive times

praktik-i, to put into practice; -a, practical

pram-o, ferry-boat

prav-a, right, true; mal—a, wrong; -igi, to justify

precip-e, principally, mainly
preciz-a, precise, accurate
predik-i, to preach
prefer-i, to prefer
preĝ-i, to pray; -ejo, church
prem-i, to press, squeeze; man—o, handshake
premi-o, prize, premium; -ito, prize-winner
pren-i, to take; parto—i, to take part
prepar-i, to prepare; -a, preliminary
pres-i, to print; -aĵo, printed matter
preskaŭ, almost
pret-a, ready; -igi, to make ready; -iĝi, to get ready
pretekst-o, excuse, pretext
preter, past, by, beyond
prez-o, price; -aro, price-list
prezent-i, to present; to introduce (a person); re—i, to represent; re—anto, representative
prezid-i, to preside; -anto, president
pri, about, concerning; -paroli, to speak about; -skribi, to describe
princ-o, prince (sovereign)
princip-o, principle
printemp-o, spring(time)
privat-a, private
pro, because of, on account of, for
proced-i, to proceed; -o, procedure
procent-o, percentage; -aĵo, commission
proces-o, lawsuit; -i, to be at law, litigate
produkt-i, to produce, yield
profesi-o, profession
profesor-o, professor
profit-i, to profit, gain, benefit
profund-a, deep
program-o, program
progres-i, to progress, advance
projekt-o, project, plan, scheme
prokrast-i, to procrastinate, delay, put off
proksim-a, near; -ume, approximately; al—iĝi, to approach, draw near; mal—a, distant, far

promen-i, to go for a walk
promes-i, to promise
propon-i, to propose, suggest, offer; -o, proposition, offer
propr-a, one's own; -avorte, in one's own words
prospekt-o, prospectus
prosper-i, to prosper, succeed
protekt-i, to protect
protest-i, to protest; -anto, protestant
prov-i, to try, attempt, test; pres—aĵo, printer's proof
provinc-o, province
proviz-i, to provide, supply; -o, stock, provision
proz-o, prose
prun-o, plum
prunt-i, to loan; -epreni, to borrow; -edoni, to lend
prus-o, Prussian; -a, Prussian (adj.)
pruv-i, to prove (tr.)
psalm-o, psalm
psikolog-o, psychologist; -io, psychology
publik-o, public; -igi, to publish
puding-o, pudding
pudr-o, powder (toilet, face)
pugn-o, fist
pul-o, flea
pulm-o, lung
pulv-o, gunpowder
pump-i, to pump
pun-i, to punish; mon—o, fine
punkt-o, point, dot, period; -okomo, semicolon
punt-o, lace
pup-o, doll
pupitr-o, desk (school, etc.)
pur-a, clean, pure; -ega, spotless; -igi, to clean
purpur-o, purple
pus-o, pus, matter
puŝ-i, to push; -veturilo, wheel-barrow
put-o, well (water)
putr-i, to putrefy, rot

R

rab-i, to rob, plunder

rabat-o, rebate, discount

raben-o, rabbi

rabot-i, to plane (wood, etc.)

raci-o, reason, logical faculty

rad-o, wheel; **-radio**, spoke; **-rando**, rim of wheel; **-ringo**, tire

radi-o, ray, beam; radio (wireless)

radar-aparat-o, radar

radik-o, root; **en—igi**, to implant, root in; **el—igi**, to root out, eradicate

rafin-i, to refine; **-ejo**, refinery

rajd-i, to ride (horse, bicycle)

rajt-o, right to something; **-igi**, to authorize

rakont-i, to tell, relate; **-o**, story

ramp-i, to crawl, creep; **-aĵo**, reptile

ran-o, frog

ranc-a, rancid

ranĉ-o, ranch

rand-o, edge, rim, brim

rang-o, rank, grade

rapid-a, rapid, quick, fast; **-i**, to hasten (intr.); **-igi**, to hurry, hasten (tr.)

raport-i, to report

ras-o, race, breed

rast-i, to rake

rat-o, rat

raŭk-a, hoarse

raŭp-o, caterpillar; **silk—o**, silkworm

rav-i, to delight, enrapture

raz-i, to shave (tr.); **-ilo**, razor; **-isto**, barber; **-klingo**, razor-blade

re-, (pref. den. again, back); **reiri**, to go back, return; **ree**, again

reakci-o, reaction (pol.)

real-a, real, actual, realistic

recenz-i, to review (a book, etc.)

reciprok-a, mutual, reciprocal; **-i**, to reciprocate; **ili amas sin reciproke**, they love one another.

redakci-o, editorial offices and staff

redakt-i, to edit; **-isto**, editor

redaktor-o, = **redaktisto**

redukt-i, to reduce to elements (chem.)

reg-i, to rule, govern; **-istaro**, government

regal-i, to entertain, regale

region-o, region, district

registr-i, to register (tr.)

regn-o, the State, realm

regul-o, rule; **-a**, regular

reĝ-o, king

reĝim-o, regime (pol.)

reklam-o, advertisement; **-i**, to advertise

rekomend-i, to recommend; **-ita letero**, registered letter

rekompenc-o, reward

rekt-a, straight, direct

rel-o, rail (of train, tramway, etc.); **-kruciĝo**, junction

religi-o, religion

rem-i, to row; **-ilo**, oar

rembur-i, to stuff, pad

ren-o, kidney

rendevu-o, rendezvous, meeting, date

renkont-i, to meet, encounter (tr.)

rent-o, income (from investment or property); **-umo**, interest

renvers-i, to upset, overthrow (tr.)

respekt-o, respect; **-inda**, respectable

respond-i, to answer, reply

respublik-o, republic

rest-i, to stay, remain

restoraci-o, restaurant

ret-o, net; **-aĵo**, netting

reŭmatism-o, rheumatism

rev-i, to daydream, fancy; **el—igi**, to disillusion

revoluci-o, revolution

rezerv-i, to reserve, hold back (tr.)

rezign-i, to give up; to resign oneself to

rezist-i, to resist, withstand

rezult-i, to result, follow

ribel-i, to rebel, revolt

ricev-i, to receive, get

riĉ-a, rich

rid-i, to laugh; -eti, to smile; -inda, ridiculous

rifuĝ-i, to take refuge; -ejo, shelter, asylum

rifuz-i, to refuse

rigard-i, to look at; ek—o, glance

rigl-i, to bolt (mech.)

rikolt-i, to harvest (tr.)

rilat-i, to relate to, have reference to; -e al, with reference to

rim-o, rhyme

rimark-i, to notice; -igi, to call attention to

rimed-o, means, resources

rimen-o, belt (mech.), strap

ring-o, ring

rip-o, rib

ripar-i, to repare (tr.)

ripet-i, to repeat

ripoz-i, to rest, take a rest

riproĉ-i, to reproach, scold, upbraid

risk-i, to risk (tr.)

risort-o, spring (mech.)

ritm-o, rhythm

river-o, river, stream; -eto, brook

riz-o, rice

rok-o, a rock

rol-o, part in a play, rôle

roman-o, novel

romanc-o, musical romance

romp-i, to break (tr.)

rond-o, circle, group of people; -a, round

ronk-i, to snore

ros-o, dew

rost-i, to roast; -bovaĵo, roast-beef

roz-o, rose

rub-o, rubbish, rubble

ruband-o, ribbon

ruĝ-a, red

ruin-o, a ruin; -igi, to ruin

rukt-i, to belch

rul-i, to roll (tr.); -kurteno, window-shade, blind

rus-o, Russian; -a, Russian (adj.); -ujo, Russia

rust-o, rust

ruz-a, cunning, clever

S

sabat-o, Saturday

sabl-o, sand

sag-o, arrow

saĝ-a, wise; mal—ulo, fool

sak-o, sack, bag

sal-o, salt

salajr-o, salary, wages

salat-o, salad

sald-i, to balance, settle (account)

salik-o, willow

salm-o, salmon

salon-o, sitting room, large elegant room

salt-i, to jump

salut-i, to salute, greet; Saluton! Hello!

sam-a, same; -ideano, fellow-thinker; -tempe, at the same time

san-a, healthy, well; -iga, healthful; mal—ulejo, hospital; Kiel vi sanas? How are you?

sang-o, blood

sankt-a, sacred, holy

sap-o, soap

sardin-o, sardine

sark-i, to weed

sat-a, satisfied; mal—a, hungry

saŭc-o, sauce, gravy

sav-i, to save (tr.), rescue; -zono, life-belt

scen-o, scene; -ejo, stage

sci-i, to know (tr.); -igi, to let know, inform; -vola, curious, inquisitive; -voli, to wonder

scienc-o, science

sciur-o, squirrel

se, if

sed, but

seg-i, to saw

seĝ-o, chair

sek-a, dry; -igi, to dry (tr.); -iĝi, to dry (intr.)

sekal-o, rye

sekc-i, to cut up, dissect
sekci-o, section
sekret-o, secret
sekretari-o, secretary
seks-o, sex
sekund-o, second
sekur-a, sure, safe
sekv-i, to follow (tr.); **-anta**, following; **sin—e**, consecutively
sel-o, saddle; **sur—iĝi**, to mount
sem-i, to sow; **-o**, seed
semajn-o, week; **ĉiu—e**, weekly
sen, without; **-igi je**, deprive of; **-brua**, quiet, still; **-dube**, undoubtedly
senc-o, sense, meaning
send-i, to send (tr.); **-ilo**, transmitter; **-aĵo**, message; **-ito**, messenger; **-stacio**, transmitting station (rad.)
sent-i, to feel (tr.); **-ema**, sensitive
sep, seven
Septembr-o, September
serĉ-i, to look for, search
serĝent-o, sergeant
seri-o, series
serioz-a, serious
serpent-o, snake, serpent; **-umi**, to meander, wind around
serur-o, a lock (on a door, etc.)
serv-i, to serve, attend; **-istino**, maid
ses, six
sezon-o, season (of the year)
si, -self (refers back to subject of sentence); **-ndeteno**, self-restraint
sibl-i, to hiss
sid-i, to sit; **-iĝi**, to sit down
sieĝ-i, to besiege
sigel-o, a seal; **-i**, to seal
sign-o, sign
signal-o, signal
signif-i, to signify, mean
silab-o, syllable
silent-i, to be silent; **-o**, silence
silk-o, silk
simbol-o, symbol
simi-o, monkey

simil-a, similar, like; **-i**, to be like, resemble
simpati-o, sympathy
simpl-a, simple
sin-o, bosom
sincer-a, sincere
sindikat-o, syndicate, union, "trust"
sinjor-o, S-ro, gentleman, Mr.; **-ino**, S-ino, lady, Mrs.
sirop-o, syrup
sistem-o, system
sitel-o, bucket
situaci-o, situation, circumstances
skal-o, scale (measure); **laŭ—e**, according to scale
skandal-o, scandal
skapol-o, shoulder-blade
skatol-o, box
skelet-o, skeleton
skiz-o, sketch
sklav-o, slave
skolt-o, Scout
skrap-i, to scrape
skrib-i, to write; **pri—i**, to describe; **sub—i**, to sign; **-maŝino**, typewriter
sku-i, to shake (tr.)
skulpt-i, to sculpture
smerald-o, emerald
sobr-a, sober, temperate
soci-o, society (as a whole); **-a**, social; **-eto**, a society
sociolog-o, sociologist; **-io**, sociology
sof-o, sofa
soif-i, to thirst, be thirsty
sojl-o, sill, threshold
sol-a, alone, sole
soldat-o, soldier
solen-a, solemn, ceremonious
solid-a, solid
solv-i, dissolve (tr.); solve (problem)
somer-o, summer
son-i, to sound (intr.), **-o**, sound
sonĝ-o, dream; **-i**, to dream
sonor-i, to ring (intr.)
sopir-i, to sigh, long for

sopran-o, soprano
sorb-i, to absorb, suck up; **-a papero,** blotting-paper
sorĉ-i, to practice sorcery, to bewitch
sort-o, fate, lot, destiny
sovaĝ-a, wild, savage
spac-o, space, room
spec-o, species, kind, sort
special-a, special
specimen-o, specimen, sample
spegul-o, mirror, looking-glass
spert-a, experienced; **-i,** to experience; **-ulo,** expert
spez-o, money turnover; **en—oj,** receipts; **el—oj,** expenditures
spic-o, spice; **-i,** to spice, season
spik-o, ear (of corn)
spin-o, spine, backbone
spinac-o, spinach
spion-o, spy
spir-i, to breathe; **el—i,** to exhale
spirit-o, spirit, mind; **-ismo,** spirit-(ual)ism
spit-e, in spite (of); **-i,** to spite
spong-o, sponge; **-eca,** spongy
sport-o, sport
sprit-a, witty; **mal—a,** stupid, dull
spron-o, spur
sput-i, to spit up (blood, etc.)
stab-o, staff (mil.)
staci-o, station; **-domo,** railway-station
stal-o, stable, barn, shed (for cattle, etc.)
stamp-i, to stamp, mark
stan-o, tin
standard-o, standard, flag
stang-o, pole, staff
star-i, to stand, be standing; **kontraŭ—i,** to resist
stat-o, state, condition
statu-o, statue
steb-i, to stitch, to quilt
stel-o, star
stenograf-i, to write shorthand; **-isto,** stenographer

step-o, steppe, plains, prairie
sterk-o, manure, dung
stern-i, to spread or lay out (tr.)
stil-o, style
stok-o, stock (of goods, books, etc.)
stomak-o, stomach
strab-i, to squint
strang-a, strange, peculiar
strat-o, street
strategi-o, strategy
streb-i, seek or strive (after)
streĉ-i, to stretch (tr.); to wind up (watch, etc.); **mal—a,** loose
strek-i, to make a streak, to line; **-eto,** hyphen; **for—i,** to delete, **sub—i,** to underline
stri-o, stripe
strik-o, strike (of workers)
strof-o, verse, strophe
struktur-o, structure
stud-i, to study
student-o, student (university, etc.)
stuk-i, to plaster
stult-a, stupid, dull, silly; **-ulo,** dunce
sub, under, beneath; **-aĉeti,** to bribe; **-skribi,** to sign; **-vesto,** underwear; **-teni,** to support
subit-a, sudden
subjekt-o, subject
suĉ-i, to suck
sud-o, south
sufer-i, to suffer, endure
sufiĉ-a, enough, sufficient; **-i,** to suffice
sufok-i, to suffocate, choke (tr.)
sugest-i, to suggest
suk-o, juice
sukces-i, to succeed; **mal—i,** to fail
suker-o, sugar
sulk-o, furrow, wrinkle
sum-o, sum, total amount; **-igi,** to add up; **re—o,** summary, resumé
sun-o, sun
sup-o, soup
super, above, over; **-i,** to exceed, surpass; **-jaro,** leap-year; **-ŝuti,** to

overwhelm, to cover (with work, etc.)

superstiĉ-o, superstition

supoz-i, to suppose, assume

supr-e, on top, above; **-a,** upper; **-o,** top, summit; **-en,** upwards, **-eniri,** to go up, ascend; **mal—eniri,** to go down, descend

sur, on, upon; **-meti,** to put on (clothes, etc.); **-teriĝi,** to land

surd-a, deaf

surpriz-i, to surprise (tr.)

surtut-o, overcoat

suspekt-i, to suspect

sven-i, to faint, swoon

sving-i, to swing (tr.); to brandish

svis-o, a Swiss (person); **-ujo,** Switzerland

Ŝ

ŝaf-o, sheep; **-aĵo,** mutton; **-ido,** lamb; **vir—o,** ram

ŝajn-i, to appear, seem; **-igi,** to pretend

ŝak-o, chess; **-i,** to check (at chess)

ŝakal-o, jackal

ŝal-o, shawl

ŝanc-o, chance; **bon—o,** good luck

ŝancel-i, to shake (tr.); **-iĝi,** to waver, to hesitate

ŝanĝ-i, to change, alter (tr.)

ŝarĝ-i, to burden, charge, load

ŝat-i, to appreciate, to like; **mal—i,** to despise

ŝaŭm-o, foam, froth

ŝel-o, shell, husk; bark (of tree)

ŝelk-o, suspenders, braces

ŝerc-i, to joke, jest

ŝi, she; **-a,** her, hers; **-n,** her

ŝild-o, shield

ŝiling-o, shilling (British)

ŝim-i, to mould, mildew

ŝink-o, ham

ŝip-o, ship

ŝir-i, to tear (tr.); **for—i,** to tear out

ŝirm-i, to shelter, protect

ŝlim-o, slime

ŝlos-i, to lock (tr.); **-ilo,** key

ŝmac-i, to kiss noisily, to smack

ŝmir-i, to smear

ŝnur-o, rope; **-eto,** string, twine

ŝose-o, highway, main road

ŝov-i, to shove

ŝovel-i, to shovel

ŝpar-i, to spare, save, economize; **-ema,** thrifty

ŝpin-i, to spin (silk, cloth, etc.)

ŝpruc-i, to spout out, gush

ŝrank-o, cupboard, closet

ŝraŭb-o, screw; **-ingo,** nut

ŝtal-o, steel

ŝtat-o, state (pol.)

ŝtel-i, to steal

ŝtip-o, block of wood

ŝtof-o, material, fabric; **sub—o,** lining

ŝton-o, stone; **-ego,** rock, boulder

ŝtop-i, to stop up, plug

ŝtrump-o, stocking; **-eto,** sock

ŝtup-o, step (of stair); **-aro,** stairway; **-etaro,** ladder

ŝu-o, shoe

ŝuld-i, to owe; **-o,** debt; **-atesto,** promissory note

ŝultr-o, shoulder

ŝut-i, to pour out (grain, sand, powder, etc. not fluids)

ŝveb-i, to float in the air, to soar, hover

ŝvel-i, to swell (intr.); **-igi,** to inflate

ŝvit-i, to sweat, perspire

T

tabak-o, tobacco

tabel-o, table, index

tabl-o, table (furniture)

tabul-o, plank, board; **nigra —o,** black-board

taĉment-o, detachment (mil.)

tag-o, day; **-iĝo,** dawn; **-mezo,** noon; **-ordo,** agenda; **-libro,** diary; **ĉiu—e,** daily

tajlor-o, tailor
taks-i, to estimate the value of
tali-o, waist
tambur-o, drum
tamen, nevertheless, however, still, yet
tank-o, tank (mil.)
tapet-o, tapestry
tapiŝ-o, carpet
tas-o, cup
task-o, task; hejm—o, home-work
taŭg-i, to be fit for
tavol-o, layer, stratum
te-o, tea; -kruĉo, teapot; -manĝo, tea (the meal)
teatr-o, theatre; -aĵo, a play
ted-i, to bore, (tr.)
teg-i, to cover over; to overlay; -ilo, tarpaulin, cover
tegment-o, roof
teknik-o, technics; -a, technical
teks-i, to weave
tekst-o, text, wording
telefon-o, telephone
telegraf-o, telegraph; -ado, telegraphy
telegram-o, telegram
teler-o, plate, dish
teleskop-o, telescope
televid-o, television
tem-o, subject, theme, topic
temp-o, time; liber—o, vacation, holidays (British)
tempi-o, temple (anat.)
templ-o, temple (building)
ten-i, to hold; -ilo, handle; sin—ado, bearing, attitude
tend-o, tent; -aro, camp
tendenc-o, tendency
tenis-o, tennis
tent-i, to tempt
teori-o, theory
ter-o, earth, ground; sub—a, underground; sub—vojo, subway, underground
teritori-o, territory

termin-o, term (word); -aro, terminology
tern-i, to sneeze
terur-o, terror; -a, terrible
testament-o, will, testament
testud-o, tortoise, turtle
tia, that kind of, such; — kia, such as
tial, for that reason, therefore
tiam, at that time, then
tie, there, yonder; ĉi —, here
tiel, in that way, thus, so; tiel . . . kiel, as . . . as
ties, that one's
tigr-o, tiger
tikl-i, to tickle
tim-i, to fear, be afraid (tr.)
tine-o, moth, clothes moth
tint-i, to tinkle, jingle (intr.)
tio, that (thing)
tiom, so much, as much or many
tip-o, type
tir-i, to pull, draw; al—i, to attract; for—i, to draw away
tiran-o, tyrant
titol-o, title
tiu, that (one); ĉi —, this (one)
tol-o, linen cloth; -aĵo, laundry, linen (in general)
toler-i, to tolerate, bear, stand (tr.)
tomat-o, tomato
tomb-o, tomb; -ejo, cemetery
tond-i, to shear; -ilo, scissors
tondr-o, thunder
torĉ-o, torch
tord-i, to twist (tr.)
torn-i, to turn (with lathe)
tornistr-o, knapsack
tors-o, trunk (body)
tort-o, tart, fruit pie
tost-i, to toast (health)
tra, through; -irejo, passage
trab-o, a beam (wood); -aro, rafters, scaffolding
traduk-i, to translate
traf-i, to hit, strike (the mark); mal—i, to miss

trafik-o, traffic
tragedi-o, tragedy
trajt-o, trait, feature
trake-o, windpipe
trakt-i, to treat, deal with; **-aĵo,** treatise
tram-o, tram, street-car; **—vojo,** tramway
tranĉ-i, to cut; **-ilo,** knife
tranĉe-o, trench (mil.)
trankvil-a, tranquil, quiet, still
trans, across; **-doni,** to hand over; **-iri,** to cross
tre, very, very much
trem-i, to tremble, shiver
tremp-i, to dip (tr.)
tren-i, to drag, tow, trail (tr.); **-ŝipo,** tugboat
trezor-o, treasure
tri, three; **-a,** third
trik-i, to knit
trink-i, to drink; **-mono,** tip
tritik-o, wheat
triumf-o, triumph
tro, too, too much
tromp-i, to deceive
tron-o, throne
trot-i, to trot
trotuar-o, sidewalk, pavement
trov-i, to find; **-iĝi,** to be found or situated
tru-o, hole
trud-i, to impose upon, intrude
trunk-o, trunk (of tree, etc.)
trup-o, troop, troupe (mil., theat.)
tub-o, tube, pipe
tuberkuloz-o, tuberculosis
tuf-o, tuft, bunch, tassel
tuj, immediately, at once; **— kiam,** as soon as
tuk-o, a cloth; **tablo—o,** tablecloth; **lit—o,** sheet
tun-o, a ton
tur-o, tower
turism-o, tourism; **turisto,** tourist
turment-i, to torment; **-ego,** torture
turn-i, to turn (tr.)

tus-i, to cough
tuŝ-i, to touch
tut-a, entire, whole, complete; **-e ne,** not at all; **en—e,** as a whole

U

-u, (end. den. imperative mood of verb, expressing an order, will, necessity); **Foriru!** Go away!; **Mi deziras, ke vi foriru,** I desire that you go away.
-uj-, (suff. den. a container, receptacle); **monujo,** purse
-ul-, (suff. den. a being characterized by idea of the root); **dikulo,** fat person
-um-, (indefinite suff.); **plenumi,** to fulfill; **aerumi,** to aerate
umbilik-o, navel
unc-o, ounce
ung-o, nail (finger, toe)
uniform-o, uniform
univers-o, universe
universal-a, universal
universitat-o, university
unu, one; **-a,** first; **-voĉe,** in unison; **-iĝi,** to unite
uragan-o, hurricane
urani-o, uranium
urb-o, city; **-estro,** mayor; **ĉef—o,** capital
urĝ-i, to urge (tr.); to be urgent (intr.)
urin-o, urine; **-i,** to urinate
urs-o, bear (animal)
-us, (end. den. conditional mood or verb); **Se mi estus riĉa, mi aĉetus ŝipon.** If I were rich, I would buy a ship.
Uson-o, United States of North America; **-ano,** citizen of United States
uter-o, uterus, womb
util-a, useful; **-i,** to be useful; **sen—a,** useless
uz-i, to use

V

vad-i, to wade

vafl-o, waffle

vag-i, to wander, roam

vagon-o, (railway) coach, car, wagon; -aro, train

vaker-o, cowboy

vak-i, to be vacant

vaks-o, wax; -tolo, oilcloth

val-o, valley

valid-a, valid

valiz-o, valise, brief-case

valor-i, to be worth, to have value; sen—a, worthless

vals-o, waltz

van-a, futile, in vain

vang-o, cheek; -oharoj, whiskers; post—o, buttock

vant-a, frivolous, shallow

vapor-o, vapor, steam

var-o, commodity; -oj, goods, wares

varb-i, to enlist, enroll (tr.)

varm-a, warm; -o, warmth; -ega, hot; mal—umo, a cold

vart-i, to look after (a child)

vast-a, vast, spacious; dis—igi, to spread abroad, to propagate

vaz-o, vase, vessel

ve, woe!; ho ve!, alas!

veget-i, to vegetate, merely exist

vejn-o, vein

vek-i, to awaken, arouse (tr.); -horloĝo, alarm-clock; -iĝi, to wake up

vel-o, a sail; -veturi, to sail

velk-i, to fade, wither, wilt (intr.)

velur-o, velvet

ven-i, to come; al—i, to arrive; de—o, origin; kun—o, meeting

vend-i, to sell (tr.); -ejo, market; -isto, salesman

vendred-o, Friday

venen-o, poison

venĝ-i, to avenge

venk-i, to conquer, vanquish, defeat

vent-o, wind; -umi, to fan

ventol-i, to ventilate

ventr-o, abdomen, belly

ver-a, true; -o, truth

verand-o, veranda

verb-o, verb

verd-a, green

verg-o, rod, switch; -i, to punish by switch, etc.

verk-i, to compose, write (a work); -o, (literary) work; -isto, author, writer

verm-o, worm

vers-o, a line of verse; -aĵo, a piece of verse

verŝ-i, to pour (liquids)

veruk-o, wart

vesp-o, wasp

vesper-o, evening; -manĝo, supper

vespert-o, bat (zool.)

vest-i, to clothe, dress; -o, dress, clothes; sen—iĝi, to undress

veŝt-o, waistcoat, vest

vet-i, to bet, wager

veter-o, weather

veteran-o, veteran

vetur-i, to travel by vehicle, to drive, ride (Amer.)

vezik-o, bladder

vi, you; -a, your

viand-o, meat

vibr-i, to vibrate

vic-o, rank, row; turn; sia—e, in turn

vid-i, to see; -o, sight; -aĵo, view; -punko, viewpoint; tra—ebla, transparent

vidv-o, widower; -ino, widow

vigl-a, alert, vigorous, wide-awake

viktim-o, victim

vil-a, shaggy, hairy

vilaĝ-o, village

vin-o, wine; -bero, grape

vinagr-o, vinegar

vind-i, to wind, swaddle

vintr-o, winter

violon-o, violin

vip-o, whip, lash

vir-o, man, male; -ino, woman, female; -bovo, bull

virg-a, virginal; -ulino, virgin
virt-o, virtue
viski-o, whiskey
vist-o, whist
viŝ-i, to wipe; for—i, to wipe away
vitamen-o, vitamin
vitr-o, glass (material)
viv-i, to live; -o, life
viz-o, visa
vizaĝ-o, face
vizi-o, vision
vizit-i, to visit; -adi, to frequent
voĉ-o, voice; -doni, to vote
voj-o, way, road
vojaĝ-i, to travel, make a journey;
    -o, journey, trip
vok-i, to call, to summon; al—o, ap-
    peal
vol-i, to will, wish; -o, will; laŭ—e,
    at will, as one pleases
volont-e, willingly; -ulo, volunteer

volv-i, to roll up, wrap up (tr.);
    dis—i, to develop (tr.)
vom-i, to vomit
vort-o, word
vost-o, tail
vual-o, veil
vulp-o, fox
vund-i, to wound, hurt, injure (tr.)

Z

zebr-o, zebra
zigzag-o, zigzag
zingibr-o, ginger
zink-o, zinc
zon-o, belt, girdle
zoolog-o, zoologist; -io, zoology
zorg-i, to care (about, for), be
    mindful of, -ema, careful; pri--i,
    to take care of
zum-i, to hum, buzz; -ilo, buzzer

ENGLISH-ESPERANTO
DICTIONARY

****

ENGLISH - ESPERANTO

A

a, an, (indefinite article, not expressed)

abandon, forlasi; cedi

ability, kapableco, kapablo; scipovo,
lerteco

able, kapabla, lerta; povanta; (as
affix) -ebla; -inda; **to be —,** povi

abnormal, nenorma, eksternorma

about, ĉirkaŭ; pri; proksimume

above, super; supre, pli alte ol;
— all, antaŭ ĉio; super ĉio

abroad, alilande

absent, for, forestanta; **to be —,**
foresti

absolute, absoluta; **-ly,** absolute

absorb, sorbi

absurd, absurda

abundance, abundeco

abuse, misuzi, trouzi; insulti

accent, akcento; supersigno; el-
parolmaniero; **-uate,** akcenti

accept, akcepti; konsenti

accident, (rail, etc.) akcidento;
hazardo; **-al,** hazarda

accompany, akompani, kuniri

accomplish, plenumi; efektivigi; **-ed,**
klera, sperta, kapabla

accord, akordo, akordi; konsento;
-ing to, laŭ

account, konto, kalkulo, kalkuli;
rakonto; raporto, raporti; **-able
for,** responda pri; **-ant,** kontisto,
kalkulisto; **on — of,** kaŭze de,
pro

accurate, ĝusta; preciza; (punctual)
akurata

accuse, akuzi

accustomed; be —, kutimi; **get —,**
alkutimiĝi

ace, (at cards) aso

ache, dolori

acid, acida, acido

acquaint, sciigi, informi; **-ance,** scio;
kono; konato

acquire, akiri

acre, akreo

across, trans, transe; **— from,** kontraŭ; **to go —,** transiri

act, agi, ago; (theat.) ludi, akto;
(leg.) akto; **-ion,** agado; proceso;
-or, (theat.) aktoro; **-ive,** aktiva

actual, reala; efektiva; (of present
time) aktuala

add, aldoni; aldiri; (math.) adicii;
— up, sumigi; **in -ition to,** aldone
al, plue

address, (of letter) adreso; (speech)
parolado

adjective, adjektivo

administer, administri; **administration,** administrado, administrejo

admit, enlasi; konfesi

adore, adori; amegi

adorn, ornami

adult, plenaĝa, plenaĝulo; plenkres-
ka, plenkreskulo

adultery, adulto; **commit —,** adulti

adventure, aventuro

advertise, reklami; anonci

advice, konsilo; **advise,** konsili; **advisable,** konsilinda

affair, afero

affect, influi, efiki sur; koncerni;
kortuŝi

afford, povi elspezi; produkti

afraid, timema; **be —,** timi

Africa, Afriko

after, post, poste; sekve; **— all,** fine,
malgraŭ ĉio; **-noon,** posttagmezo;
—wards, poste

again, ree, denove; plue; **once —,** ankoraŭ unufoje

against, kontraŭ

age, aĝo; epoko; maljuneco; maljuniĝi

agent, agento, peristo; rimedo

ago, antaŭ; **long —,** antaŭlonge; **two years —,** antaŭ du jaroj

agree, (inter) konsenti; akordi; **-able,** agrabla, plaĉa; **-ment,** interkonsento, kontrakto

agriculture, terkulturo

ah! ha!

aid, helpi, helpo

aim, celo, celi; intenci; pafceli

air, aero; mieno; maniero; aerumi; **-force,** aerkorpuso; **-plane,** aeroplano; **-ing,** promenado; aerumo; **-tight,** perfekte fermita

alarm, alarmi, alarmo; timigi; **-clock,** vekhorloĝo

alas! ho ve!

alcohol, alkoholo

ale, biero

alien, fremda, fremdulo; alilandano

alike, simila

alive, viva, vivanta

all, tuta, tute, tuto, ĉio; ĉiuj; **— the more** des pli; tiom pli; **not at —,** tute ne; **— right,** bone, tute bone

alley, strateto

alliance, interligo, alianco

alligator, aligatoro

allow, permesi, lasi; **-ance,** stipendio

almost, preskaŭ

alone, sola; sole, nur

along, laŭ, laŭlonge de; antaŭen; pluen; flanke de; **— with,** kune kun

aloud, laŭte

already, jam

also, ankaŭ

although, kvankam

altogether, tute, kune

aluminum, aluminio

always, ĉiam

am, estas

amateur, amatora, neprofesia

amaze, mirigi; **-ment,** mirego

ambulance, ambulanco

amen, amen

America, Ameriko; Usono (U.S.A.); **-n,** amerikano, amerika

among, inter, meze de

amount, kvanto; sumo; nombro

amuse, amuzi

an, (see **a**)

analyse, analizi

ancestor, prapatro

ancient, antikva

and, kaj; **— so on,** kaj tiel plu, k.t.p.

angel, anĝelo

anger, kolero, **angry,** kolera

animal, besto; **(of the — kingdom)** animala

ankle, maleolo

anniversary, datreveno

announce, anonci; **-ment,** anonco

annoy, ĝeni; ĉagreni; **to be -ed by,** esti ĝenata de

anonymous, anonima

another, alia; aliulo; **one —,** unu la alian

answer, respondi, respondo

ant, formiko

anthem, himno

anthropology, antropologio

antique, antikva; **antiquity,** antikveco; pratempo

antiseptic, kontraŭsepsa

anxiety, maltrankvilo; **anxious,** maltrankvila; dezira

any, (kind of) ia, kelka; (quantity) iom (da); **— at all,** iom ajn; **-body,** iu; **-body's,** ies; **-how,** iel; almenaŭ; **-one,** iu; **-thing,** io; **-where,** ie; **-way,** almenaŭ, ĉiuokaze

apart, aparta, aparte; dise; **— from,** krom; **-ment,** apartamento

ape, simio; **to —,** imiti

apiece, (each) ĉiu; (for each) por ĉiu; po; (to each) al ĉiu

apologize, pardonpeti

190]

apparent, videbla, evidenta
appeal, alpeti, alpeto; alvoki; allogi; (leg.) apelacii
appear, aperi; troviĝi; (seem) ŝajni; **-ance**, aspekto, mieno
appetite, apetito
applaud, aplaŭdi
apple, pomo
apply, apliki; peti (pri, por)
appoint, nomi; **-ment**, ofico; rendevuo
appreciate, estimi; ŝati; plivaloriĝi
approach, alproksimiĝi, alproksimiĝo; aliri
approve, aprobi
approximately, proksimume
April, Aprilo
apron, antaŭtuko
arch, arkajo
are, estas
area, areo; distrikto
argue, diskuti; argumenti
arithmetic, aritmetiko
arm, brako; armi, armilo; **-ament**, armilaro, milit-provizo; **-chair**, brakseĝo; **-pit**, akselo; **-y**, armeo, militistaro
around, ĉirkaŭ
arrange, aranĝi; ordigi
arrest, aresti, kapti
arrive, alveni
arrow, sago
art, arto; **-ificial**, artefarita; nenatura; **-ist**, artisto
article, objekto, ajo; (newspaper, etc.) artikolo
artillery, artilerio
as, kiel; (so) tiel; (because) ĉar; (while) dum; — **if**, kvazaŭ; — **to**, pri, rilate al; **as ... as ...** , tiel ... kiel ..
ascend, supreniri
ash, cindro
ashamed, to be, honti
Asia, Azio
ask, demandi; peti
asleep, dormanta; **fall —**, ekdormi

ass, azeno; stultulo
assemble, kunveni; kolekti; **arigi**, ariĝi; **-y**, kunsido, kunsidantaro
assist, helpi; **-ant**, helpanto
association, asocio; societo; kuniĝo
assume, supozi; preni sur sin
assure, certigi; (insure) **asekuri**; **assurance**, aplombo, memfido
astonish, nirigi; **be -ed**, miri
at, en, ĉe; (near) apud; (time) **je**; (price) por, po; — **the rate of**, po
athlete, atleto; **athletic**, atleta
atmosphere, atmosfero
atom, atomo; — **bomb, atoma bombo**
attack, ataki
attain, atingi, trafi; **-ments**, akirajo
attempt, provi, provo; (criminal) atenci, atenco
attend, ĉeesti; apudesti; (wait for) atendi; viziti; servi
attention, atento; **pay — to**, atenti
attract, altiri; allogi
August, Aŭgusto
aunt, onklino
author, aŭtoro, verkisto; **-ity, aŭtor**-itato, rajtigo
automobile, aŭtomobilo
autumn, aŭtuno
avenue, avenuo, aleo
average, meza
aviation, aviado
avoid, eviti
await, atendi
awake, maldorma; vigla; veki, **vekiĝi**
away, for, de
awkward, mallerta
axe, hakilo
axle, akso

B

baby, infaneto, bebo
bachelor, fraŭlo; (of arts, science, etc.) bakalaŭro
back, dorso; malantaŭa, malantaŭe; ree, poste; **in — of**, malantaŭ;

-bone, spino, vertebraro; -ward, neprogresa, neinteligenta; nevola; -wards, reen, malantaŭen; to —, subteni
bacon, lardo
bad, malbona; putra
bag, sako; -gage, pakajo, pakajoj; -pipe, sakfajfilo
bake, baki, bakiĝi
balance, (swing) balanco, balanci, balanciĝi, balancilo; egalpezo; ekvilibro; (accounts) saldo, saldi; (-sheet) bilanco; (remainder) restajo
bald, kalva; senhara
ball, (toy) pilko; (of earth, snow, etc.) bulo; (dance) balo
ballet, baleto
balloon, balono
ballot, baloto, baloti
ban, malbeno, malpermeso
banana, banano
band, aro; (troop, gang) bando; (mus.) muzikistaro
bandage, bandaĝo, bandaĝi
bank, banko; enbankigi; (river, etc.) bordo; (slope) deklivo; -note, bankbileto, banknoto
bankrupt, bankrota; become —, bankroti
banner, flago, standardo
banquet,, festeno, festeni
bar, bari, barilo, baro; malpermesi; (leg.) advokataro; trinkejo
barber, razisto, barbiro; -shop, frizejo, razejo
bare, nuda, senkovra, kruda; -ly, apenaŭ
bargain, kontrakti, kontrakto, interkonsenti, marĉandi
bark, (of tree) ŝelo; (of dog) bojo, boji
barn, grenejo, fojnejo
barracks, soldatejo, kazerno
barrel, barelo; — organ, gurdo
barren, senfrukta; sennaska; dezerta

base, bazi, bazo; fundamento; malnobla, malvirta; falsa; -ball, basbalo; -ment, subetaĝo
bashful, timema; malaplomba
basin, pelvo
basis, bazo, fundamento; principo
basket, korbo
bat, (zool.) vesperto; bati
bath, bano, bankuvo; -e, bani, baniĝi; -ing-place, banejo, banloko; -room, banĉambro
battle, batalo, batali
bay, golfo; boji; at —, en danĝero, sin defendanta
be, esti; ekzisti
beach, marbordo; banejo
beak, beko
beam, (light) radii, radio; (wood) trabo
bean, fabo
bear, elteni, toleri; porti; naski; produkti; (zool.) urso
beard, barbo
bearing, sintenado; rilato; (mech.) aksingo
beast, besto
beat, bati, frapi; gajni, venki, superi; (mus.) takto
beauty, beleco, belulino, belajo; beautiful, bela; beautify, beligi
because, ĉar; pro tio ke; tial ke; — of, pro
become, iĝi
bed, lito; (flower, etc.) bedo; (river) fluejo; -stead, litkadro; go to —, enlitiĝi; -bug, litcimo, cimo
bee, abelo; (bumble) burdo
beef, bovajo; -steak, bifsteko
been, estis, estinta
beer, biero
beet, beto
before, antaŭ, antaŭe; (time, before a verb) antaŭ ol
beg, peti; almozpeti; -gar, almozulo
begin, komenci, komenciĝi; — again, rekomenci
behalf of, on, pro

behave, konduti; bonkonduti
behind, malantaŭ; post
behold, jen! rigardi
being, estajo; human —, homo
Belgium, Belgujo; Belgian, belgo
belief, kredo
believe, kredi; make —, ŝajnigi
bell, sonorilo, tintilo
belly, ventro
belong to, aparteni al
beloved, karega, karegulo; amata, amat(in)o
below, malsupre; sub, sube; pli mal-alta ol
belt, zono; (strap) rimeno
bench, benko; juĝistaro
bend, fleksi, fleksiĝi, klini, kliniĝi
beneath, sub, malsupre de
benefit, profiti, profito; (theat.) benefico
berry, bero
berth, kuŝejo; lito
beside, apud; proksime de; ĉe; -s, krom, krome
best, plej bona
bet, veti
betray, perfidi; evidentigi
betrothal, fianĉ(in)iĝo
better, pli bona, pli bone; plibonigi
between, inter
beware, sin gardi kontraŭ; atentu!
beyond, (across) trans; (going past) preter; (farther) pli malproksime
bib, antaŭtuko
Bible, Biblio
bicycle, biciklo
bid, ordoni; proponi
big, granda; ampleksa
bill, kalkulo; monbileto; (bird's) beko; (placard) afiŝo; (leg.) leĝ-propono; -fold, monujo
bind, ligi; vindi; (books) bindi
bird, birdo
birth, naskiĝo; give —, naski; -day, naskiĝtago
biscuit, (Amer.) panbuleto; (Brit.) biskvito

bit, peceto, malmulto, iom; a little —, iomete; — by —, iom post iom
bite, mordi, mordo
bitter, maldolĉa, amara, acida
black, nigra; -board, nigra tabulo; -mail, minac-postuli; -smith, forĝisto
blame, kulpigi; riproĉi
blank, senskriba; senrima
blanket, (lan)kovrilo
bleed, sangi (intr.)
bless, beni; -ed, benita, feliĉega
blind, blinda, blindigi; window —, rulkurteno; venetian —, tabulet-kurteno
blister, (haŭt)veziketo
block, bloki; stratparto; (of wood) ŝtipo; -ade, blokado
blonde, blonda, blondulino
blood, sango
bloom, flori, floro
blot, makuli, makulo; — out, forigi; -ting paper, sorba papero
blouse, bluzo
blow, blovi; bato; sonigi
blue, blua, bluigi
blush, ruĝiĝi, ruĝiĝo
board, tabulo; nutri; suriri; direk-tantaro, konsilantaro; -ing-house, pensiono, loĝejo
boast, fanfaroni
boat, boato
body, korpo; substanco; anaro
boil, boli, boligi; (med.) furunko
bold, kuraĝa, maltimema; troriskema; elstara
bolt, rigli, riglilo; fulmofajro; forkuri; rapidgluti
bomb, bombo
bombard, bombardi
bond, ligilo; kontrakto; (fin.) obligacio
bone, osto; senostigi
book, libro; antaŭmendi; -keeping, librotenado; -worm, studemulo
boot, boto

border, landlimo; borderi, bordero; — upon, limtuŝi; simili
bore, bori; tedi, tedulo
born, naskita; to be —, naskiĝi
borrow, prunti, pruntepreni
bosom, brusto, sino
boss, estro, estri, ĉefo
both, ambaŭ; — A and B, kaj A kaj B
bother, ĝeni
bottle, botelo; enboteligi
bottom, fundo; malsupro
bound, salti; ligita; -ary, limo, landlimo
bouquet, bukedo
bow, saluti, sin klini, kliniĝi; riverenci; arko; (ribbon) banto; -legged, kurbkrura
bowels, intestoj; internajo
bowl, pelvo; pilkruli
box, skatolo; (sport) boksi, pugnobati; (theat.) loĝio
boy, knabo
boycott, bojkoti
braid, plekti, plektajo
brain(s), cerbo; rack one's —, cerbumi
brake, haltigilo, bremso
branch, branĉo; fako; filio
brave, brava, kuraĝa; spiti
bread, pano
break, rompi, rompiĝi; -fast, matenmanĝo
breast, brusto; mamo
breath, spiro; -e, spiri
breeze, venteto
bribe, subaĉeti, subaĉetajo
bride, novedzino; -groom, novedzo
bridge, ponto; (game) briĝo
brief, mallonga; (leg.) instrukcio; -ly, malmultvorte
bright, hela, brila, luma; gaja, vigla, sprita
bring, alporti, alkonduki; — together, kunigi; — about, okazigi; — up, eduki

Britain, Britujo; British, brito (person), brita (adj.)
broad, larĝa; -cast, dissendi, disaŭdigi
broil, kradrosti
brook, rivereto
broom, balailo
broth, buljono, supo
brother, frato; -hood, frateco, fratularo
brown, bruna
bruise, kontuzi, kontuzo; premegi
brush, brosi, broso
bubble, veziko; ŝaŭmeti; bobelo
bucket, sitelo
bud, burĝoni, burĝono
budget, buĝeto
bug, insekto, cimo
build, konstrui; -ing, konstruajo
bulb, bulbo; elektra bulbo
bullet, kuglo
bulletin, bulteno
bunch, aro, fasko, tufo
bungalow, dometo
bungle, fuŝi
bureau, oficejo; -cracy, burokrateco; -crat, burokrato
burn, bruli, bruligi; brulvundo; -er, flamingo
burst, krevi; disrompiĝi; eksplodi
bury, enterigi; kaŝi
bus, aŭtobuso
bush, arbeto; -y, densa
business, afero; negoco, komerco
busy, okupata
but, sed; krom; kun la escepto de; nu; nur
butcher, buĉisto
butter, butero
button, butono, butonumi; -hook, butonumilo
buy, aĉeti
by, (agency) de, per; (according to) laŭ; (at the rate of) po; (past) preter; close —, apude, proksime; — and —, baldaŭ, poste

C

cab, fiakro
cabbage, brasiko
cabin, kabano; (of ship) kajuto
cable, kablo; ŝnurego; -gram, kablogramo
cafe, kafejo
cage, kaĝo
cake, kuko
calendar, kalendaro
calf, bovido; (of leg) tibikarno
call, voki; krii; nomi; vizito
calm, trankvila, kvieta
came, venis
camel, kamelo
camera, foto-aparato
camp, tendaro, tendejo
can, povas; metala ujo, lada ujo
canal, kanalo
canary, kanario
candle, kandelo
candy, dolĉaĵo, bombonoj
cane, kano; bastoneto
cannot, ne povas
cannon, kanono
cap, ĉapo; kapsulo (mil.)
capable, kapabla
capital, (fin.) kapitalo; (city) ĉefurbo
captain, (mil.) kapitano; (ship) ŝipestro
capture, kapti; captive, kaptito
car, (Amer.) aŭtomobilo; ĉaro; (railroad) vagono
card, karto; -board, kartono; post —, poŝtkarto
care, zorgo; — about, prizorgi; -ful, zorgema; -less, senzorga; take —, atenti
career, kariero
caress, karesi, kareso
carpenter, ĉarpenti, ĉarpentisto
carpet, tapiŝo
carriage, veturilo, vagono; sinteno
carrot, karoto

carry, porti; — out, efektivigi, plenumi
cart, ŝarĝveturilo
case, (box) skatolo, kesto; ingo, ujo; (leg.) proceso; (gram., med.) kazo; (event) okazo; in that —, tiuokaze
cash, mono, monigi; -ier, kasisto; ready —, kontanto
casket, ĉerko; skatoleto
casual, hazarda, okaza; -ty, akcidento, malfeliĉaĵo
cat, kato
catch, kapti; infektiĝi per
cathedral, katedralo
catholic, katolika, katoliko
cattle, bovoj, bovaro
cauliflower, florbrasiko
cause, kaŭzo; (movement) movado; to —, igi, kaŭzi
caution, singardemo; averti, averto
cease, ĉesi; ĉesigi
celebrate, celebri; festi; solenigi
cell, ĉelo; (prison) karcero
censor, cenzuristo; act as —, cenzuri
cent, cendo; per —, procento
center, centro; centralize, alcentrigi
centimeter, centimetro
century, jarcento
ceremony, ceremonio; ceremonious, solena, ceremonia
certain, certa; neduba; a — one, iu; -ly, certe
certificate, atesto; certify, atesti
chain, ĉeno
chair, seĝo; -man, prezidanto; ĉefseĝulo
chalk, kreto
champagne, ĉampano
chance, ŝanco; hazardo, hazarda; by —, hazarde
change, ŝanĝi, ŝanĝiĝi; monero, monerigi
chapter, ĉapitro
character, (personal) karaktero, ecaro; (letter) litero; (theat.) rolulo

charge, (load) ŝarĝi; (exhort) admoni; (accuse) akuzi

charm, ĉarmo, ĉarmi; ensorĉi

charter, ĉarto, ĉarti

chase, ĉasi, postkuri; — away, forpeli

chat, babili

cheap, malmultekosta

cheat, trompi

check, (fin.) ĉeko; (meal) kalkulo; haltigi; (chess) ŝaki

cheek, vango; impertinenteco

cheer, aplaŭdi; kuraĝigi; -fulness, gajeco

cheese, fromaĝo

chemistry, kemio; chemical, kemiajo; chemist, kemiisto; (Brit.) drogisto

cherry, ĉerizo

chest, kesto; kofro; brusto; -of-drawers, komodo, tirkestaro

chew, maĉi; — cud, remaĉi

chicken, koko, kokino, kokido; -pox, varioleto

chief, ĉefo, ĉefa; estro; superulo; -ly, precipe

child, infano, ido; -ren, infanoj

chimney, kamentubo

chin, mentono

China, Ĉinujo; Chinese, ĉino (person), ĉina (adj.)

chocolate, ĉokolado

choice, elekto; elektinda

choir, koruso

choke, sufoki, sufokiĝi

choose, elekti

chop, haki; kotleto

Christ, Kristo; -ian, Kristano; christian name, baptonomo

Christmas, Kristnasko

chum, kunulo, kamarado

church, (building) preĝejo; (body) eklezio

cigar, cigaro; -ette, cigaredo

circle, rondo; (geom.) cirklo; to —, rondiri

circular, ronda; (a paper) cirkulero; circulate, cirkuli

circumstance, cirkonstanco

circus, cirko

cistern, akvujo, cisterno

citizen, civitano

city, urbo

civil, ĝentila; (not mil.) civila

claim, pretendi, pretendo; postuli

clam, tridakno

class, klaso; kurso; -ify, enklasigi

clean, pura, purigi

clear, klara; evidenta; certa; simpla

clerk, komizo, vendisto, skribisto

clever, lerta

climate, klimato

climb, grimpi; suprenrampi

clock, horloĝo

close, proksima; aermanka; — by, apude, proksime; to —, fermi

closet, ŝranko; kamero; vestejo

cloth, ŝtofo, drapo; a —, tuko

clothe, vesti; -s, vesto, vestaro

cloud, nubo

club, (society) klubo; (stick) bastonego; -s, (cards) trefo

co-, kun

coal, karbo

coarse, maldelikata, maleleganta, malĝentila

coast, marbordo

coat, mantelo; jako; vesto

cock, (fowl) koko

cockroach, blato

cocoa, kakao

coconut, kokoso

code, kodo

coffee, kafo

coffin, ĉerko

coin, monero; monerfabriki

cold, malvarma; senfervora, senpasia; a —, malvarmumo; catch —, malvarmumi

collar, kolumo; -bone, klaviklo

collect, kolekti, kolektiĝi; -ion, monkolekto

college, kolegio

colony, kolonio; colonize, koloniigi

color, koloro, kolorigi; -ing matter, farbo

column, kolono

comb, kombi, kombilo; (fowl) kresto

come, veni; -ing, venonta; — in, envenu! — back, reveni; — toward, alproksimiĝi

comfort, komforto; konsoli; -able, komforta

comma, komo

command, ordoni, ordono; estri; (mil.) komandi

commerce, komerco

commission, komisii; ĝomisiono

common, komuna, ĝenerala, ordinara, publika; — sense, prudento

companion, kunulo; akompananto

company, anaro; asocio, societo; (com.) kompanio; (mil.) roto

compare, kompari; -d with, kompare kun

compete, konkuri; competition, (com.) konkurado; (for prize) konkurso

complain, plendi

complete, kompleta, tuta; kompletigi

compose, kunmeti; verki; (mus.) komponi; trankviligi

comrade, kamarado

concern, koncerni, rilati; maltrankvileco; firmo; afero; -ing, pri, koncerne al, rilate al

concert, (mus.) koncerto

condemn, kondamni; mallaŭdi

condition, kondiĉo, stato

conduct, konduki, gvidi; administri, direkti; -or, (rad.) kondukilo; (train, etc.) konduktoro, kondukisto; (behavior) konduto

confer, konsiliĝi (kun); doni; -ence, konferenco

confess, konfesi

confirm, konfirmi; certigi

congress, kongreso

connect, kunigi, kunligi

conscious, konscia; be — of, konscii pri

consent, konsenti, konsento

consider, konsideri, pripensi; -ate, pripensema, malsevera

consist of, konsisti el

constant, konstanta, fidela; daŭra

constipation, mallakso

constitution, (pol.) konstitucio

contain, enhavi, enteni

content, kontenta, kontentigi; -ment, kontento

contest, konkurso; pridisputi; kontraŭstari

continent, kontinento

continue, daŭri, daŭrigi; continuous, senĉesa, seninterrompa

contract, (leg.) kontrakto; (disease) infektiĝi per

control, regi, estri; (checking) kontroli; — oneself, sin regi

convention, kunveno

conversation, konversacio, interparolo

convince, konvinki

cook, kuiri, kuirist(in)o

cookie, kuketo

co-operate, kunlabori; kunhelpi

copy, kopii, kopio; ekzemplo, modelo; (of book, etc.) ekzemplero; -right, kopirajto

cord, ŝnuro; (of mus.) kordo

corn, (Amer.) maizo; greno

corner, angulo; -stone, bazangula ŝtono

corporal, kaporalo; korpa

corporation, korporacio, kompanio

corpse, kadavro

correct, korekta, korekti; senerara, ĝusta

correspond, korespondi

cost, kosti, kosto; -ly, multekosta

costume, kostumo

cosy, komforta

cottage, dometo

cotton, kotono; (cloth) katuno

couch, kanapo, sofo

[197

cough, tusi, tuso
could, povis
council, konsilantaro; counsel, konsili, konsilo
count, kalkuli; taksi; grafo
counter, montrotablo
country, lando; kamparo
county, konteo
couple, paro, parigi; (mech.) kupli
coupon, kupono
courage, kuraĝo
course, direkto; vojiro; kurso;
in the — of, en la daŭro de; of —,
kompreneble
court, korto; amindumi
cousin, kuz(in)o
cover, kovri, kovrilo; ŝirmi
cow, bovino; -boy, (Amer.) vakero;
brutzorgisto
coward, timulo, malkuraĝulo
cradle, lulilo
cramp, spasmo
crawl, rampi
cream, kremo
crease, faldeto
create, krei; creature, kreito
credit, (com.) kredito; estimo,
honoro
creep, rampi
crime, krimo; criminal, krimulo
cripple, kripla, kriplulo, kripligi
crisis, krizo
crochet, kroĉtriki
crook, (Amer.) krimulo; kurbaĵo;
-ed, kurba, malrekta
crop, rikolto; (of bird) kropo
cross, kruco, krucigi, kruciĝi; transiri; malafabla, kolera; -wise, kruce
crowd, homamaso; amasigi, amasiĝi
crown, krono, kroni
crude, kruda
cruel, kruela
crumb, panero, panpeceto; -le, pecetiĝi, pecetigi
crush, premegi; subpremi
crust, ŝelo, krusto
crutch, lambastono

cry, krii; plori; (of animals) bleki
cucumber, kukumo
cuff, manumo; frapi
cultivate, kulturi
cunning, ruza
cup, taso; pokalo; -board, ŝranko
cure, resanigi, resanigo; kuracilo;
(pickle) pekli; (smoke) fumaji
curious, stranga; kurioza; scivola
curl, buklo, bukligi; frizi
curse, malbeni, malbeno; blasfemo
curtain, kurteno
curve, kurbo, kurbigi, kurbiĝi
custom, kutimo; -house, dogano
cut, tranĉi; tondi; (print) kliŝo
cute, ĉarmeta; ruzema
cyclone, ciklono
cylinder, cilindro

D
dabble, dileti
dagger, ponardo
daily, ĉiutage
dairy, lakt(vend)ejo
daisy, margarito, lekanteto
dam, digo
damage, difekti; -s, kompenso
damn, kondamni; malbeni
damp, malseketa
dance, danci, danco, balo
dandy, dando
danger, danĝero
dare, kuraĝi; defii
dark, malluma; malhela; sekreta
darling, karul(in)o
date, dato; datumi; (fruit) daktilo;
up to —, ĝisdata, aktuala
daughter, filino
dawn, tagiĝo
day, tago; -dream, revo
dead, seniva, mortinta; -ly, mortiga
deaf, surda; -mute, surdmutulo
deal, negoci; (cards) disdoni; —
with, trakti pri
dear, kara; multekosta
death, morto; -ly, morte

debate, diskuti; diskutado
debit, debeti; debeto
debt, ŝuldo; -or, ŝuldanto
decay, putriĝi; ruiniĝi
deceive, trompi
December, Decembro
decent, deca
decide, decidi (tr.); — to, decidiĝi
decimal, decimalo
decision, decido; juĝo
deck, (ship) ferdeko
declare, deklari; aserti
decorate, ornami
decoration, ornamo; ordeno
decrease, malpli-igi, -iĝi
decree, dekret-i, -o
dedicate, dediĉi
deed, faro, ago; (leg.) akto
deep, profunda
deer, cervo
defeat, malsukceso; venki (conquer)
defect, manko, difektaĵo
defence, defendo
defend, defendi; -ant, (leg.) pri-
   plendanto, akuzito
defer, prokrasti; — to, cedi al
deficit, deficito
define, difini
definite, difinita, definitiva
defy, spiti; malobei
degree, grado; rango; diplomo
delay, prokrasti, prokrasto; mal-
   fruigi
delegate, delegi, delegito
delicate, delikata
delicious, bongust(eg)a
delight, plezur(eg)o, ĝojo; ĉarmi,
   plezurigi
deliver, liveri; liberigi, savi; eldiri
demand, postuli
demi- (prefix) duon-
democracy, demokrateco
demolish, detrui; malkonstrui
demonstrate, demonstracii; demon-
   stration, demonstracio
denial, ne(ad)o; rifuzo
denounce, denunci

dense, densa; stulta
dentist, dentisto; dental, denta
deny, nei, rifuzi
depart, foriri, forlasi
department, fako; (pol.) departe-
   mento; — store, magazeno
depend (on, upon), dependi (je); fidi
   (je)
deposit, demeti; deponi, depono
deprive (of), senigi (je)
depth, profund(aĵ)o, profundeco
derive, devenigi; derived from, de-
   venis de
descend, malsupreniri, subiri; deveni
descent, deklivo; deveno
describe, priskribi; rakonti; desegni
desert, dezerto; forlasi; merito
deserve, meriti
design, elpensi; desegni, desegnajo;
   projekti
desire, deziri, deziro; voli, volo
desk, (writing-) skribtablo; (read-
   ing-) pupitro
despair, malesperi, malespero
despatch, ekspedi; rapideco; (communication) depeŝo
desperado, bandito
desperate, riskega; furioza; senespera
despise, malestimi; malŝati
despite, spite de; malgraŭ
dessert, deserto
destine, destini; destiny, destino;
   sorto
destination, vojaĝcelo; vojaĝfino
destroy, detrui; pereigi
detail, detalo
detect, eltrovi; detekti (rad.)
detective, kaŝpolicano; detektivo
determine, decidi; determini; difini
detour, deturniĝo, ĉirkaŭiro
deuce (cards, etc.) duo
develop, disvolv(iĝ)i; evolui; (phot.)
   riveli
deviate, deflankiĝi; devious, malrekta; erara
device, devizo; ilo; elpensaĵo; ruzo

devil, diablo
devote, dediĉi; (sin) doni (al); -d, sindona
devour, manĝegi
devout, pia
dew, roso
diagnose, diagnozi
diagram, desegnajo; plano
dial, ciferplato
dialect dialekto
dialogue, dialogo
diameter, diametro
diamond, diamanto; (cards) karoo
diaper, vindo, bebotuko; desegnita lintolo
diarrhea, lakso
diary, taglibro
dice, jetkuboj
dictate (to writer) dikti; (command) ordoni; dictator, diktatoro
dictionary, vortaro
die, morti; stampilo; (matrix) matrico
diet, dieto, nutrado; deputitaro; kunsido
differ, diferenci, malsimili; malkonsenti
different, malsama, diversa
difficult, malfacila; -y, malfacilajo
dig, fosi
digest, resumi, resumo; (food) digesti
dignified, digna, dignoplena
dike, digo
diligent, diligenta
dilute, plimaldensigi
dim, malhela; malklara
dime, dekcendo; dek cendoj
dimension, amplekso; dimensio (math.)
dimple, kaveto
din, bruego
dine, manĝi, ĉefmanĝi
dinner, ĉefmanĝo
dip, trempi; mallev(iĝ)i
diploma, diplomo

diplomacy, diplomatio; diplomat, diplomat(ist)o
direct, direkti, gvidi; ordoni; administri; rekta; senpera; -or, direktoro, direktisto; -ory, adresaro; -ion, direkto
dirt, koto, malpurajo; -y, kota, malpura
disagree, malkonsenti; -able, malagrabla
disappear, malaperi
disappoint, malkontent(ig)i; ĉagreni; -ed, malkontenta
disapprove, malaprobi
disarm, senarmigi, senarmiĝi
disbelieve, malkredi
disc, disko
discharge, eksigi; plenumi; eligi, elverŝi; malŝargi (elec.)
disciple, disĉiplo
discipline, disciplino
discomfort, malkomforto; ĝeno
disconnect, malkunigi; apartigi
discontent, malkontento
discount, rabato; (a bill) diskonti
discourage, senkuraĝigi; malhelpi
discover, eltrovi, ektrovi; malkovri
discuss, diskuti; trakti
disease, malsano
disgrace, malhonori, malhonoro; hontindajo
disgust, naŭzi, naŭzo
dish, plado
dishonest, malhonesta
disinfect, malinfekti, seninfektigi
dislike, malŝati
disloyal, mallojala
dismal, malgaja
dismay, konsterno, konsterni
dismiss, maldungi, eksigi; forsendi
disobey, malobei
disorder, malordo, konfuzo; malsano
dispatch, = despatch
display, elmontri, elmontro
displease, malplaĉi al
disprove, malpruvi, refuti
dispute, disputi, disputo

disregard, ignori; malobservi
dissect, sekci
distance, malproksim(ec)o; distanco; distant, malproksima
distinct, klara; aparta
distinguish, distingi
distribute, disdoni, dissendi
district, distrikto, regiono; kvartalo
distrust, malfidi, malfido
disturb, interrompi; maltrankviligi;
malordigi
ditch, fosajo
dive, subakviĝi
diverse, diversa, malsama; mult-
forma
divide, dividi, dividiĝi
divine, dia; teologo; diveni; — service, Diservo
division, divid(ad)o; part(ig)o;
fako; malakordo; (mil.) divizio
dizzy, kapturna, kapturniĝa
do, fari; farti; taŭgi; sufiĉi; (em-
phatic) ja
dock, doko
doctor, kuracisto; (title) doktoro
document, dokumento
dog, hundo
doll, pupo
dollar, dolaro
dome, kupolo
domestic, doma, hejma; servist(in)o
donate, donaci
donkey, azeno
doom, sorto; kondamno; pereo
door, pordo; -keeper, pordisto
dope, narkoti, narkotajo
dose, dozo
dot, punkto
double, duobla, duobligi, duobliĝi
doubt, dubo; -ful, duba, dubema;
without —, sendube
dough, pasto
dove, kolombo
down, malsupre(n); lanugo; -heart-
ed, malgaja
doze, dormeti
dozen, dekduo

draft, (draught) trablovo; skizi;
(com.) trato, ĉeko
drag, tren(iĝ)i
dragon, drako; -fly, libelo
drain, dreni, dreniĝi, drenilo; (sewer) kloako
drake, anaso, viranaso
drama, dramo
draw, tiri; desegni; (water, etc.)
ĉerpi; (com.) trati; (lots) loti;
—along, kuntiri; — away, fortiri
(sin); -bridge, levponto; — near,
alproksimiĝi; — up, alproksimiĝi
drawer, tirkesto; -s, kalsono
drawing room, salono
dread, timegi, timego
dream, songi, songo; (day-) revi
dress, vesti; vesto; kostumo; robo;
(wound) bandaĝi; -coat, frako
drift, blovajo; blovpeliĝi
drill, bori, borilo; ekzercado
drink, trinki, trinkajo; (to excess)
drinki
drive, veturi, veturigi; pel(iĝ)i
drop, faligi, lasi fali; guto, guti
drought, sekegeco, pluvmanko
drown, dron(ig)i
drowsy, dormema
drug, drogo, medikamento
drum, tamburo; (of ear) timpano
drunk, ebria; -ard, ebriulo, drinkulo
dry, seka
duck, anas(in)o; ekklin(iĝ)i
dude, dando
due, ŝuldata, pagota; ĝusta, deca;
meritajo; -s, kotizo
duel, duelo
duet, dueto
duke, duko
dull, malhela, malklara; malakra;
stulta, malsprita; enuiga
dumb, muta; malinteligenta
dunce, stultulo, mallertulo
dung, sterko
dungeon, subtera malliberejo; kel-
karcero
duplicate, kopio, duplikato

[201

during, dum
dusk, krepusko, vesperiĝo; -y, malpala
Dutch, nederlanda, holanda; -man, nederlandano
duty, devo; imposto, limimposto; be on —, dejori
dwarf, pigmeo, malgrandegulo
dwell, loĝi; restadi
dye, tinkturi, tinkturo

E

each (one), ĉiu; — other, unu la alian
eager, avida
eagle, aglo
ear, orelo; (corn) spiko; -drum, timpano; -ring, orelringo
earl, grafo
early, frue, frua; antaŭa
earn, (labor) gajni; -ings, salajro
earth, tero; mondo; -quake, tertremo; -ly, monda, surtera
ease, facileco; trankvileco; -y chair, apogseĝo
east, oriento
Easter, Pasko
eat, manĝi; -able, manĝebla; -ables, manĝaĵoj
echo, eho
economic, ŝparema; -s, ekonomio
edge, rando; bordo; two —d, dutranĉa
edit, redakti; -ion, eldono; -or, redaktisto
educate, eduki; -ion, eduk(ad)o
effect, rezulto; efiko; efektivigi; (mental) impreso; -ive, efektiva; -ual, efika
efficient, kapabla, kompetenta
effort, peno, klopodo
egg, ovo; to — on, instigi
eh! he!
eight, ok; -h, oka; -y, okdek
eighteen, dek-ok
either, aŭ; — ... or, aŭ...aŭ

elastic, elasta, elastajo
elbow, kubuto; — room, movospaco
elder, pliaĝa
elect, elekti
electric, elektra; -ity, elektro; electrify, elektrigi
elegant, eleganta
element, elemento; -ary, elementa; (school) unuagrada
elephant, elefanto
eleven, dek-unu
elf, elfo
eliminate, forigi; (sc.) elimini
elope, amforkuri
else, alia, alie; krome; -where, aliloke
embarrass, embarasi
embassy, ambasadorejo
embers, ardajo
embezzle, ŝteli monon konfiditan
emblem, emblemo
embrace, ĉirkaŭpreni; enteni
embroider, brodi
emerald, smeraldo
emigrate, elmigri
emotion, emocio
emperor, imperiestro
empire, imperio
employ, okupi; uzi; dungi; -ee, dungito; -er, dunginto
empty, malplena; vanta
enable, ebligi; povigi
enamel, emajlo, emajli
enchant, ĉarmi, ravi; sorĉi
encircle, ĉirkaŭi
enclose, enfermi, enmeti; -ure, enmetajo
encore, bis!; bisajo
encourage, kuraĝigi
encyclopedia, enciklopedio
end, fino, fin(iĝ)i; celo; -less, senfina
endorse, aprobi, konsenti (kun), konfirmi; (com.) ĝiri
endure, daŭri; toleri
enemy, malamiko
energy, energio; energetic, energia
enforce, efikigi, devigi, efektivigi

engage, promesi; dungi; **-d,** okupata; fianĉ(in)iĝinta; **-ment,** rendevuo; batalo; fianĉ(in)iĝo

engine, maŝino; (of train) lokomotivo; **-er,** inĝeniero

England, Anglujo; **English,** anglo (person), angla (adj.)

engrave, gravuri

enjoy, ĝui; posedi

enlarge, (pli)grandigi

enlightened, klera

enlist, varbi, varbiĝi; enskribi

enormous, grandega, eksternorma

enough, sufiĉa, sufiĉe; **to be —,** sufiĉi

enquire, demandi; enketi; esplori

enroll, enskribi, registri; varbi

entangle, impliki; konfuzi

enter, eniri, enveni

entertain, amuzi, distri; gastigi; regali; konsideri; **-ment,** amuzprezentado, regalo

enthusiasm, entuziasmo

entire, tuta; sendifekta

entitle, titoli; rajtigi

entrance, enir(ej)o

entrance, ravi

entrust (one with something), komisii (al iu ion); **— to,** alkonfidi al

envelop, envolvi, kovri; **-e,** koverto

environment, medio; ĉirkaŭajo

envoy, sendito

envy, envio, envii

epic, epopeo

epidemic, epidemio

epoch, epoko

equal, egala, egalulo, egali

equator, ekvatoro

equip, ekipi

era, epoko

erase, forviŝi, forfroti, trastreki

erect, rekta; starigi, konstrui

err, erari

errand, komisio

escape, liberiĝi, forkuri, sin savi; eviti

essence, esenco

establish, fondi, establi, starigi; pruvi, firmigi

esteem, estimo, estimi

estimate, taksi; antaŭkalkuli

et cetera, kaj ceteraj, k.c.; kaj tiel plu, k.t.p.

eternal, eterna; **eternity,** eterneco

ether, etero

ethics, etiko

etiquette, etiketo

evade, eviti

eve, antaŭvespero; **-ning,** vespero; **-ning-dress,** frako, festrobo

even, ebena, glata; eĉ (adv.); (of numbers) para

event, okazo; rezulto; **at all -s,** ĉiuokaze; almenaŭ

eventual, rezultanta; (possible) eventuala

ever, ĉiam; iam ajn; **-green,** ĉiamverda; **-lasting,** ĉiamdaŭra, eterna

every, ĉiu; **-body, -one,** ĉiu; **-one's,** ĉies; **-thing,** ĉio; **-where,** ĉie; **— kind of,** ĉia; **— time,** ĉiufoje, ĉiam

evil, malbono, malbona

evolution, evolu(ad)o

ex-, (former) eks-

exact, postuli; ĝusta, preciza; (math.) ekzakta

exaggerate, troigi

examine, ekzameni; esplori; kontroli

example, ekzemplo; ekzemplero; **for —,** ekzemple

excel, superi

excellent, bonega

except, escepti; krom, kun escepto de; **-ion,** escepto

exchange, interŝanĝi, interŝanĝo; **bill of —,** transpagilo; **rate of —,** kurzo; **stock —,** borso

excite, eksciti

exclaim, ekkrii

excuse, senkulpigi, pardoni; preteksto

execute, plenumi; (criminal) ekzekuti; (document) subskribi

executive, administra, administrant-(ar)o; agada; plenuma
exercise, ekzerci; uzi; praktiki; — **book**, kajero
exhibit, elmontri, elmontrajo; ekspozicii, ekspozicio
exhort, admoni; kuraĝigi
exist, ekzisti
expand, etendi, etendiĝi; plivastiĝi
expect, atendi; esperi, anticipi, supozi
expensive, multekosta
experience, sperto, sperti; travivajo; **-d**, sperta
experiment, eksperimento
expert, sperta, spertulo; lerta, kompetenta
explain, klarigi
explore, esplori
export, eksporti
express, esprimi; (com.) ekspresa; **-ion**, esprimo; mieno; **-ly**, intence
extend, etendi; plidaŭrigi; **extensive**, vasta, ampleksa; **extent**, vasteco, amplekso; **to some —**, iagrade, iomete
extinguish, estingi
extra, ekstra
extra-, ekster-
extravagance, malŝparemo
extreme, ekstrema; **-ly**, ekstreme, plejege
eye, okulo; **to —**, okulumi; **-ball**, okulglobo; **-brow**, brovo; **-glasses**, okulvitroj; **-lashes**, okulharoj; **-lid**, palpebro; **-sight**, vidkapablo; **-witness**, memvidinto

F

fable, fablo; **fabulous**, fabla
fabric, ŝtofo; teksajo, fabrikajo
face, vizaĝo; antaŭajo
fact, fakto; **in —**, fakte, efektive, ja
faction, partio; malpaco
factory, fabriko
faculty, kapablo; (of school, medicine) fakultato

fad, kaprico
fade, paliĝi, senkoloriĝi; malaperi; velki
fail, malsukcesi; maltrafi; bankroti; manki; **a -ing**, kulpo, malforto; **without —**, nepre
faint, sveni, sveno; laca, malforta; nedifinita
fair, blonda; bela; justa; senpluva; foiro (market)
fairy, fe(in)o
faith, fido; kredo; **-ful**, fidela
fake, falsi, falsajo
fall, fali, falo; aŭtuno (autumn)
false, malvera, mensoga, trompa; artefarita (teeth, etc.); falsa; **-hood**, mensogo; **falsify**, falsi
falter, ŝanceliĝi
fame, famo, gloro; **-ous**, fama
familiar, familiara; intima
family, familio; idaro; parencaro
famine, manko; malsatego
fan, ventumi, ventumilo; admiranto
fancy, revi; imagi; kaprico, emo
fang, dentego
fantasy, fantazio
far, malproksima, malproksime, distance; **-seeing**, sagaca; **as — as Boston**, ĝis Bostono; **as — as I know**, laŭ mia scio
fare, farti; veturpago; **-well!** adiaŭ!; **bill of —**, manĝkarto, menuo
farm, farmi, farmbieno
farther, pli malproksime; plie; plue
fascinate, ĉarmi; ravi; ensorĉi
fashion, modo; (cut) fasono; maniero; **-able**, laŭmoda
fast, rapida; firma, daŭrema, fiksita; diboĉema; fasti; **— asleep**, profunde dormas; **the watch is —**, la horloĝo antaŭiĝas
fasten, ligi; fiksi
fat, grasa, graso; dika
fate, destino; fatalo, sorto; **fatal**, fatala; mortiga
father, patro; **-hood**, patreco
fatigue, laceco, laciĝo, lacigi

fault, kulpo; eraro, difekto; **at —,** kulpa; **-finding,** grumblema

favor, favoro, komplezo; **-able,** favora; **-ite,** favorato; preferata

fawn, cervido; flavbruna; **— upon,** sklave flati

fear, timi, timo; **-ful,** timema, timiga; terura; **for — that,** pro timo ke; timante ke

feast, festeno, festeni; bankedo

feather, plumo

feature, trajto; karakterizajo; prezenti

February, Februaro

federal, federa; **federate,** federi

federation, federacio

fee, pago, honorario

feeble, malforta, senenergia; **-minded,** idiota

feed, nutri; paŝti

feel, senti; (by touch) palpi; **-ing,** sento, sentema, kortuŝa

feet, piedoj

fell, faligi; falis

fellow, kunulo, fratulo; (as prefix) kun-, sam-; **-thinker,** samideano

felt, felto

female, ino, ina; virino

feminine, virina, virinseksa

fence, barilo; barilumi; skermi (sport)

fender, (car, etc.) ŝirmilo

fern, filiko

ferry, transirejo; **-boat,** pramo

fertile, fruktodona

festival, festo

fetch, alporti, alkonduki; venigi

feudal, feŭda

feud, malpacado, interbatalo

fever, febro

few, kelkaj, nemultaj

fiancé, fianĉo; **-e,** fianĉino

fiasco, fiasko

fib, mensogeto

fiction, fikcio

fictitious, fikcia

fiddle, violono; **-bow,** arĉo

field, kampo; sfero; **-glass,** lorno

fierce, furioza, kolerega

fiery, fajra, arda

fife, fajfilo

fifteen, dek-kvin; **-th,** dek-kvina

fifth, kvina; (mus.) kvinta

fifty, kvindek

fight, batali, batalo

figure, figuro; staturo; cifero

file, fajli, fajlo; dokumentaro, dokumentujo; (soldiers, etc.) vico; registri

fill, plenigi; satigi; plenumi

film, filmo

filth, malpurajo

fin, naĝilo

final, fina, lasta; decida

finance, financo

find, trovi; konstati, decidi

fine, bela, delikata; malgrandpeca; senpluva; monpuno

finger, fingro, fingrumi

finish, fini, finiĝi, fino

fire, fajro; brulo; pafi; **-engine,** fajrestingilo; **-escape,** fajrsavilo; **-fly,** fulgoro; **-place,** kameno; **-proof,** nebruligebla

firm, firma, fortika, senmova; (com.) firmo

first, unua; ĉefa; **-rate,** bonega, unua-klasa; **at —,** unue, komence

fish, fiŝo; fiŝkapti

fist, pugno

fit, deca, konvena, oportuna, taŭga; konvulsio, sveno, atako, spasmo; **— out,** ekipi

five, kvin

fix, fiksi, starigi; determini; ripari; firmigi

flag, flago

flame, flamo, flami; **to — up,** ekflami, flagri

flannel, flanelo

flap, bati

flash, ekbrili, ekbrilo

flat, plata, ebena; unutona; sengusta: **-iron,** gladilo

[205

flatter, flati
flavor, aromo; gusto; spici
flea, pulo
flee, forkuri
fleet, ŝiparo; rapida; -ing, nedaŭra
flesh, karno
flight, flugo; forkuro; -y, ŝanĝiĝema
flimsy, nesolida
flirt, koketul(in)o; flirti
flit, flirti
float, naĝi, ŝvebi
flood, diluvo, superakvego; inundo
floor, planko; etaĝo
flour, faruno
flow, flui, fluo
flower, floro, flori
fluid, fluajo, fluida
flush, ruĝiĝi; traakvumi; ebena, samnivela
flutter, flirti
fly, flugi; forkuri; muŝo; -wheel, reguliga rado
foam, ŝaŭmi, ŝaŭmo
foe, malamiko
fog, nebulo; -horn, sireno
fold, faldi, faldaĵo
foliage, foliaro
folk, popolo; homoj; -lore, folkloro
follow, sekvi; atenti; rezulti; -ing, sekvanta
food, nutraĵo
fool, malsaĝulo; trompi; (prof.) ŝercisto; -hardy, troriskema
foot, piedo; futo (measure); (verse) silabo; -ball, piedpilko; (the game) futbalo; -note, subnoto; -path, vojeto; -print, pied-signo; -step, piedpaŝo
for, por, pro, anstataŭ, (rilate) al, pri, de, malgraŭ; ĉar; dum
forbid, malpermesi
force, forto; devigi; trudi
fore, antaŭa; -cast, antaŭkalkuli; -fathers, prapatroj; -finger, montra fingro; -ground, antaŭajo; -head, frunto; -most, ĉefa; -noon, antaŭ-

tagmezo; -sight, sagaco; -tell, antaŭdiri, profeti
foreign, fremda, alilanda
forest, arbaro
forget, forgesi; malatenti
forgive, pardoni
fork, forko
form, formi, formo; figuro; (of book) formato; (of application) aliĝilo, abonilo; -al, laŭforma, ceremonia
former, antaŭa, pasinta
forsake, forlasi
fort, fortikaĵo; -ify, fortikigi
forth, for; antaŭen; -coming, aperonta, venonta, okazonta; -with, tuj
fortune, sorto, ŝanco; riĉaĵo, riĉeco
forty, kvardek
forward, antaŭe; malmodesta, trudema; ekspedi
found, fondi, starigi; (melt and cast) fandi; -ation, fundamento, bazo, grundo, fondo
fountain, fontano; -pen, fontplumo
four, kvar; (mus.) kvarto
fourteen, dek-kvar; -th, dek-kvara
fox, vulpo
fraction, frakcio; (math.) ono
fragile, rompiĝema; malfortika
fragrant, bonodora
frame, kadro, enkadrigi; (of mind) stato
franc, franko
France, Francujo
frank, nekaŝema, sincera
fraud, malhonestaĵo, trompaĵo
freckle, lentugo
free, libera, liberigi; kvita, senkondiĉa; senpage; -dom, libereco
freeze, frosti, frostiĝi; glaciiĝi
freight, ŝarĝo, ŝarĝpago
frequent, ofta; vizitadi
fresh, freŝa; nova; sensala
Friday, vendredo
friend, amiko
fright, ektimo, teruro; -en, timigi

frivolous, frivola
fro, to and, al kaj de; tien kaj reen
frog, rano
from, de, el
front, antaŭajo; fasado; (mil.) fronto; **in — of,** antaŭ
frontier, landlimo
frost, frosto; **-bite,** frostovundo
frown, sulkigi la frunton
fruit, frukto; **-ful,** fruktodona; **-less,** senfrukta, vana
fry, friti; **-ing pan,** pato
fuel, hejtajo
-ful, -plena; -ema
fulfil, plenumi
full, plena; tuta
fun, gajo, ŝerco; **-ny,** ŝerca, komika stranga
fund(s), kaso, kapitalo, mono
fundamental, fundamenta
funeral, enterigo
funereal, funebra
funnel, funelo
fur, felo; **a —,** pelto
furious, furioza
furnace, forno
furnish, mebli, ekipi; liveri, provizi
furniture, meblaro
furrow, sulko
further, pli malproksima; plu, plua
fuss, ekscitiĝo
future, estonta, estonteco

G
gab, babiladi
gag, buŝoŝtopilo; ŝerco
gain, gajni, gajnajo; profiti, profito; atingi
gala, festa
gale, ventego, blovado
gall, galo; ĉagreni
gallant, brava, bravulo
gallery, galerio
gallop, galopi, galopo
galosh(es), galoŝo(j)
gamble, vetludi

game, ludi, ludo
gang, bando, aro
gangway, ponteto; transirejo
garage, aŭtomobilejo
garden, ĝardeno
garland, girlando
garlic, ajlo
garment, vesto
garter, ŝtrumpligilo
gas, gaso; (Amer. gasoline) benzino; **-burner,** gasflamingo; **-meter,** gasmezurilo
gasp, spiregi, spasme spiri
gate, pordego
gather, kolekti, kolektiĝi; amasigi; rikolti; faldeti
gauze, gazo
gay, gaja
gaze, rigardadi
gazette, gazeto
gem, gemo
general, ĝenerala; (mil.) generalo
genius, genio, geniulo
gentle, milda, delikata; **-man,** sinjoro; **-manly,** ĝentilhoma
genuine, malfalsa; sincera
geographer, geografo; **geography,** geografio
geologist, geologo; **geology,** geologio
geometry, geometrio
germ, mikrobo; ĝermo; **-inate,** ĝermi
Germany, Germanujo; **German,** germano (person); germana (adj.)
gesture, gesto
get, ricevi, akiri; havigi, venigi; (become) iĝi; **— up,** ellitiĝi, leviĝi, stariĝi, supreniri
ghost, fantomo, spirito; **Holy —,** Sankta Spirito
giant, giganto, grandegulo
gift, donaco; **-ed,** naturdotita
giggle, subridi
gin, (liquor) ĝino
ginger, zingibro
gipsy, cigano
giraffe, ĝirafo

girl, knabino
give, doni, donaci, transdoni; — up, ĉesi, ĉesigi, forlasi, cedi
glacier, glaciejo
glad, ĝoja; -den, ĝojigi
glamour, ĉarmo, allogeco
glance, ekrigardo
gland, glando
glare, brilego; fikse rigardi
glass, glaso (drinking); vitro; -es, okulvitroj (spectacles)
glimpse, ekvido
glisten, glitter, brili, ekbrili
globe, globo, sfero
glory, gloro; glorious, glorinda; belega; glorify, glori
glove, ganto
glow, ardi; ardo; morning —, matenruĝo
glue, gluo, glui
gnat, kulo
gnaw, mordeti
go, iri; (machine) funkcii; — away, foriri; — back, reiri; — down, malsupreniri; — forward, antaŭeniri; — in, eniri; — out, eliri; — toward, alproksimiĝi; — up, supreniri; — with, akompani
goal, celo; (sport) golo
goat, kapro
God, Dio; godliness, pieco
godfather, baptopatro; godson, baptofilo
goggles, okulŝirmiloj
gold, oro; -en, ora; -fish, orfiŝo; -smith, orajisto
golf, golfludo; -links, golfejo
good, bona, bono, bone!; -bye, adiaŭ!; -day!, bonan tagon!; -for-nothing, sentaŭga, sentaŭgulo; — looking, belaspekta; -luck, bonŝanco; -s, varoj, komercajoj; -will, bonvolo
Good Friday, Sankta Vendredo
goose, anser(in)o
gorgeous, grandioza, luksega, belega (Amer.)

gospel, evangelio
gossip, klaĉi, klaĉo
govern, regi; direkti; -ess, guvernistino; -ment, registaro, regado
gown, robo
grace, gracieco, ĉarmeco; Difavoro, korfavoro; -ful, gracia; (figure) svelta; Your Grace, via . . . moŝto
gracious, afabla, bonkora, pardonema
grade, grado, rango
gradually, iom post iom
graduate, gradigi; (university, etc.) diplomiĝi
graft, korupto, subaĉeto, subaĉeti
grain, greno (wheat, oats, etc.); (particle) -ero (as grenero, sablero)
gram, gramo
grammar, gramatiko
granary, grenejo
grand, glora; grandioza, impona; -eur, majesteco; -father, avo; -son, nepo
granite, granito
grant, permesi; cedi; donaci; monhelpo; take for -ed, akcepti kiel fakton
grape, vinbero; -fruit, pampelmo
grasp, ekpreni; premteni, tenegi; ekkapti; kompreni
grass, herbo; -hopper, lokusto
grate, raspi; grinci; knari; krado; fajrujo
grateful, dankema
grating, krado
grave, tombo; grava, serioza
gravel, gruzo, sablego
gravy, saŭco, viandsuko
gray, griza
graze, paŝti (sin)
grease, graso; grasoŝmiri
great, granda; eminenta, glora; grava; (as prefix for relationship) pra-
greedy, avida

Greek, greko (person); greka (adj.)
green, verda
greet, saluti
grey, griza; **-hound,** ĉashundo
griddle, platbakilo
grief, malĝojo, aflikto
grill, kradrosti
grin, ridetaĉi
grind, (corn) mueli; (sharpen) akrigi; grinci
grip, manpremo; premteni
groan, ĝemi, ĝemo
ground, tero, grundo; kaŭzo, motivo; — floor, teretaĝo
group, grupo, grupigi, grupiĝi; aro
grow, kreski, kreskigi; — old, maljuniĝi; -n up, maturaĝa; -th, kresk(ad)o; kreskajo
growl, grumbli
guarantee, garantii, garantiajo
guard, gardi, gardisto; protekti; (mil.) gvardio; -ian, zorganto
guess, konjekti, diveni, diveno; — right, ĝuste diveni
guest, gasto
guide, gvidi, gvidanto, konduki, kondukanto
guilt, kulpo; -y, kulpa
guitar, gitaro
gulf, golfo; profundejo
gull, mevo
gum, macĝumo, gumo; dentokarno
gun, pafilo; kanono; -boat, kanonŝipo; -powder, pulvo
gush, elŝpruci
gymnasium, gimnastikejo

H
ha!, ha!
habit, kutimo; (rajd)vesto; -ual, laŭkutima
hag, virinaĉo
hail, hajlo; saluti; aklami; alvoki
hair, haro, haroj, hararo
half, duona, duone; -hearted, nefervora

hall, ĉambrego, halo
halt, halti, haltigi; lama
halter, kolŝnuro, kolbrido
halve, duonigi
ham, ŝinko
hammer, martelo, marteli
hammock, hamako
hamper, malhelpi; ĝeni, embarasi; korbego
hand, mano; (of clock) montrilo; -cuff, fermanumo; -ful of, plenmano de; -icraft, metio; -kerchief, poŝtuko, naztuko; — over, transdoni; -shake, manpreno; -y, lerta; oportuna; at —, apuda, ĉemana, proksima; on the other —, kontraŭe
handle, tuŝi, palpi, manipuli; anso, tenilo; -bar, (bicycle) gvidilo
handsome, bela, belaspekta
hang, pendi, pendigi; (paper) tapeti
hangar, aeroplanejo, veturilejo
happen, okazi
happy, feliĉa, kontenta; **happiness,** feliĉo
harbor, haveno; rifuĝejo; kaŝe gastigi, enloĝigi
hard, malmola; malfacila; peniga; -en, malmoliĝi, malmoligi, hardi; -ship, malfacilajo; -ware, metalvaroj; -working, laborema; " — labor," punlaboro; — up, monmanka
hare, leporo
hark! aŭskultu!
harm, difekti, malutili, dolorigi
harness, jungi, jungajo
harp, harpo; — upon, aludaĉi
harvest, rikolti, rikolto
hash, viandmiksajo; fuŝmiksajo
haste, rapideco; senpripenseco; -n, rapidigi; **hasty,** koleretema
hat, ĉapelo
hatch, elkovi; konspiri; -way, aperturo
hatchet, hakileto

hate, malami, malamo; -ful, malaminda
haul, treni; transporti
haunt, vizitadi; fantomviziti
have, havi; posedi; — to, devi
hay, fojno; -stack, fojnamaso
he, li; — who, tiu kiu
head, kapo, supro; estro, ĉefo; estri; -quarters, ĉefsidejo; -strong, obstina; -way, progreso
heal, resanigi, resaniĝi
health, sano; tosto; (state of) farto, sanstato; -ful, saniga
hear, aŭdi; -ing, aŭdado, aŭdanta, aŭdkapablo
heart, koro; mezo; -burn, pirozo; -ily, kore; -s, kero (cards); -y, bonkora; by —, memore, parkere
heat, varmeco, varmigi; (stoke) hejti
heaven, ĉielo
heavy, peza, ŝarĝa; malvigla; seninteresa
Hebrew, Hebreo (person); hebrea (adj.)
hedge, kreskajbarilo; eviti demandon
heed, priatenti, atenti
heel, kalkano; (of boot), kalkanumo
height, alteco; -en, plialtigi
heir, heredonto
hell, infero
hello!, saluton!
helm, ŝipdirektilo
helmet, kasko
help, helpi, helpo; -ful, helpema; cannot — (laughing), ne povas ne (ridi)
hem, borderi; — in, ĉirkaŭi
hen, kokino; birdino (female bird)
her, ŝia, ŝin; -self, ŝi mem, si mem
herb, herbo
herd, grego, brutaro; paŝti
here, ĉi tie; -after, poste, estonte; -with, ĉi kune; — is, jen
hermit, ermito
hero, heroo
herring, haringo

hesitate, ŝanceliĝi; (mental) heziti
hiccup, singulto
hide, kaŝi; felo, haŭto
high, alta; eminenta, ĉefa; altpreza; -er, pli alta; -school, altlernejo, gimnazio; -way, ĉefvojo
hill, monteto
him, lin; -self, li mem, si mem
hinder, malhelpi
hinge, ĉarniro; — on, dependi de
hint, aludi
hip, kokso
hippopotamus, hipopotamo
hire, (house) lui; (servant) dungi
his, lia
hiss, sibli, siblo
history, historio
hit, frapi; (a mark) trafi
ho!, ho!
hoarse, raŭka
hobby, flankokupo
hoe, sarkilo
hog, porko
hold, teni; enhavi (contains); persisti; festi; (of ship) holdo; — back, rezervi
hole, truo
holiday, libertago, libertempo; festtago
hollow, kava; malsolida
holy, sankta
Holy Ghost, Sankta Spirito; — Virgin, Dipatrino, Sankta Virgulino; — Writ, Sankta Skribo
home, hejmo; domo; -land, patrolando; -less, senhejma; -ly, malluksa; malbela; -sickness, nostalgio; -stead, farmdomo, farmbieno (Amer.); — rule, aŭtonomeco; at —, hejme
honest, honesta
honey, mielo; -moon, mielmonato
honor, honoro; -able, honorinda; -s, (exam.) distingo, honoro; your —, via moŝto
hood, kapuĉo
hoof, hufo

hook, hoko; (clasp) agrafo, agraf-umi; **—to,** alkroĉi al
hop, salteti
hope, esperi, espero; **-ful,** esperplena; **-less,** senespera
horizon, horizonto; **-tal,** horizontala
horn, korno
horrible, terura, terurega
horrid, terura, naŭza
horse, ĉevalo; **-power,** ĉevalforto; **-shoe,** hufferajo
hose, fleksebla tubo; ŝtrumpoj
hospitable, gastigema, gastama
hospital, malsanulejo, hospitalo
host, gastiganto; mastro (hotel, etc.); arego
hostile, malamika
hot, varmega; **-house,** (flor)varmejo; **-tempered,** kolerema
hotel, hotelo
hound, ĉashundo
hour, horo; **-glass,** sablohorloĝo; **-ly,** ĉiuhore
house, domo; firmo; **-hold,** doman-aro; **-holder,** domposedanto; **-keeping,** mastrumado; **-wife,** domestrino
how, kiel, kiamaniere; **-ever,** kiel ajn, ĉiuokaze, tamen; **— many,** kiom
howl, kriegi; blekegi
hug, ĉirkaŭpreni
huge, grandega
hull, ŝipkorpo; ŝelo; senŝeligi
hum, zumi; **-ming bird,** kolibro
human, homa, homo; **-race,** homaro
humble, humila, humiligi
humid, malsekeca
humor, humoro
hump, ĝibo; **-back,** ĝibulo
hundred, cent
hunger, malsato, malsati
hunt, ĉasi, ĉaso; serĉi
hurrah! hura!
hurricane, uragano
hurry, rapidi, rapidigi

hurt, dolorigi, vundi; ofendi; difekti; **-ful,** malutila
husband, edzo; konservi
hush, silenti, silentu!
hut, kabano
hygiene, higieno
hymn, himno
hysteria, histerio

I
I, mi
ice, glacio; glaciigi; sukerkovri; **an —,** glaciaĵo; **-cream,** kremglaciaĵo; **-berg,** glacimonto
icicle, pendglacio
idea, ideo
ideal, idealo, ideala; **-ist,** idealisto
identical, identa
idiom, (language) idiomo; (peculiar form) idiotismo, idiomaĵo
idiot, idioto
idle, senokupa, mallaborema; vana, bagatela
idol, idolo
if, se; (whether) ĉu
ignore, ignori
ill, malsana; **-bred,** malĝentila; **-feeling,** malamikeco; **-luck,** malbonŝanco, malbonsorto; **-will,** malbonvolo
illegal, kontraŭleĝa
illegible, nelegebla
illegitimate, bastarda, eksteredzeca; senrajta
illusion, iluzio
illustrate, ilustri; klarigi
image, bildo, figuraĵo; portreto
imagine, imagi; **imaginary,** imaga, fiktiva, neekzistanta, fantazia
imitate, imiti
immediate, tuja; **-ly,** tuj
immigrate, enmigri
immortal, senmorta
immune, imuna
impact, kunfrapo
impart, komuniki; doni; sciigi

impartial, senpartia
impel, antaŭenpuŝi, instigi
imperfect, neperfekta, nekompleta
impetuous, ardega, impulsema, senbrida
import, importi; signifo, senco
important, grava; to be —, gravi
impose, trudi, devigi; imponi
imposter, trompanto
impress, impresi; stampi; -ion, impreso
impudent, malĝentila, malrespekta, senhonta, aŭdaca
impulse, impulso
in, en; — order to, por
in-, sen-, mal-, ne-
inner, interna; inside, interno
incapable, nekapabla, nekompetenta; nepovanta
incense, incenso
inch, colo
incite, inciti, provoki; kuraĝigi
incline, kliniĝi; inklini; deklivo
income, enspezo, rento; — tax, imposto
increase, kreski; pliiĝi, pligrandiĝi
indebted, be, ŝuldi
indeed, ja, efektive, vere
index, indekso, tabelo; — finger, montra fingro
Indian, (Amer.) indiano; (Asia) hindo
indicate, montri, indiki, signi
indifferent, indiferenta; mezkvalita
indignant, indigna
indirectly, nerekte, pere
individual, individua, individuo
indoctrinate, endoktrinigi
industrial, industria; industrious, diligenta, laborema; industry, industrio (manufacture)
infant, infano; (in law) neplenaĝulo
infantry, infanterio
infect, infekti; -ion, infekto
infer, konkludi; (imply) supozigi
inferior, suba, malsupera
inflame, flamigi, eksciti, incitegi

inflammation, inflamo
influenza, gripo
inform, informi, sciigi
inhabit, loĝi; -ant, loĝanto
inhale, enspiri
inherit, heredi
initial, komenca; ĉeflitero
initiate, iniciati, enkonduki, komenci
injure, vundi, difekti; injury, vundo, difekto
ink, inko
inn, gastejo, hoteleto; trinkejo
innocent, senkulpa; naiva
inquest, enketo
inquire, demandi; enketi, esplori
insane, freneza
insect, insekto
inside, interne
insignia, insigno
insist, insisti; -ent, insistema
inspect, inspekti
inspire, inspiri; enspiri
instal, instali, enoficigi
instalment, partopago
instance, okazo; ekzemplo
instant, momento; urĝa, tuja, rapida, subita
instead, anstataŭe; — of, anstataŭ
instinct, instinkto
institute, instituto; fondi, starigi
institution, institucio; fondo
instruct, instrui; ordoni; sciigi; "-ions," instrukcio
instrument, instrumento, ilo; muzikilo; (leg.) akto
insulin, (med.) insuleno
insult, insulti, insulto; ofendi
insurance, asekuro; to insure, asekuri
intelligence, inteligenteco; intelligent, inteligenta
intelligible, klara, komprenebla
intend, intenci; intention, intenco
intense, intensa, ega
intent, celo
inter, enterigi
interchange, interŝanĝi, interŝanĝo
intercourse, interrilato; kuniĝo

212]

interest, intereso, interesi; (com.)
rentumo; to be -ed in, interesiĝi
pri; -ing, interesa
interfere, entrudi sin; malhelpi
intern, internigi; -ment camp, in-
ternigejo
interpret, interpreti; klarigi
intersect, interkruciĝi
interview, intervjuo (jour.)
intestine, intesto
into, en (with -n showing direction
towards)
intra-, inter-
introduce, prezenti; enkonduki
invade, invadi
invalid, malsanulo, malfortulo; nula,
senvalora; -ate, nuligi
invaluable, altvalora, netaksebla
invent, inventi, elpensi; -ion, invento,
inventajo
investigate, esplori
invite, inviti
invoice, fakturo
involve, envolvi; impliki
inward, interna; -ly, interne
iodine, jodo
iota, iometo, joto
I.O.U., ŝuldatesto
iron, fero; gladi, gladilo; -clad, fer-
kovrita; — foundry, ferfandejo;
-s, katenoj
irony, ironio
irritate, ĝeni, kolerigi
is, estas
Islam, Islamo
island, insulo
ism, ismo; doktrino
Israel, Izraelo
issue, elflui, elfluo; deveni; rezulto;
eldono, eldoni; idaro; decidotajo
it, ĝi; -self, ĝi mem, si mem; -s, ĝia,
sia
Italian, italo (person); itala (adj.)
italic, kursiva
itch, juki, juko; (med.) skabio
item, ero
ivory, eburo

ivy, hedero

J
jack, levilo; (cards) bubo; -ass,
azeno; stultulo
jacket, jako
jade, (min.) jado; virinaĉo
jail, malliberejo
jam, konfitajo, fruktajo; premegi
janitor, domzorganto; dompurigisto
January, Januaro
Japan, Japanujo; -ese, japano (person), japana (adj.)
jar, ujo, konservujo, poto, mala-
kordi, knari
jaw, makselo; -s, faŭko, buŝego
jazz, jazo
jealous, jaluza, to be —, jaluzi
Jehovah, la Eternulo
jelly, gelateno, gelatenajo
jerk, ekskui, ekskuo
jersey, trikotjako
jest, ŝerci, ŝerco
Jesuit, Jesuito
Jesus, Jesuo
jet, ŝprucajo
Jew, judo; -ish, juda
jewel, juvelo
job, komisio, ofico, posteno; tasko
join, kunigi, unuigi; aliĝi, kuniĝi;
ligi
joint, artiko; viandpeco (Brit.); -ly,
kune; — stock company, akcia
societo
joke, ŝerci, ŝerco
jolly, gaja
journal, gazeto; jurnalo (newspaper); taglibro
journey, vojaĝo
joy, ĝojo; -ful, ĝoja
judge, juĝi, juĝisto; -ment, juĝo;
prudento
jug, kruĉo
juice, suko
July, Julio
jump, salti, salto

[213

June, Junio
jungle, junglo
junior, pli juna; malsupera
jurisprudence, juro
jury, juĝantaro
just, (fair) justa; (exactly) ĝuste,
precize; (immediately) jus
justice, justeco

K

keen, vigla, agema; akra
keep, teni, gardi; deteni; konservi;
daŭri; -sake, memorajo; — house,
mastrumi
keg, bareleto
kennel, hundejo
kerchief, (kap)tuketo
kernel, kerno
kettle, kaldrono, bolilo; -drum, tam-
bureto
key, ŝlosilo; (mus.) gamo; (of instrument) klavo; -board, klavaro
kick, piedbati
kidnap, ŝteli homon, infanŝteli
kidney, reno
kill, mortigi; buĉi; nuligi
kilogram, kilogramo
kilometer, kilometro
kimono, kimono
kin, parencaro
kind, speco; afabla, bonkora, bon-
vola, kompleza
kindle, ekbruligi
king, reĝo; -dom, reĝolando
kiss, kisi, kiso; (smack) ŝmaci
kitchen, kuirejo
kite, flugludilo
kitten, katido
knead, knedi
knee, genuo; -cap, patelosto; -l,
genuiĝi; bend the —, genufleksi
knife, tranĉilo
knight, kavaliro
knit, triki; kunigi; — the brows,
sulkigi la frunton
knob, tubero; door-, anso; tenilo

214]

knock, frapi, frapo
knot, nodo; (wood) tubero; -ty,
tuberhava; malsimpla
know, scii, koni; -ing, scianta, ruza;
-ledge, scio, kono; -n, konata
kodak, manfotografilo

L

label, (package) adresmarko;
(bottle, etc.) enhavmarko
labor, laboro, labori; naskdoloro;
"hard —", punlaboro
laboratory, laborejo
lace, punto; (shoe, etc.) laĉo, laĉi
lack, manko; to be -ing, manki;
-ing, mankanta
lad, knabo, junulo; bubo
ladder, ŝtupetaro
ladle, kulerego
lady, sinjorino; nobelino
lag, malrapidiri; sin trenadi
laid, kuŝigita, metita
lake, lago
lamb, ŝafido; ŝafidajo (meat)
lame, lama, lamigi
lament, lamenti
lamp, lampo; (of temple) lucerno
land, lando; tero; bieno; alteriĝi;
-lord, luiganto; -owner, bienulo;
-scape, pejzaĝo
language, lingvo
lantern, lanterno
lap, lektrinki; genuoj; kurrondo
lapel, refaldaĵo
lard, porkograso
large, granda, vasta; -ly, grandparte,
grandmezure, precipe; at —, libera
lash, skurĝi, skurĝilo; vipŝnuro;
ligi
lass, knabino
last, lasta; pasinta; fina; daŭri;
resti freŝa; next to the —, antaŭ-
lasta; at —, fine
late, malfrua, malfrue; mortinta;
eks-; -ly, antaŭnelonge; -est, lasta,
freŝdata

lather, sapŝaŭmo
Latin, latina (lingvo)
latter, ĉi tiu
Latvia, Latvujo, -n, latvo
laugh, ridi, rido; -able, ridinda; —
at, ridi je
laundress, lavistino; laundry, tolajo,
tolajlavejo
lavatory, lavejo; necesejo
law, leĝo; (science of) juro; —
court, juĝejo; -ful, laŭleĝa, per-
mesata; -less, kontraŭleĝa; -suit,
proceso; -yer, leĝisto, advokato;
go to —, procesi
lawn, herbejo; tolmuslino
lay, meti, surmeti; kuŝigi; demeti
ovojn; kanto; poemo; -man, laiko
layer, tavolo; (metal, thin) lameno
lazy, mallaborema
lead, konduki, gvidi; antaŭiri, direkti,
estri; superi; -er, ĉefo, estro
lead, (metal) plumbo
leaf, folio
league, ligo, interligiĝi
leak, traflueto; fendeto
lean, malgrasa; sin klini; — against,
apogi sin al; a -ing, emo
leap, salti; -year, superjaro
learn, lerni; sciiĝi; -ed, klera, instru-
ita; -ing, klereco
lease, lu-kontrakto; luigi; take on —,
lui; farmi
least, malplej; at —, almenaŭ
leather, ledo
leave, lasi; forlasi; forpermeso;
foriri; — off, ĉesi; — out, ekster-
lasi
leavings, restajo
lecture, prelego, parolado; admono
ledge, breto
ledger, ĉeflibro
left, maldekstra; forlasis, lasis;
-handed person, maldekstrulo
leg, kruro; -gings, tibiumoj
legacy, testamentajo
legal, laŭleĝa

legend, legendo; moto
legion, legio
legislate, leĝdoni; legislature, parlamento
leisure, libera tempo
lemon, citrono; -ade, limonado
lend, pruntedoni
length, longeco; -en, plilongigi;
-wise, laŭlonge; at —, fine, detale
Lent, granda fasto
less, malpli; -en, malpliigi
lesson, leciono
let, lasi; permesi; luigi; — go, liberigi; — in, enlasi
letter, letero; litero (of alphabet);
literumi; -box, leterkesto; -of-
credit, kredit-letero; capital —,
majusklo; small —, minusklo
lettuce, laktuko
level, nivelo, nivelilo; ebena, ebenigi
liabilities, ŝuldoj; liable for, responda
pri
liar, mensoganto
liberal, malavara, donacema; libera;
(pol.) liberala
liberty, libereco
library, (building) biblioteko;
(books) libraro
license, koncesio; rajtigilo; trolibe-
reco
lick, leki; venki
lid, kovrilo
lie, kuŝi; mensogi, mensogo; —
down, kuŝiĝi
lieutenant, leŭtenanto
life, vivo, vivdaŭro; vivmaniero;
vigleco; biografio; -belt, sav-zono;
-boat, sav-boato; — insurance, viv-
asekuro
lift, levi; (Brit.) lifto
light, lumo, lumigi; ekbruligi (fire,
cigar, etc.); (weight) malpeza;
(color) hela; -hearted, facilkora,
gaja; -house, lumturo
lightning, fulmo; —conductor, -rod,
fulmoŝirmilo

like, simila; (as) kiel; ŝati; **-ly,** kredeble; **-n,** kompari; **-ness,** simileco; portreto; **-wise,** ankaŭ, same
lily, lilio
lime, kalko; (fruit) limedo
limit, limo, limigi
line, linio; ŝnuro; (fer)vojo; vico; streko; **-r,** oceanŝipo
linen, (cloth) lintolo; (in general) tolajo
linguist, lingvisto; **-ics,** lingvoscienco
lining, subŝtofo
link, ĉenero; kunigi, kunigilo; **-s,** (golf) golfludejo
lion, leono; **-ize,** honoregi, trakti kiel heroo; **"-'s share,"** pliparto
lip, lipo
liquefy, fluidigi, fluidiĝi; **liquid,** fluida, fluidajo
liquidate, likvidi
list, listo, listigi
listen, aŭskulti
liter, litro
literary, literatura
litter, best-idaro; pajlajo; homportilo; senorde disjeti
little, malgranda, malmulta; **a —,** iom da, iomete; **— by —,** iom post iom
live, vivi; loĝi; viva, vivanta; **-lihood,** viv-rimedoj; **-ly,** gaja, viveca, vigla; **-stock,** bestaro
liver, hepato
lizard, lacerto
lo! jen!
load, ŝarĝi, ŝarĝo; (gun) ŝargi
loaf, panbulo; mallabori
loan, prunto
lobster, omaro
local, loka
lock, ŝlosi, seruro; (sluice) kluzo; (hair) buklo, hartufo; **— up,** ŝlosi, enkarcerigi
locomotive, lokomotivo
lodge, loĝi; dometo; (fraternal, etc.) loĝio
log, ŝtipo; (naut.) vojaĝlibro

lonely, soleca
long, longa; sopiri (por); **-er,** pli longa; plu; **— ago,** antaŭlonge
look, rigardi, rigardo; aspekti; sajni. ŝajno; mieno; **— after,** prizorgi; **— at,** rigardi; **— for,** serĉi; atendi; **— like,** simili; **— out!** atentu!; **— over,** ekzameni; **-ing-glass,** spegulo
loose, malstreĉa, malfirma; malpreciza; (clothing) malstrikta; **-n,** liberigi, elkatenigi, malligi
lord, nobelo, sinjoro, mastro; **the Lord,** la Sinjoro, la Eternulo; **the Lord's Supper,** la Sankta Vespermanĝo
lose, perdi, malgajni; (train, bus, etc.) maltrafi; (opportunity) preterlasi; **— one's way,** perdi la vojon, perdiĝi
lot, sorto, ŝanco; lotajo; parto; **a —,** multo, multe; (of land) parcelo
loud, laŭta; (showy) parada; **— speaker** (rad.) laŭtparolilo
louse, pediko
love, ami, amo; **-ly,** bela; **-r,** amant(in)o; **-d one,** amat(in)o; **fall in — with,** enamiĝi kun; **make — to,** amindumi
low, malalta; mallaŭta; malsupera; bovbleki; **-er,** pli malalta; malsupra; mallevi; malaltigi; malpliigi; **-ly** humila
loyal, lojala
luck, ŝanco, sorto; **-y,** bonŝanca, bonsorta, feliĉa; **bad —,** malbonŝanco, **good —,** bonŝanco
luggage, pakajoj, pakajaro
lumber, ŝtipligno, ligno
lump, ŝvelajo; bulo, maso
lunatic, frenezulo; **— asylum,** frenezulejo
lunch, tagmezmanĝo; manĝeto, lunĉo
lung, pulmo
lust, avidi; volupto, voluptemo

M

macaroni, makaronio

machine, maŝino; **-ry**, maŝinaro

mad, freneza; **-house**, frenezulejo; **-man**, frenezulo

Madam, Sinjorino

made, faris; farita

magazine, gazeto

magic, magio; **-ian**, magiisto, sorĉisto

magnet, magneto; **-ic**, magneta

magnificent, belega, grandioza, pompa

magnify, pligrandigi; glori; laŭdegi

maid, servistino

maiden, fraŭlino; junulino; virgulino; **-hood**, virgeco; **-name**, fraŭlina nomo

mail, poŝto, enpoŝtigi; **coat of —**, maŝkiraso

maim, kripligi

main, ĉefa, precipa; oceano; **-land**, kontinento; **-ly**, precipe

maintain, konservi; subteni; daŭrigi; pretendi, aserti; nutri

majestic, majesta, grandioza

major, pligranda; plenaĝa; (mil.) majoro; **-ity**, plimulto; plenaĝo

make, fari; igi; devigi; okazigi; formi; gajni; fabriki; **-believe**, ŝajnigi; **— haste**, rapidi; **— known**, proklami; sciigi; **— up one's mind**, decidiĝi; **— fun of**, moki

male, viro, virseksulo

mamma, panjo

mammal, mambesto

man, viro; (species) homo; **-hood**, vireco; plenaĝeco; **-ikin**, kvazaŭhomo; **-kind**, homaro; **to —**, virprovizi

manage, administri, direkti; **— a house**, mastrumi; **-r**, administranto

mandate, mandato

mane, kolhararo, kolharoj

manner, maniero; modo; kutimo, stilo; **-s**, moroj; **in some —**, iel; **well -ed**, ĝentila, bonmora

mansion, domego

mantelpiece, kamenbreto

mantle, mantelo

manual, mana; lernolibro

manufacture, fabriki

manure, sterko

manuscript, manuskripto

many, multaj; multe da

map, geografia karto

mar, difekti, malbonigi

marble, marmoro

march, marŝi, marŝo

March, Marto

margarine, margarino

margin, marĝeno; (stockbroker's) aĝio

marine, mara; marsoldato; **-r**, maristo

mark, marki, marko; signi, signo; celo

market, vendejo; komercado; **-able**, vendebla

marmalade, marmelado

marriage, edziĝo, edzeco

marry, edzigi, edzinigi; edziniĝi, edziĝi

Mars, Marso

marsh, marĉo; **-mallow**, alteo

marvel, miri, mirindaĵo

mask, maski, masko

mason, masonisto; **free-**, framasono

mass, amaso, maso; meso; plimulto; **the -es**, la homamaso; vulgarularo

massacre, masbuĉi

massage, masaĝi, masaĝo

master, mastro; estro; (in his profession or trade) majstro; ellerni; **— of arts**, magistro; **-piece**, ĉefverko

mat, mato; **-ted**, konfuzplekta; **-ting**, mataĵo

match, alumeto; konkuro; svato; pariĝo

mate, kunulo, kolego; parigi; pariĝi

material, ŝtofo; materialo; esenca, grava; **-ism**, materiismo

mathematics, matematiko

matinee, tagprezentado
matrimony, edzeco
matter, afero; materio; teksto; puso;
   it doesn't matter, ne gravas;
   what's the matter?, kio okazas?
mattress, matraco
mature, matura
maximum, maksimuma
May, Majo
may, povas; eble povos; **-be**, eble,
   povas esti; — **I?** ĉu estas perme-
   sate, ke mi . . . ?
mayor, urbestro
me, min; al mi
meadow, herbejo; paŝtejo
meal, mangô; grio; — **check**, kalkulo
mean, signifi; intenci, voli; malnobla,
   malgrandanima; avara; **-ing**, signifo; **-s**, rimedoj; monhavo; **by -s**
   of, per
measure, mezuro, mezurigi, mezurilo; grado; **-s**, rimedoj; **take -s to**,
   klopodi
meat, viando
mechanic, maŝinisto, mekanikisto;
   -s, mekaniko
medal, medalo; **-ion**, medaliono
meddle, enmiksiĝi, sin intermeti
medicine, (science) medicino; medikamento (remedy)
medieval, mezepoka
medium, meza; perilo, perulo;
   (phys.) medio; (spiritualism)
   mediumo
meet, renkonti, renkontiĝi; kunveni;
   -ing, renkonto; kunveno
melody, melodio
melon, melono
melt, degeli; fluidigi, fluidiĝi; fandi,
   fandiĝi
member, ano, membro; **-ship**, aneco,
   anaro; **-ship form**, aliĝilo
memory, memoro; **memorial**, memorajo; **memorize**, lerni parkere,

memorlerni; **memorable**, memorinda
men, viroj; homoj
mend, fliki, ripari, rebonigi
menstruate, menstrui
mental, mensa, spirita
mention, citi; mencii; nomi
menu, menuo, mangôkarto
merchandise, komercajo; **merchant**,
   komercisto, negocisto
mercy, kompato, korfavoro
mere, simpla, nura; **-ly**, nure
merit, meriti, merito; **-orious**, merita,
   laŭdinda
merry, gaja; **-go-round**, karuselo
mesh, maŝo
mess, malordo; miksajo; (mil.) kun-
   mangô
message, sendajo; komuniko, kom-
   unikajo
messenger, sendito, komisiito
metal, metalo
meter, (gas-, akvo-) mezurilo
method, metodo; **-ism**, Metodismo
mew, miaŭi
microbe, mikrobo
microphone, mikrofono
microscope, mikroskopo
mid, meza; meze de; **-day**, tagmezo;
   -dle, mezo, meza; **-dle ages**,
   mezepoko; **-dle classes**, burĝaro;
   -night, noktomezo; **-wife**, akuŝist-
   ino
might, povo, potenco, forto; povus;
   — **and main**, per ĉiuj fortoj
mild, milda
mildew, ŝimo
mile, mejlo
militant, militema; **militarism**, mili-
   temo, militismo; **military**, militista,
   milita
milk, lakto; melki; **-y Way**, Lakta
   Vojo
mill, mueli, muelilo, muelejo; **-er**,
   muelisto
million, miliono; **-aire**, milionulo

mind, menso, spirito; atenti, obei; zorgi; **-ful,** atenta, zorgema; **absent -ed,** senatenta, vagpensa; **make up one's —,** decidiĝi

mine, mia; mini, minejo; eksplodilo; **-r,** ministo

mineral, mineralo, minerala

minister, servi; (state) ministro; (church) pastro

mink, lutreolo

minor, neplenaĝa, neplenaĝulo; malsupera; (mus.) minora; **-ity,** malplimulto

minute, minuto (time); detalega; **-s** (of meeting) protokolo

miracle, miraklo

mirror, spegulo, speguli

mis-, (prefix), mis- (used in the sense of wrongly, improperly)

miscarriage, aborto; maltrafo, malsukceso; **— of justice,** juĝeraro

miscellaneous, miksita, diversa

mischief, petolado; malbono; **mischievous,** petola, malutila, malpaciga

miser, avarulo

miserable, mizera, malfeliĉega; **misery,** mizero

misfortune, malfeliĉo, malprospero

mislead, erarigi, trompi

misprint, preseraro

miss, maltrafi; manki; senti la mankon de; fraŭlino

mission, misio, misiejo; vivcelo; senditaro; **-ary,** misiisto

mistake, erari, eraro; miskompreni; **-n,** erara

mister, Mr., sinjoro, S-ro

mix, miksi, miksiĝi; **-ture,** miksaĵo

moan, ĝemi, ĝemo

mob, popolamaso; popolaĉo; atakeme svarmi

mock, moki; nevera; falsa; **-ing bird,** mimo

mode, modo

model, modelo, modeli, modelul(in)o

modern, moderna

modest, modesta, sinretirema; ĉasta

modify, modifi

moist, malseketa

moment, momento; graveco; **-ary,** momenta; **-ous,** gravega; **One —!** Momenton!

monarch, monarko; **-y,** monarkeco

monastery, monakejo

Monday, lundo

money, mono; **ready —,** (cash) kontanto; **-order,** mandato, poŝtmandato

monk, monako

monkey, simio

monologue, monologo

monopoly, monopolo; **monopolize,** monopoligi

monster, monstro; eksternorma

month, monato; **-ly,** ĉiumonate

mood, humoro, animstato; (gram.) modo; **-y,** malgaja, melankolia

moon, luno; **-beam,** lunradio; **-light,** lunbrilo

mop, viŝilo

moral, morala; leciono; **-ity,** moraleco; **-s,** moroj

more, pli, plia; plu, plua; **-over,** plie, plue; **— or less,** plimalpli; **— than,** pli ol; **the —. . . , the —. . .,** ju pli . . . ,des pli . . .

morning, mateno

mortgage, hipoteko, hipoteki

mosquito, moskito; **-net,** kontraŭmoskitoreto

moss, musko

most, plej, plejmulto; **-ly,** pleje, plejparte

moth, tineo

mother, patrino; **-country,** patrinlando; **-hood,** patrineco; **-in-law,** bopatrino; **-tongue,** nacia lingvo

motion, movo, movado; impulso; propono; signi; **-less,** senmova

motive, motivo, kaŭzo; moviga

motor, motoro

motto, moto

mount, supreniri; surseliĝi; munti

mountain, monto; — chain, montaro;
-eer, montarano
mourn, malĝoji; priplori; funebri
mouse, muso
moustache, lipharoj
mouth, buŝo; faŭko; (river) enfluejo,
elfluejo; -ful, plenbuŝo; by word
of —, parole
move, movi, moviĝi; eksciti, emocii,
kortuŝi; proponi; transloĝiĝi;
-ment, movado
movie, kinofilmo
mow, falĉi
Mr., Sinjoro, S-ro; — and Mrs.,
Gesinjoroj, Ges-roj
Mrs., Sinjorino, S-ino
much, multo, multa, multe da; as
— as, tiom kiom; how —, kiom
da; make — of, dorloti; too —, tro
da
mucilage, gumajo
mud, koto
muff, mufo
muggy, varme malseketa
mule, mulo
multiple, oblo, obla; multiply, mul-
tigi, obligi; (math.) multipliki
municipal, urba; -ity, urbo, civito
murder, murdi, murdo; -er, mur-
danto, murdinto
murmur, murmuri
muscle, muskolo; muscular, fort-
muskola
museum, muzeo
mush, kaĉo
mushroom, agariko, fungo
music, muziko; -al, muzika; -al instrument, muzikilo; -ian, muzikisto
must, devas, devos; necesas ke;
estas necese ke; nepre
mustard, mustardo; —plaster, mus-
tarda kataplasmo
mutter, murmuri, parolaĉi
mutton, ŝafajo
muzzle, buŝumo, buŝumi
my, mia; -self, mi mem

mystery, mistero; mysterious, mistera
myth, mito; -ology, mitologio

N

nail, najlo, najlfiksi; (finger, toe)
ungo
naked, nuda
name, nomo, nomi; -less, sennoma;
-sake, samnomulo; what is your
name? kiel vi nomiĝas?; good —,
bonfamo
nap, dormeto; harajo
nape of neck, nuko
napkin, buŝtuko
narcotic, narkota, narkotilo
narrow, mallarĝa; -minded, bigota
nasty, aĉa; malagrabla, malpura,
naŭza
nation, nacio; -al, nacia; -ality, na-
cieco
native, indiĝena, indiĝeno; enland-
ana, enlandano; natura; — country, patrolando
nature, naturo; ecaro, karaktero;
natural, natura; senafekta; naturally, nature; natural history, natur-
scienco
naughty, malbonkonduta; petolema;
malmoraleta, nedeca
nausea, naŭzo; -te, naŭzi
naval, ŝipa
navel, umbiliko
navy, mararmeo; militmaristaro,
militŝiparo
near, proksime, proksima; apude;
-ly, preskaŭ; -sighted, miopa
neat, orda, ordema; belforma; lerta
necessary, necesa; necessity, neceso,
necesajo
neck, kolo; -erchief, koltuko; -lace,
kolringo; -tie, kravato
nectar, nektaro
need, bezoni, bezono; malriĉeco
needle, kudrilo

neglect, malatenti, malprizorgi; ne-zorgeco

negligence, malatento

negro, negro

neighbor, najbaro; -hood, ĉirkaŭajo, apudeco; -ing, apuda

neither, nek; — A nor B, nek A nek B

nephew, nevo

nerve, nervo; **nervous,** nerva, ner-vema

-ness, -eco

nest, nesto, nesti; -le, nestumi

net, reto, retkapti; sen-rabata (com.); -ting, -work, retajo, reto

neutral, neŭtrala, senpartia; -ize, senefikigi

never, neniam; -theless, tamen; malgraŭe

new, nova, freŝa, neuzita

news, novajo; -paper, jurnalo

next, venonta; sekvinta, sekvonta

nice, agrabla; delikata; preciza

nickel, nikelo

nickname, ŝercnomo, moknomo

niece, nevino

night, nokto; pass the —, tranokti; -ly, ĉiunokta, ĉiunokte; -mare, inkubo; last —, hieraŭ nokte

nightingale, najtingalo

nine, naŭ; -teen, dek-naŭ; -ty, naŭdek; -pins, kegloj

ninth, naŭa

no, ne; -body, neniu; -doubt, sen-dube; — (kind of), nenia; — longer, ne plu, jam ne; — one, neniu; — one's, nenies; -where, nenie; in — way, neniel; on — account, nenial

no., numero, n-ro

noble, nobla; (rank) nobela; -man, nobelo

nod, kapklini; kapjesi

noise, bruo; -y, brua

none, nenio, neniom

nonsense, sensencajo

noon, tagmezo

noose, kaptilo, maŝkaptilo

nor, nek; **neither** A — B, nek A nek B

norm, normo; -al, norma, normala

north, nordo, norda; -east, nordori-enta; -wards, norden

nose, nazo; **nostril,** naztruo

not, ne; —at all, tute ne; — quite, ne tute

notary, notario

note, noto, noti; atenti, observi; bonfamo; -d, famkonata; -worthy, notinda; **bank-,** bank-bileto, bank-noto

nothing, nenio; nulo

notice, rimarki, rimarko; atento; anonco, avizo, sciigo; averto

notify, anonci; sciigi; informi

notwithstanding, malgraŭ, malgraŭe, tamen

noun, substantivo

nourish, nutri; eduki

novel, romano; nova; -ette, novelo

November, Novembro

now, nun; jam; nu, do; -adays, nun-tempe, nune

nucleus, kerno

nude, nuda

nuisance, ĝenajo, ĝenulo

numb, sensenta

number, numero, numeri; (quantity) nombro; -less, sennombra

nun, monakino

nurse, (infants) vartistino; (sick persons) flegistino, flegi; -ry, vartejo, infanejo; plantkultivejo

nut, nukso; ŝraŭbingo; **hard — to crack,** malfacila problemo

O

O!, ho!

oak, kverko

oar, remilo

oat, aveno; -meal, grio; "sow wild —s," diboĉi

oath, juro; malbeno, blasfemo

obedient, obeema
obey, obei
object, objekto (thing); celo (aim); (gram.) komplemento; malkonsenti; kontraŭstari; ion, kontraŭstaro, malkonsento; -ionable, naŭza; malplaĉa
obligation, devo; ŝuldo
oblige, fari komplezon; devigi
observe, observi; observatory, observejo
obstinate, obstina; be —, obstini
obstruct, bari; malhelpi; (med.) obstrukci
obtain, akiri, ricevi, havigi
occasion, fojo; okazo; -al, okaza
occupation, okupo; ofico, profesio, metio
occupy, okupi
occur, okazi; troviĝi; -rence, okazajo, okazintajo
ocean, oceano
October, Oktobro
oculist, okulisto
odd, stranga; nepara; -s, ŝanco; -s and ends, diversajoj
odor, odoro
of, de; da; pri; el
off, for; — and on, intermite; carry —, forporti; -hand, senhezite, senprepare; -shoot, flankajo, ido; elkreskajo
offend, ofendi; peki
offer, proponi, propono, (sacrifice) oferi, ofero
office, ofico, oficejo; -r, oficisto; (mil.) oficiro
official, oficiala
often, ofte
oh! ho!
oil, oleo, oleumi; -y, olea, oleeca
ointment, ŝmirajo
O.K.! Bone! Korekte!
old, maljuna, malnova; antikva; -er, pliaĝa
olive, olivo
omelette, ovajo

omit, ellasi
on, sur; je; -ward, antaŭen
once, iam; unufoje; foje; — for all. unufoje por ĉiam; — more, ankoraŭ unufoje; — upon a time, foje; at —, tuj
one, unu; iu; oni; — by —, unuope; -ness, unueco; — says, oni diras; -self, si mem; — moment! momenton!
onion, bulbo, cepo
only, nur; sola, sole; (but) sed
open, malfermi; komenci; nefermita; nekaŝema; -ing, malfermajo; breĉo, aperturo; -minded, senantaŭjuĝa
opera, opero; -glass, lorneto
operate, funkcii, funkciigi; (surg.) operacii
opinion, opinio
opportune, oportuna; opportunity oportunajo, okazo
oppose, kontraŭstari; opposite, kontraŭa; mala, malo
oppress, subpremi
optimism, optimismo; optimist, optimisto
or, aŭ; either A — B, aŭ A aŭ B
orange, oranĝo; oranĝkolora
orchard, fruktarbejo
orchestra, orkestro
orchid, orkideo
ordeal, severa provo
order, ordo, ordigi; rango, klaso, vico; ordoni, ordono; mendi mendo; ordeno; -ly, ordema; servsoldato
ordinary, ordinara
ore, mineralo, minmetalo
organ, organo; (mus.) orgeno
organization, organizo; organize, organizi
orient, oriento; -al, orienta, orientano
origin, deveno, origino; -al, originala; originate, deveni, devenigi
ornament, ornami; ornamajo
orphan, orfo

other, alia; **-wise,** alie
ought, devi
ounce, unco
our, nia; **-selves,** ni mem
out-, el-, super-
out, ekstere; (fully) tute; **-cast,** elpelito, pario; **-come,** rezulto; **-er,** ekstera; **-fit,** ekipo; **-house,** kromdometo; **-ing,** ekskurso; **-law,** eksterleĝulo; **-lay,** elspezo; **-line,** konturo; **-look,** elrigardo, perspektivo; **-of-date,** malnovmoda; — **of,** el; **-put,** produkto; **-side,** ekstere; **-wards,** eksteren
oval, ovoforma
ovary, ovujo
oven, forno, bakforno
over-, super-, trans-, tro-
over, super; trans; finita; — **again,** denove; — **and** — **again,** ripete; **-board,** elŝipe; **-coat,** surtuto, palto; **-come,** venki; **-due,** malfrua, posttempa; **-hear,** subaŭdi; **-look,** observi; kontroli; pardoni; preterlasi; **-night,** dumnokta, tranokta; **-take,** (kur)atingi; **-throw, -turn,** renversi; **-time,** ekstra tempo
owe, ŝuldi; **owing to,** pro, sekve de
owl, strigo
own, posedi; propra
ox, bovo
oyster, ostro

P
pace, paŝi, paŝo, paŝadi; rapideco
pacific, pacema, paciga; **pacifism,** pacifismo
pack, paki; bestaro; kartaro; **-age,** pakaĵo
pad, remburi, remburaĵo; kuseneto; kompreso
paddle, padeli, padelilo
padlock, pendseruro
page, paĝo; (boy) paĝio; **to** — (Amer.) alvoki per paĝio

pail, sitelo
pain, doloro, dolori, dolorigi; puno; **-ful,** doloriga; **-less,** sendolora; **-s,** penoj
paint, kolorigi; kolorigilo; (art) pentri; **-ing,** pentrajo; pentrado, pentrarto; — **brush,** peniko; — **the face,** ŝminki
pair, paro, parigi; pariĝi; duo
pal, kamarado
palace, palaco
pale, pala, paliĝi; paliso
palm, manplato; (tree) palmo; — **off,** trompe transdoni
pamper, dorloti, troindulgi
pamphlet, broŝuro
pan, kaserolo; "— **out**" rezulti
pan-, tut-
pancake, patkuko, krespo
pane, fenestra vitraĵo
panic, paniko
pants, pantalono
papa, paĉjo
paper, papero; raporto, traktajo; (ekzamena) demandaro; tapeti
parachute, falombrelo; paraŝuto
parade, paradi, parado
paradise, paradizo
paragraph, paragrafo
parcel, pakaĵo
pardon, pardoni, pardono; **Pardon me! Pardonu min!**
parent, patr(in)o; **-al,** gepatra; **-s,** gepatroj
park, parko
parliament, parlamento
parlor, saloneto
parole, honorpromeso
parrot, papago
parsley, petroselo
part, parto, porcio; (theat.) rolo; (of serial) kajero, numero; **for the most** —, plejparte; **take** —, partopreni
participate, partopreni
particle, ero, parteto; (gram.) partiklo

particular, aparta, speciala, detala, detalo; preciza; elektema

partner, partoprenanto; firmano; kunulo; kunludanto, kundancanto

party, festo, amika kunveno; persono; partoprenanto; (pol., etc.) partio

pass, pasi, pasigi; superi; plenumɪ; trapasejo; for-, pas-permeso; -able, tolerebla; -age, trairo, trairejo, koridoro; vojaĝo; frazo; -port, pasporto; -word, signaldiro; bring to —, okazigi; let —, preterlasi

passenger, pasaĝero

Passover, Pasko

past, pasinta, estinta; preter; the —, pasinteco

paste, farungluo; (dough) pasto; -board, kartono

pastel, paŝtelo

pastor, pastro

pastry, pastaĵo

pasture, paŝti, paŝtigi, paŝtejo, herbejo

pat, manfrapeto

patch, fliki, flikajo; (ter)peceto

patent, patenti, patento

path, vojo, vojeto

patience, pacienco; patient, pacienca; (med.) paciento, kuracato

patrol, patroli, patrolo

patron, patrono; -ize, favori; -s, klientaro

pattern, modelo, modela; desegno; ekzemplo

pause, paŭzi, paŭzo

pave, pavimi; -ment, pavimo; — the way, pretigi vojon

paw, piedo, piedego; mano

pay, pagi; doni; rekompenci; profiti; puni; salajro; -able, pagota; -ee, alpagoto

pea, pizo

peace, paco; -able, pacema; -ful, paca, serena; -maker, pacigisto

peach, persiko

peak, pinto; montsupro

peanut, arakiso

pear, piro

pearl, perlo; mother of —, perlamoto

peasant, kamparano

peck, bekpiki

peculiar, stranga; aparta; — to, propra

pedal, pedalo, pedali

peddle, kolporti; -r, kolportisto

peel, ŝelo; senŝeligi

pen, plumo; enbari, enbarejo; -holder, plumingo; -knife, tranĉileto

pencil, krajono; skizi; (slate) grifelo

peninsula, duoninsulo

penis, peniso

penny, penco; penniless, senmona

pension, pensio; (boarding house) pensiono; -er, pensiulo

people, homoj; popolo; oni

pepper, pipro; surĵeti; red —, papriko

per, per; laŭ; -cent, procento

percolate, trafiltriĝi

perfect, perfekta, perfektigi; -ion, perfekteco

perform, plenumi; (actor) ludi; -ance, prezentado

perfume, parfumo

perhaps, eble

peril, danĝero, risko

period, periodo; epoko; punkto

perish, perei; -able, putrema

permanent, konstanta, daŭra

permit, permesi, permeso

perpetual, ĉiama, senĉesa, eterna

persecute, persekuti; turmenti

persist, persisti; -ence, persisto, persistado; daŭremo

person, persono; homo; -age, eminentulo; -al, persona, propra; -ality, personeco; -ate, reprezenti, imiti; -nel, personaro

perspire, ŝviti

persuade, konvinki, influi, instigi

pest, pesto; ĝenulo

pet, dorloti; favorato, favorata

petal, petalo
petroleum, petrolo
petticoat, subjupo
petty, malgranda, malgrava; bagatela
phantom, fantomo
philately, filatelo
philosopher, filozofo; philosophy,
filozofio
phonetic, fonetika; -s, fonetiko
phonograph, fonografo
photograph, fotografi, fotografajo
phrase, frazeparto, frazero
physic, kuracarto; laksigilo
physician, kuracisto
physicist, fizikisto; physics, fiziko
piano, piano; pianist, pianisto
pick, elekti; kolekti; -axe, pioĉo
pickle, pekli; -s, peklajo
picnic, pikniko
picture, bildo; pentrajo; figuri;
-sque, pentrinda
pie, pasteĉo, torto
piece, peco; monero; teatrajo; fliki;
— together, kunligi; -work, laŭ-
peca laboro
pier, kajo
piety, pieco
pig, porko; -headed, obstina; -iron,
ferfandajo
pigeon, kolombo
pigmy, pigmeo
pile, amaso; — up, amasigi
pill, pilolo
pillar, kolono
pillow, kapkuseno
pilot, piloto, piloti
pin, pinglo; pinglefiksi
pinch, pinĉi
pine, sopiri; (tree) pino; -needle,
pinglofolio
pineapple, ananaso
pink, rozkolora; (bot.) dianto
pint, kvartoduono
pioneer, pioniro
pious, pia
pipe, (tobacco) pipo; tubo; fajfi

piracy, piratado; pirate, pirato
pistol, pistolo
piston, piŝto
pit, kavajo, kavo; minejo; (theat.)
partero
pitcher, kruĉo
pity, kompato, kompati; pitiful, kompatinda
place, loko, loki; meti; ejo; rango;
vico; take —, okazi
plain, ebeno, ebenajo; ebena; klara,
evidenta; senornama, neluksa; -s,
stepo, ebenajo
plan, plano, plani, projekto, projekti;
metodo
plane, (Amer.) aeroplano; raboti,
rabotilo; (geom.) ebeno
plank, tabulo, tabulego
plant, kreskajo, vegetajo; planti,
planto
plaster, stuki, stuko; (med.) plastro;
-of-Paris, gipso
plastic, plastika, plastiko
plate, telero; (engraved) kliŝo; (thin
metal) lameno
platform, podio, estrarejo; (rail)
perono; (pol.) programo, princi-
paro
play, ludi; teatrajo; movlibereco;
-mate, kunludanto; -thing, ludilo
plea, petego; petegi; (law) pledo
pleasant, agrabla; plaĉa
please, plaĉi al; kontentigi; mi petas;
se plaĉas al vi; bonvolu
pleasure, plezuro
plenty, abundo, sufiĉo
pliers, prenilo
plot, konspiri, konspiro; intrigo;
(ter)peco
plow, plugi, plugilo
plug, ŝtopi, ŝtopilo
plum, pruno
plumber, plumbisto
plural, pluralo
pocket, poŝo; enpoŝigi
poem, poemo
poet, poeto

point, montri; punkto; esenco; (tip) pinto; (in games) poento; **to the —**, trafe, alcele; **— of view**, vidpunkto

poison, veneno, veneni

polar, polusa

pole, stango; (geog., elec.) poluso

police, polico; **-man**, policano; **-station**, policejo

policy, administra sistemo; politiko; (insurance) poliso

polish, poluri, polurilo; ĝentileco; **shoe —**, ciro

polite, ĝentila; komplezema

politic, saĝa, lerta, sagaca; **-s**, politiko

poll, enketo; voĉdoni; baloti

pond, lageto

pony, ĉevaleto

pool, lageto: kombini, kombinajo

poor, malriĉa; sensprita; kompatinda; bedaŭrinda

pope, papo

porch, verando, enirejo

pork, porkajo

port, haveno: **-er**, portisto; pordisto

portion, porcio, parto; porcii, dividi

portrait, portreto

position, pozicio; ofico; rango; loko

possess, posedi

possibility, ebleco, eblajo; **possible**, ebla

post, ofico; posteno; stango; (mails) poŝto, enpoŝtigi; **-age**, poŝtkosto; **-age stamp**, poŝtmarko; **-free**, afrankita; **-man**, leterportisto; **-mark**, poŝta stampo; **-master**, poŝtestro; **-office**, poŝtoficejo; **-paid**, afrankita; **by return —**, poŝtrevene

poster, afiŝo

postscript, postskribo

postpone, prokrasti

pot, poto; enpotigi

potato, terpomo

poultry, kortbirdoj

pound, pisti; funto; (English money) pundo

pour, (liquids) verŝi; (solids) ŝuti

poverty, malriĉeco

powder, (toilet) pudro; (dust) polvo; (med., chem.) pulvoro; (gun) pulvo

power, povo; potenco; forto; **rajto**

practice, ekzerci; praktiki; kutimo; **practical**, praktika; utila

prairie, stepo

praise, laŭdi, laŭdo; **-worthy**, laŭdinda

pray, preĝi; petegi; **-er**, preĝo

pre-, antaŭ-

preach, prediki; **-er**, predikisto, pastro

precede, antaŭi, antaŭiri

precious, altvalora, multekosta; karega; **— stone**, gemo

precise, preciza; **-ly**, precize; (time) akurate

predict, antaŭdiri, profeti

prefer, preferi; **-ably**, prefere

prefix, prefikso

pregnant, graveda; multsignifa

prejudice, antaŭjuĝo; **-d**, partiema

prepare, pretigi, pretiĝi; prepari; **-d to**, preta por

prepay, antaŭpagi; (post) afranki

prescription, (med.) recepto

presence, apudesto, ĉeesto

present, estanta, nuntempa; donaci, donaco; (introduce) prezenti; **at the — time**, nuntempe; **of — interest**, aktuala; **be —**, ĉeesti

preserve, gardi; konservi; (fruit) konfiti; **-s**, konfitaĵo

preside, prezidi; **president**, prezidanto

press, premi, premilo; presejo; (be urgent) urĝi; (the Press) gazetaro, ĵurnalaro

pretend, ŝajnigi; preteksti; (claim) pretendi

pretty, beleta, ĉarma; **— much**, preskaŭ

prevent, malhelpi, malebligi
previous, antaŭa; -ly, antaŭe
price, prezo; -less, multvalora, netaksebla; -list, prezaro
prick, piki, pikilo
pride, fiereco, malhumileco
priest, pastro
primary, unua; origina, elementa,
praa; ĉefa
primeval, praa
prince, princo, princido
principal, ĉefa; ĉefo, estro; precipa;
kapitalo
principle, principo
print, presi, presaĵo; bildo, gravur-
aĵo; -er, presisto; -er's proof, presprovaĵo; -ing press, presilo; out of
—, elĉerpita
prison, malliberejo; -er, malliberulo;
-er of war, militkaptito
private, privata; simpla soldato
privilege, privilegio, privilegii
privy, necesejo; sekreta; privata
prize, premio; kaptaĵo; ŝati; -fight,
bokskonkurso; -fighter, boksisto
probable, kredebla; (math.) probabla
problem, problemo
proceed, antaŭeniri; procedi; -s,
ricevaĵo
process, procedo; (law) proceso
produce, produkti, produktaĵo;
kaŭzi; montri
profit, gajno; profito, profiti; -able,
profitdona
progress, progresi, progreso; -ive,
progresema, progresemulo
prohibit, malpermesi; -ion, malpermeso
project, elstari; projekti, projekto
promise, promesi, promeso; -ing,
promesplena; esperiga; promissory note, ŝuldatesto
promote, favori, antaŭenigi; iniciati
prompt, tuja; akurata; senhezita;
instigi; (theat.) suflori
pronoun, pronomo
pronounce, elparoli, prononci

proof, pruvo; provo; presprovaĵo
propaganda, propagando
proper, propra; ĝusta; konvena,
deca; -ty, proprajo, havajo, pose-
dajo
proprietor, posedanto
prose, prozo; piece of —, prozaĵo
prosecute, persekuti; procesi kontraŭ
prospect, vidaĵo, aspekto; serĉi, esplori; -ive, atendata, estonta
prospectus, prospekto
prosper, prosperi
prostitute, prostitui, prostituulino,
publikulino
protect, protekti, ŝirmi; -ion, pro-
tekto
protest, protesti, protesto; -ant, pro-
testanto
proud, fiera; malhumila; aroganta
prove, pruvi, pruviĝi; konstati;
(test) provi
provide, provizi; -d that, kondiĉe ke
province, provinco; (Russian) gu-
bernio
prune, ĉirkaŭtranĉi; (seka) pruno
psalm, psalmo
psychologist, psikologo; psychology,
psikologio
public, publiko, publika
publish, eldoni, publikigi; proklami
pudding, pudingo
pull, tiri; (oar) remi
pulse, pulso; -beat, pulsbato
pump, pumpi, pumpilo
pumpkin, kukurbo
pun, vortludo
punch, (drink) punĉo; (fist) pugnobati; (tickets) trui
punish, puni; -ment, puno
puppy, hundido
pupil, lernanto; (eye) pupilo
purchase, aĉeti, aĉeto
pure, pura; simpla, nura; purify,
purigi; purity, pureco, ĉasteco
purple, purpura
purpose, celo, celi; intenco, intenci;
for the — of, por

[227

purse, monujo; — **the lips,** kunpremi la lipojn
pursue, sekvi, postsekvi; persekuti; daŭrigi
pus, puso
push, puŝi, puŝo; — **along,** ŝovi
put, meti; — **in order,** ordigi; — **off,** demeti, prokrasti; — **on,** surmeti; — **out,** estingi; elpeli; — **up with,** toleri
puzzle, enigmo; konfuzi; cerbumi pri
pyramid, piramido

Q

quack, kvaki; ĉarlatano
quail, kaŭri; tremi; koturno (bird)
quaint, kurioza, stranga
quake, tremi; **earth-,** tertremo
Quaker, Kvakero
quality, kvalito; (trait) eco
quantity, kvanto
quarrel, kverelo, kvereli; disputo
quarter, kvarono, kvaronigi; kvartalo, regiono
quay, kajo
queen, reĝino; (cards) damo
queer, stranga, kurioza; duba, suspektinda
question, demando, demandi; temo; disputo; esprimi dubon pri; **-naire,** demandaro
quick, rapida; viva; facilmova; **-en,** vigligi; **-lime,** kaŭstika kalko; **to the —,** ĝis la koro
quiet, kvieta, trankvila, paca, silenta, senbrua
quilt, stebi, kunstebi; litkovrilo (stebita)
quit, kviti; forlasi
quite, sufiĉe; tute
quiz, demandi; kontrolo; moke demandi
quote, citi; proponi prezon; **quotation,** citajo

R

rabbi, rabeno
rabbit, kuniklo
race, konkurso, kurkonkurso; raso; **human —,** homaro
radar, radar-aparato
radiant, brila
radical, radikala, radikalulo; radika
radio, radio-aparato; **radiate,** radiĺ
radish, rafano
radium, radiumo
rag, ĉifono; tukpeco; **-amuffin,** ĉifonulo
rage, kolerego; furiozo; modo
rail, relo; **-road,** fervojo; — **at,** insulti; moki
railway, relvojo, fervojo; **-carriage,** vagono; **-station,** fervojo-stacio; **-train,** vagonaro
rain, pluvo; **-coat,** pluvmantelo
raise, levi; kreskigi; produkti; plialtigi
raisin, sekvinbero
rake, rasti, rastilo; diboĉulo
ranch, ranĉo, brutbieno
random, sencela; **at —,** hazarde
range, amplekso; vico, envicigi; ĉirkaŭvagi; vidlimo, paflimo; (rad.) trafpovo; **-r,** (arbar-, park-) zorgisto; **kitchen-,** kuirforno; **mountain-,** montaro
rank, rango; vico, grado; multkreska; malbonodora
rap, frapeti, frapeto
rapid, rapida; **-s,** rapidfluejo
rare, malofta; maldensa; bonega
rascal, fripono
raspberry, frambo
rat, rato
rate, taksi; klasigi; imposto; rapideco; — **of exchange,** kurzo; **at any —,** ĉiaokaze, iaokaze; **at the — of,** po
rather, prefere, plivole
ration, porcio
rattle, klaki; (in the throat) stertoro; (toy) tintilo; **-snake,** sonserpento

raw, kruda; nekuirita
ray, radio
razor, razilo
re-, re-
reach, atingi; etendiĝi ĝis
react, reagi, kontraŭagi; -ion (poɪ., rad.) reakcio
read, legi; —aloud, laŭtlegi; -able, legebla, leginda
ready, preta; -made, jamfarita; — money, kontanto; get —, pretiĝi make —, pretigi
real, efektiva; reala, malfalsa; -ize, efektivigi
reap, rikolti
rear, eduki, nutri; konstrui; (as a horse) ekleviĝi; postajo
reason, motivo, kaŭzo; kialo; prudento; racio; (argue) rezoni; -able, racia, prudenta; justa, modera; for every —, ĉial; for no —, nenial
rebel, ribeli, ribelanto; -lion, ribelo
recall, revoki; rememori
receipt, ricevo; enspezo; recepto; (com.) kvitanco
receive, ricevi; (guests, ideas, etc.) akcepti; -r. aŭskultilo, ricevilo; kolektisto, likvidisto
recent, freŝdata; antaŭnelonga
recipe, recepto
recite, deklami; rakonti; recital, (muzika, deklama) prezentado
reckless, senzorga, riskema
recognize, rekoni; konstati; konfesi
recommend, rekomendi; konsili
record, registri, registrolibro; enskribi; muzikdisko; (sport) rekordo; -office, arkivejo
recover, rericevi, retrovi, reakiri; rekovri; resaniĝi
recruit, rekruto, rekrutigi; varbi, varbito
red, ruĝa; -den, ruĝigi, ruĝiĝi; -hot, brulruĝa; -tape, rutino
reduce, malpliigi; maldikiĝi; (in

rank) degradigi; (chem., math.) redukti
reed, kano; junko; (mus.) ŝalmo
reef, (rocks) rifo
refer, resendi; direkti; transdoni; — to, turni sin al; rilati al; aludi al; -ee, decidonto, arbitronto; -ence, aludo; (character) referenco
reflect, rebrili, speguli; resendi; pripensi
reform, reformi; plibonigi
refreshment, manĝeto, trinketo; — bar, bufedo
refrigerator, malvarmigilo
refuge, rifuĝo, rifuĝejo, -e, rifuĝinto; take —, rifuĝi
refund, repagi
refuse, rifuzi; rubo, forĵetajo
regard, rigardi; observi; estimi, respekti; taksi; ŝati; as —s, with — to, rilate al, pri; kind regards! saluton! bondeziron!
regime, reĝimo
regiment, regimento
region, regiono
register, registri; (letter) rekomendi; (voice) skalo
regret, bedaŭri; domaĝi
regular, regula, laŭregula; regulate, reguligi
reign, regi, regado
rein, bridi. bridrimeno
reject, malakcepti, rifuzi
relate, rakonti; -d, parenca; — to, rilati al
relax, malrigidigi, malrigidiĝi; malstreĉi; -ation, distrado
release, liberigi, liberigo
reliable, fidinda
religion, religio; religious, pia, religia
rely on, fidi al
remain, resti; -der, restajo; cetero; -ing, restanta, cetera; -s, kadavro
remark, rimarki, rimarko; dirajo; -able, rimarkinda

remedy, rimedo; kuracilo, rebonigi; ripari
remember, memori
remind, rememorigi
remove, translokigi; formovi, forpreni; (from office) eksigi
rendezvous, rendevuo, renkonto; renkontejo
rent, lupago; lui, luigi; ŝirajo
repair, ripari; rebonigi
repeat, ripeti
repent, penti
reply, respondi, respondo
report, raporti, raporto; pafbruo; -er, raportisto
represent, reprezenti; prezenti; figuri; -ation, reprezentado; -ative, reprezenta, reprezentanto
reproach, riproĉi, riproĉo
reptile, rampaĵo, rampulo, reptilio
republic, respubliko; -an, respublika, respublikano
request, peti, peto
require, (need) bezoni; (demand) postuli
rescue, savi, savo; liberigi, liberigo
research, serĉado, esplorado, studo
resemble, simili
reserve, rezervi, rezervo; reteni; sindeteno
reside, loĝi; restadi; -nce, loĝejo; -nt, loĝanto
resign, forlasi; (office) eksiĝi el; rezigni pri (or je); -ation, eksiĝo
resist, kontraŭstari, rezisti; -ance, (rad.)rezistanco
respect, respekti, respekto; -able, respektinda; -ful, respektema; -ive, respektiva; in — of, pro; in some -s, en kelkaj rilatoj; with — to, rilate al, pri
respond, respondi; -ent, respondanto, defendanto; response, respondo; responsible, responda
rest, ripozi, ripozo; (remain) resti, restaĵo; (support) apogilo; (mus.)

paŭzo; -ful, ripoziga; at —, senmova; the —, cetero, ceteraj
restaurant, restoracio, manĝejo
restore, restarigi, rebonigi, redoni; revivigi
result, rezulti, rezulto; -ant, (math.) rezultanto
retail, podetala, podetale vendi
retired, emerita
return, reveni; reiri; redoni, repagi; resendi; profito; -ticket, duvoja bileto
reveal, malkaŝi, aperigi, revelacii
revenge, venĝi, venĝo
reverse, mala, malo; renversi; nuligi
review, ekzameni, inspekti; rekonsideri; (literary work) recenzi; (gazette) revuo; (mil.) revui, parado
revolt, ribeli, ribelo; -ing, naŭzega
revolution, (pol.) revolucio; turniĝo, turno
reward, rekompenci, rekompenco
rhyme, rimi, rimo
rhythm, ritmo
rib, ripo
rice, rizo
rich, riĉa; altvalora; luksa
rid, liberigi; get — of, liberiĝi el
ride, rajdi; (in vehicle) veturi
ridicule, moki, moko; ridiculous, ridinda
rifle, pafilo; rabi
right, prava; ĝusta; korekta; akurata; dekstra; rajti, rajto; to the —, dekstre, dekstren; give -s to, rajtigi; -away, tuj
rim, rando
ring, ringo; sonori, sonorigi
rinse, laveti; (throat) gargari
riot, tumulti, tumulto; run —, agi senrege
rip, ŝiri, disŝiri
ripe, matura; -n, maturiĝi, maturigi
rise, leviĝi, levi sin; pligrandiĝo; deveni
risk, riski, risko

230]

river, rivero; **-bed**, riverfluejo
road, vojo; **high-**, ŝoseo
roam, vagi, ĉirkaŭvagi
roar, kriegi; blekegi; ridegi; (wind waves, etc.) muĝi
roast, rosti, rostaĵo; **-beef**, rostbovaĵo
rob, rabi, ŝteli
robe, robo
rock, roko, ŝtonego; balanci; luli; **-ing-chair**, balanc-seĝo, lulseĝo
rod, bastono, vergo, stango
roll, ruli, ruligi; ondi; volvi, volvaĵo; (bread) bulko; (names) nomaro; (drums) tamburado; **-er**, rulilo, platigilo; **-er skate**, rulglitilo
romance, romano; (mus.) romanco
romantic, romaneca; (lit.) romantika
roof, tegmento; suprajo
room, ĉambro; spaco; **-s**, ĉambraro, loĝejo; **-y**, vasta
root, radiko; bazo
rope, ŝnuro; ŝnurligi
rose, rozo
rot, putri; putrigi; **-ten**, putra
rouge, vang-ruĝo; ruĝigilo
rough, malglata, malebena; maldelikata; malserena; kruda; proksimuma
round, ronda; rondo; serio; rondkanto; ĉirkaŭ
route, vojo
row, vico, linio; remi
royal, reĝa; **-ty**, reĝeco
rub, froti; **-ber**, kaŭĉuko; **-bers** galoŝoj; **— out**, forviŝi
rubbish, rubo, forjetaĵo; sensencaĵo
rude, malĝentila; malklera; kruda, senkultura
rug, tapiŝeto; vojaĝa lankovrilo
ruin, ruino, ruinigi
rule, regulo; regi, regado; **-r**, reganto; liniilo; **as a —**, kutime
rum, rumo
rumor, onidiro

run, kuri, kuro; flui; daŭri; puŝi; **— away**, forkuri
rush, kuregi
Russia, Rusujo; **Russian**, ruso, rusa
rust, rusto, rusti
rut, (voj)sulko; rutino; seksardo
rye, sekalo

S

sack, sako; rabadi
sacred, sankta
sacrifice, oferi, ofero, oferaĵo
sad, malĝoja, malgaja; bedaŭrinda
saddle, selo, seli
safe, sendanĝera; senriska; sekura; **-guard**, protekti, protektilo
sage, saĝa, saĝulo
said, diris, dirita; **it is —**, oni diras
sail, velo; velveturi, ŝipveturi, boatveturi; **-or**, maristo, ŝipano
saint, sanktulo
sake of, for the, pro
salad, salato
salary, salajro; **salaried**, salajrata
sale, vendo; (auction) aŭkcio; **-able**, vendebla; **-sman**, vendisto
salmon, salmo
saloon, drinkejo, salono
salt, salo, sala, sali; pekli; **-cellar**, salujo; **"not worth one's —,"** sentaŭgulo; **"take with a grain of —,"** rezerve akcepti
salute, saluti, saluto
salve, (kurac)ŝmiraĵo
same, sama; **— as**, same kiel; **-ness**, sameco; unuformeco; **all the —**, tute egale; **at the — time**, samtempe; tamen
sample, specimeno; ekzemplo; provi
sand, sablo; **-bank**, sablajo
sandal, sandalo
sandwich, sandviĉo
sane, cerbo-sana; racia, prudenta
sanitary, sanitara, higiena; **sanitation**, higieno
sap, suko; stultulo

sardine, sardino; (pickled) sardelo
Satan, Satano
satisfy, kontentigi, satigi, satisfied, kontenta, sata
Saturday, sabato
sauce, saŭco; -pan, kaserolo
saucer, subtaso; tastelero
sausage, kolbaso
savage, sovaĝa, sovaĝulo; furioza
save, savi; ŝpari; krom; savings-bank, ŝparbanko
saw, segi, segilo; vidis; proverbo; -mill, segejo
say, diri; -ing, dirajo, diro; that is to —, tio estas
scab, (vundo)krusto; (disease) skabio
scald, brogi; brogvundi
scale, (measure) skalo; (mus.) gamo; (mount) suprenrampi; (weigh) pesilo
scandal, skandalo
Scandinavian, skandinava
scar, cikatro, cikatrigi
scarce, malofta, malsufiĉa; -ly, apenaŭ
scarf, koltuko
scarlet, skarlata; -fever, skarlatino
scatter, disĵeti, dissemi, disvastigi, disigi
scene, sceno; (landscape) peizaĝo
scent, odoro, odori; parfumi; flari, flaro
schedule, tabelo, listo; enlistigi
scheme, skemo, plano, plani; projekto, projekti; intrigo, intrigi
schism, skismo, disiĝo
scholar, lernanto; klerulo; -ship, stipendio; instruiteco
school, lernejo; (secondary) gimnazio, liceo; (of thought) skolo; instrui
science, scienco; scientific, scienca; scientist, sciencisto
scissors, tondilo
scold, kolere riproĉi, insulti

score, kalkulo; poentaro; dudeko; entranĉajo; gajni; trafi
Scot, skoto; -land, Skotlando; -tish, skota
scoundrel, kanajlo
scout, skolto, skolti; mokridi
scrap, peceto; eltirajo
scratch, grati, grato; skrapi
scream, kriegi
screen, skreno; ŝirmi, ŝirmilo
screw, ŝraŭbi, ŝraŭbo; (of steamship) helico, ŝraŭbego; -driver, ŝraŭbturnilo
scrub, broslavi
sculptor, skulptisto; sculpture, skulpti; skulptajo
scum, ŝaŭmo
sea, maro; -coast, marbordo; -man, maristo; -port, havenurbo
seal, sigeli, sigelo; (animal) foko
seam, kunkudrajo; (geol.) vejno; -stress, kudristino
search, serĉi, serĉo; esplori, esploro; -ing, penetrema, traesplora
season, sezono; tempo; spici; hardi; -ing, kondimento
seat, sidloko, sidejo; sidigi; postajo
second, subteni, sekvi; (in order) dua; (of time) sekundo; -hand, uzita, brokante; -rate, duaklasa, duaranga
secret, sekreto, sekreta; kaŝita; -e, kaŝi; (physiology) sekrecii
secretary, sekretario
section, sekcio; parto; fako
secure, sendanĝera, sendanĝerigi; sekura, sekurigi; firma, firmigi; akiri, kapti; security (leg.) kaŭcio; garantio
see, vidi; kompreni; — to, klopodi pri, atenti pri
seed, semo; -ling, plantido; -y, mizera, kaduka
seek, serĉi; (strive after) strebi
seem, ŝajni; -ly, deca; bela
seize, ekpreni, ekkapti, ekokupi; seizure, atako, ekpreno

seldom, malofte

select, elekti; ekskluziva; **-ion,** elektado

self, mem; si; **-command, -control,** sinregado; **-conceited,** vanta; **-confidence,** aplombo; **-conscious,** memkonscia; **-denial,** sindeteno; **-evident,** memevidenta; **-governing,** memreganta, aŭtonoma; **-ish** egoista; **-reproach,** sinriproĉo; **-taught,** meminstruita

sell, vendi

semi-, duon-

senate, senato; **senator,** senatano

send, sendi; **-back,** resendi; **— on,** ekspedi, transsendi; **a -off,** adiaŭo

sense, sento; (meaning) senco; konscio; **sensible,** prudenta; sentebla; **sensitive,** sentema

sentence, frazo; kondamno

separate, apartigi, aparta, apartiĝi; disigi, disiĝi; **-ly,** aparte, dise

September, Septembro

sergeant, serĝento; **-major,** ĉefserĝento

series, serio

serious, grava; serioza

sermon, prediko

serve, servi; dejori; utili, taŭgi; **servant,** servist(in)o; **service,** servado; (table) servico; (Divine) Diservo; **serviceable,** utila, efika, uzebla

set, meti; fiksi; firmiĝi, solidiĝi; aro, kolekto, serio; (of dishes) servico; (sun) subiri; (gems) munti; (limb, bone) enartikigi; **— aside for,** difini por; **— teeth on edge,** agaci; **— type,** komposti

settle, decidi; solvi; pagi; trankviligi; ordigi; loĝiĝi; koloniigi; **-ment,** kolonio

seven, sep; **-th,** sepa; (mus.) septo; **-ty,** sepdek

seventeen, dek-sep; **-th,** dek-sepa

several, kelkaj, kelke da, pluraj; diversaj

severe, severa, senindulga

sew, kudri; **-ing-machine,** kudromaŝino, stebilo

sewage, kloakajo; **sewer,** kloako

sex, sekso

shade, ombro, ombrumi; ŝirmilo; nuanco; **shadow,** ombro

shake, skui, ŝanceli, agiti; tremi; **— hands,** manpremi; **— off,** deskui; **shaky,** tremanta; nefidinda

shall, (future tense ending on verb) -os

shame, honto, hontigi; malhonoro; bedaŭrindajo, domaĝo

shape, formo, formi; (cut of clothes) fasono; **-ly,** belforma, gracia

share, dividi; partopreni; (fin.) akcio; **-holder,** akciulo

sharp, akra; pinta; inteligenta, vigla; neta; (mus.) dieso; **-en,** akrigi

shatter, frakasi

shave, razi

shawl, ŝalo

she, ŝi

shed, budo, kabano; deigi, dejeti; **— tears,** larmi

sheep, ŝafo; **-fold,** ŝafejo; **-ish,** timema

sheet, folio; lameno, tavolo; litotuko; **-brass,** latuno; **-iron,** ferlado

shelf, breto

shell, konko; bombo, bombardi; (eggs) ŝelo; senŝeligi; **-fish,** molusko

shelter, ŝirmi, ŝirmilo, ŝirmejo; rifuĝejo

shepherd, ŝafisto, paŝtisto

shilling, ŝilingo

shine, brili, lumi

shingle, (roof) ŝindo

ship, ŝipo; ekspedi; **-wreck,** ŝippereo; **-yard,** ŝipkonstruejo

-ship, -eco

shirt, ĉemizo

shiver, tremi, tremo

shock, skuo; frapego; ŝoki, ofendi; (med.) atako

shoe, ŝuo; -maker, ŝufaristo, ŝuriparisto; -polish, ciro

shoot, pafi; mortpafi; (bud) ĝermi; branĉeto; -ing-star, meteoro

shop, butiko; (store) magazeno; -ping, aĉetado

shore, marbordo; riverbordo; lagbordo

short, mallonga; manka; -bread, buterkuko; -coming, manko; -sighted, miopa; nesagaca

shorthand, stenografarto; write —, stenografi

shot, pafo, pafita, pafajo; kugletoj

should, (ought to) devus

shoulder, ŝultro; surŝultrigi; -blade, skapolo

shout, krieg i, kriego

shove, ŝovi, puŝi

show, montri; pruvi; montro, spektaklo; parado

shower, pluveti; surŝuti; -bath, ŝprucbano, duŝo

shrink, malpliiĝi, malpliiĝi, kuntiriĝi; — from, sin detiri (pro timo)

shut, fermi, fermita; -ter, fenestrokovrilo; (phot.) obturatoro

shy, timema; (horse) flanken salti

sick, malsana; vomema; -en, naŭzi; malsaniĝi; -ness, malsaneco

side, flanko; bordo; partio; -face, profilo; -walk, trotuaro; -ways, flanke; take -s, partianiĝi

sieve, kribrilo

sift, kribri; (evidence) esplori

sigh, ekĝemi, ekĝemo; (longing) sopiri, sopiro

sight, vido, vidajo; vidindajo; vidpovo; spektaklo; (rifle) celilo; at first —, unuavide

sign, signo, signi; gesto, gesti; subskribi; -ature, subskribo; -board, montro-tabulo; -post, vojmontrilo

signal, signalo, signali; rimarkinda

signify, signifi; esti grava; significance, graveco; signifo

silent, silenta; senbrua; .be —, silenti; silence, silento, silentigi

silk, silko; silka; -worm, silkraŭpo; -y, silkeca

silly, malsaĝa, senprudenta; stulta, malsprita

silver, arĝento

similar, simila; -ly, simile

simple, simpla; naiva, senarta; facila; simplify, simpligi; simply, simple, nur

sin, peko, peki; -ful, peka, pekema; -ner, pekulo

since, depost; ĉar; tial ke; pro tio ke; — the time, depost la tempo; two years —, antaŭ du jaroj

sincere, sincera

sing, kanti; -ing, kantado, kantarto

single, sola; senedz(in)a; -minded, unucela; singly, unuope

sink, malleviĝi; subakviĝi; lavujo; -ing-fund, amortizajo

sir, sinjoro

sister, fratino; -in-law, bofratino

sit, sidi; (as hen) kovi; — down, sidiĝi

situation, (circumstances) situacio; loko, sidejo; stato; (employment) ofico

six, ses; -th, sesa; -ty, sesdek

sixteen, dek-ses; -th, dek-sesa

size, grandeco, amplekso; mezuro; sizing, gluajo

skate, gliti, glitilo

skeleton, skeleto

sketch, skizi, skizo

ski, skii, skio

skill, lerteco; skilful, lerta

skin, haŭto, senhaŭtigi; (hide) felo; (fruit) ŝelo

skirt, jupo; limtuŝi

skull, kranio

sky, ĉielo; -blue, lazura

slam, brufermi

slang, slango

slap, manfrapi, manfrapo

Slav, slavo, slava

slave, sklavo; **-ry,** sklaveco

sleep, dormi, dormo; -er, dormanto; **-y,** dormema

sleet, hajl-pluvo, neĝ-pluvo

sleeve, maniko

sleigh, glitveturilo

slender, maldika, mallarĝa, svelta; malforta

slice, tranĉi, tranĉajo

slide, gliti; (for lantern) kliŝajo

slim, maldika; malforta

slip, gliti; faleti; erareto; (paper) slipo; (twig) detranĉajo; **-per,** pantoflo; **-pery,** glita, glitiga; **let —,** preterlasi

slow, malrapida; teda; **-down,** malrapidiĝi, malrapidigi; **go —,** malrapidi

slum, domaĉaro

sly, ruza, kaŝema

small, malgranda; negrava; **— letter** (type) minusklo

smart, lerta; sprita; eleganta; ruza; ekdoloreti

smash, frakasi, frakaso

smear, ŝmiri

smell, odori, odoro; (tr.) flari

smile, rideti, rideto

smoke, fumi, fumo

smooth, glata, glatigi; **— down,** trankviligi

smother, sufoki

smuggle, kontrabandi

snake, serpento

snap, ekrompi; kraketi

sneak, kaŝe (eniri, rigardi, etc.)

sneeze, terni

snore, ronki, ronko

snow, neĝo, neĝi; **-ball,** neĝbulo; **-capped,** neĝkovrita; **-drift,** neĝblovajo; **-flake,** neĝero; **-shoe,** glitŝuo

so, tiel; tial, do; **— as to,** por ke; **-called,** tiel nomata; **— far as,** ĝis;

— much, tiom; **— that,** tiel ke; **and — forth,** kaj tiel plu, k.t.p.

soak, trempi; malsekigi, malsekiĝi; **— up,** sorbi

soap, sapo, sapumi; **-y,** sapeca

sob, ploregi, plorĝemi

sober, sobra; **-minded,** trankvilanima, neekscitema

social, socia; (pol.) sociala; **-ism,** socialismo

society, socio; **a —,** societo

sock, ŝtrumpeto

socket, ingo

soda, sodo; **-water,** sodo-akvo; **carbonate of —,** natro

sofa, sofo; (couch) kanapo

soft, mola; mallaŭta; **-en,** moligi, malseverigi, moderigi; **-ly,** kviete, mallaŭte

soil, grundo; tero; malpurigi, makuli

sold, vendis, vendita

solder, luti

soldier, soldato, militisto

sole, sola; (of foot or shoe) plando

solid, solida, solidajo; fortika; **-arity,** solidareco

solo, solo

soluble, solvebla; **solution,** solvo; (chem.) solvaĵo

solve, solvi; **solvent** (fin.) solventa; solvebla, solvilo

some, (kind) ia; (quantity) iom; (number) kelke da; **-body,** iu; **-body's,** ies; **-how,** iel; **-thing,** io; **-time,** iam; **-times,** iafoje, okaze; **-times A, -times B,** jen A, jen B; **-where,** ie

son, filo; **-in-law,** bofilo

song, kanto

soon, baldaŭ, frue; **-er or later,** plimalpli baldaŭ; **as — as,** tuj kiam; **as — as possible,** kiel eble plej baldaŭ

soot, fulgo

sore, dolora; ĉagrenita; ulcereto, vundo

[235

sorrow, malĝojo; bedaŭro; be sorry, bedaŭri; malĝoji; be sorry for, kompati

sort, speco, klaso; enklasigi; bonordigi

soul, animo

sound, sono, soni; sonori; sana

soup, supo

sour, acida, acidiĝi

source, fonto, deveno, origino

south, sudo, suda; -wards, suden; South America, Sud-Ameriko

sow, semi

space, spaco; (time) daŭro; spacious, vasta

spade, fosilo; (cards) piko

spare, (save) ŝpari; (part with) doni; (treat leniently) indulgi; kroma; malgrasa; superflua

spark, fajrero

sparrow, pasero

speak, paroli, paroladi; -er, parolanto

special, speciala; aparta; -ist, specialisto, fakulo

specimen, specimeno

spectacles, okulvitroj

speech, parolado; lingvo

speed, rapido, rapideco; -ometer, rapidmezurilo; -y, rapida

spell, sorĉo; (words) literumi

spend, elspezi; (time) pasigi

spider, araneo

spill, disverŝi, perdeverŝi

spin, ŝpini

spinach, spinaco

spine, spino

spinster, fraŭlino

spirit, spirito; animo; viveco; energio; fantomo

spit, kraĉi; viandpikilo

spite, malico, malbonvolo; in — of, (notwithstanding) malgraŭ, (defiance) spite de

splendid, grandioza, belega, bonega

split, fendi; krevi; (splinter) spliti; (in a party) skismo

spoil, malbonigi, malboniĝi; fuŝi; trodorloti; putriĝi

sponge, spongo, sponge lavi

spool, bobeno

spoon, kulero; -ful, plenkulero

sport, sporto

spot, makulo, makuli; loko; rimarki; -less, senmakula, purega

sprain, artiktordo

spread, etendi, etendiĝi; disvastigi

spring, printempo; fonto; risorto; salto; — from, deveni de

sprinkle, surŝprucigi; (ceremonial) aspergi

spy, spioni, spiono; -glass, teleskopeto

square, kvadrato, kvadrata; (public) placo

squeeze, premegi, premego

squirrel, sciuro

stab, pikvundi

staff, (mil.) stabo; oficistaro; bastono; stango

stage, scenejo; grado; -manager, reĝisoro

stain, makuli, makulo; koloriĝi; -less, senmakula

stair, ŝtuparo

stale, nefreŝa

stamp, stampi, stampilo; marki, marko; piedbati; postage —, poŝtmarko

stand, stari, stariĝi; (at exhibition) budo, elmontrejo; toleri; -point, vidpunkto

standard, normo, norma; -ize, alnormigi; up to —, laŭnorma

stanza, strofo

star, stelo; (any heavenly body) astro

starch, amelo, amelumi

start, ekiri, ekiro; komenci; ektremi, ektremo; fondi, starigi; ekfunkciigi

starve, malsati, malsatiĝi; — to death, malsatmorti

state, stato; (pol.) ŝtato; (circum-

236]

stances) situacio; eldiri; esprimi;
-ly, majesta; -ment, dirajo
station, (railway, etc.) stacio; (job
assigned) posteno; (in life) rango;
-ary, senmova, senprogresa; fiksa;
-ery, skribpapero
statistics, statistiko
statue, statuo
stay, resti, restado; loĝadi
steady, firma, konstanta; regula;
sobra
steak, viandtrancajo, bifsteko
steal, ŝteli
steam, vaporo; (cul., etc.) vaporumi;
-engine, vapormaŝino; -ship, vap-
orŝipo
steel, ŝtalo
steep, kruta
steer, direkti, gvidi; kastrita bovo
stem, trunketo; haltigi; kontraŭagi
stenographer, stenografisto; stenography, stenografio
step, paŝi, paŝo; ŝtupo; klopodo;
-father, duonpatro; "take -s,"
klopodi
stew, (cul.) stufi; -pan, kaserolo
stick, bastono; piki; alglui; — at,
persisti pri; -y, glueca
stiff, rigida, nefleksebla
still, senmova, kvieta, trankvila; ankoraŭ; tamen
sting, piki, piko, pikdoloro
stink, odoraĉi, odoraĉo
stir, kirli; kortuŝi; inciti
stock, provizi, provizo; stoko; havajo; bestaro; raso; -broker, bors-
isto; -exchange, borso; -holder,
akciulo
stocking, ŝtrumpo
stomach, stomako
stone, ŝtono; ŝtonbati; gemo; (fruit)
kerno
stool, tabureto
stood, staris
stop, halti, haltigi; ĉesi, ĉesigi;
paŭzi; ŝtopi; (valve) klapo; -per,
ŝtopilo

store, butiko; magazeno; provizo
stork, cikonio
storm, ventego; furiozi; (mil.) atak-
egi
story, rakonto; historieto; mensogeto; (of house) etaĝo
stout, dika; solida; firma
stove, forno
straight, rekta; justa; fidinda; -for-
ward, sincera, honesta
strain, streĉi, trastreĉi; filtri; kribri;
raso
strange, stranga; fremda; neordi-
nara; -r, nekonato, fremdulo
strangle, premsufoki; strangoli
strap, rimeno
straw, pajlo; -berry, frago
stream, rivero; fluo, flui; amase iri;
down —, laŭflue
street, strato
strength, forto, forteco; -en, pli-
fortigi
stretch, streĉi, streĉiĝi; etendi, etendiĝi; -er, homportilo
strike, bati, frapi; trafi; (labor)
striki, striko; -ing, impresa
string, ŝnureto; (of violin) kordo;
(beads, etc.) laĉi
stripe, strio
strive, penadi; — for, celi, strebi al
strong, forta; -hold, fortikajo
struggle, barakti, barakto; penegi,
penego; batali, batalado
stubborn, obstina, malcedema
student, studanto; (of college, etc.)
studento
study, studi
stuff, ŝtofo, aĵo; senvalorajo; tro-
manĝi; (furniture) remburi; -y,
malfreŝaera
stumble, stumbli
stump, stumpo
stupid, stulta, malsprita; -ly, malsaĝe, stulte, malsprite
stutter, balbuti
style, stilo, maniero; modo; -ish,
bonstila, laŭmoda

subject, temo; (gram.) subjekto; subigi; regato

submit, sin cedi, submetiĝi; antaŭmeti

subscribe, kotizi; subskribi; mondoni; — to, (gazet) aboni

subscription, abono; kotizo; mondono

substance, substanco; ŝtofo; esenco

substitute, anstataŭi; anstataŭanto

suburb, eksterurbo, suburbo

subway, subtervojo

succeed, sukcesi, prosperi; sekvi; — to, heredi

success, sukceso, prospero; -ion, vico, serio; -or, posteulo

such, tia; — as, tia kia

suck, suĉi; -le, suĉigi, mamnutri

sudden, subita; -ly, subite

sue, procesi (kontraŭ)

suffer, suferi; toleri

sugar, sukero

suggest, sugesti, proponi

suit, konveni, taŭgi, akordi kun; proceso; amindumado; (cards) serio; (clothes) kompleto; -able, konvena, taŭga, deca; -case, valizo

sum, sumo; -marize, — up, sumigi

summer, somero

summit, supro, (mont)pinto

sun, suno; -beam, sunradio; -burnt, sunbrunigita; -down, sunsubiro; -rise, sunleviĝo; -stroke, sunmalsano

Sunday, dimanĉo

supper, vespermanĝo, noktomanĝo

supply, liveri, liverajo; plenigi; provizi, provizo

support, subteni, subtenilo; (lean) apogi, apogilo; -er, subtenanto

suppose, supozi; supposition, supozo

suppress, subpremi

sure, certa; nepra; fidinda; sekura, nedanĝera; -ty, certeco; garantiajo

surface, surfaco; suprajo

surgeon, kirurgo; surgery, kirurgio

surname, alnomo, familia nomo

surplus, troajo, restajo; profito

surprise, surprizi, surprizo; surprizataki

surrender, cedi, kapituli

surround, ĉirkaŭi; -ings, ĉirkaŭajo

suspect, suspekti, suspektato; suspicion, suspekto

swallow, gluti; (bird) hirundo

swamp, marĉo; (boat) subakviĝi, subakvigi

swan, cigno

swear, (an oath) juri; blasfemi

sweat, ŝviti, ŝvito; -er, (garment) trikotvesto

sweep, balai

sweet, dolĉa; freŝa; sukerajo; -heart, amat(in)o, amant(in)o

swell, ŝveli; ŝveligi; bonege

swim, naĝi; -suit, naĝvesto

swing, balanci, balanciĝi, balancilo; (brandish) svingi

Swiss, (person) sviso; (adj.) svisa

sword, glavo

syllable, silabo

symbol, simbolo

symphony, simfonio

syndicate, (trust) sindikato

syphilis, sifiliso

syrup, siropo

system, sistemo; -atize, sistemigi

T

table, tablo; surtabligi; (list) tabelo; -cloth, tablotuko; -service, servico

tablet, tabuleto; skribkajero

tack, najleto, najletfiksi; kudreti

tact, takto; -ful, taktoplena

tag, alpendajo

tail, vosto; (of coat, etc.) basko

tailor, tajloro

take, preni; akcepti; konduki; kapti; okupi; lui; —advantage of, profiti el; — off, demeti, ekiri; — part, partopreni; — place, okazi; — notice of, rimarki

talk, paroli, babilo; interparolo; -ative, parolema, babilema

tall, alta, altkreska

tame, malsovaĝa, malsovaĝigi

tank, akvujo; (mil.) tanko

tap, frapeti, frapeto; krano; ellasi fluidajon

tape, rubandeto; "red —", rutino

tapestry, tapeto

tar, gudro

tariff, tarifo

tart, torto; acida

task, tasko

taste, gusto, gusti, (tr.) gustumi; **tasty**, bongusta

tavern, trinkejo

tax, imposto, imposti; ŝarĝi

taxi-cab, fiakro, taksfiakro, taksio

tea, teo; (meal) temanĝo; -pot, tekruĉo

teach, instrui; -er, instruisto, instruanto

tear, (from eye) larmo

tear, ŝiri, ŝiriĝi; — out, forŝiri; — off, deŝiri; — up, disŝiri

teat, mampinto

technical, teknika; **technics**, tekniko

teens, in one's, dekkelkjara

teeth, dentoj

telegram, telegramo; **telegraph**, telegrafi

telephone, telefono, telefoni

telescope, teleskopo

television, televido

tell, diri, rakonti; informi; klarigi

temper, humoro; kolereto; moderigi, moligi; (metals) hardi

temperature, temperaturo

temple, templo; (anat.) tempio

tempt, tenti; -ation, tento

ten, dek; -fold, dekobla; -th, deka; one -th, dekono

tend tendenci, emi; zorgi pri; (invalid) flegi; (children) varti; -ency, tendenco

tender, delikata; amema, sentema, kompatema; dolora; proponi

tense, strečita; rigida; (gram.) tempo

tent, tendo

term, (time) templimo, periodo; (math.) termo; (definition) termino; -inology, terminaro; -s, kondiĉoj; **come to —s**, interkonsenti

terrible, terura; **terrify**, teruri; timigi; **terror**, teruro

territory, teritorio

test, provi, provo; kontroli, kontrolo; (sc.) testi, testo

testify, atesti

text, teksto; -book, lernolibro

than, ol

thank, danki; -ful, dankema; -less sendanka; -s! dankon!

that, (conj.) ke; (dem. pron.) tiu; (thing) tio; (rel. pron.) kiu; — **kind of**, tia; — one, tiu; — one's. ties

the, la; — more . . . , — more . . . ju pli . . . , des pli . . .

theater, teatro

thee, ci, cin

theft, ŝtelo

their(s), ilia, sia

them, ilin; -selves, mem, si(n)

theme, temo

then, tiam; poste; sekve; tiuokaze; do

there, tie; -abouts, apude; proksime; -after, post tio; -by, per tio; -fore, tial, pro tio, do; — **are, is**, estas, ekzistas, jen

these, ĉi tiuj

they, ili; oni; — **themselves**, ili mem

thick, dika; densa; malklara; abunda; -set, dikkorpa

thief, ŝtelisto; **thieve**, ŝteli

thin, maldika, malgrasa, maldensa; (flimsy) malsolida

thing, objekto, aĵo; afero

think, pensi; kredi; opinii

third, tria; one —, triono; (mus.) terco

thirst, soifo, soifi; -y, soifa

[239

thirteen, dek-tri; -th, dek-tria
thirty, tridek
this, (one) ĉi tiu; (thing) ĉi tio; — one's, ĉi ties
thistle, kardo
thorn, dorno
thorough, tuta, ĝisfunda; -bred, pursanga; -fare, trairejo
those, tiuj
thou, ci, vi
though, kvankam; eĉ se; tamen
thought, penso, pensado; -ful, pensema; -less, senpensa
thousand, mil
thread, fadeno; (of screw) spiralo; -bare, eluzita
threat, minaco; -en, minaci
three, tri; -fold, triobla
thresh, draŝi
threshold, sojlo
thrift, ŝparemo; -y, ŝparema
throat, gorĝo
throne, trono
through, tra; per; -out, tute tra; dum
throw, ĵeti, ĵeto
thumb, dikfingro; fingrumi
thunder, tondro, tondri; -storm, fulmo-tondro
Thursday, jaŭdo
thus, tiel, tiamaniere
ticket, bileto
tickle, tikli; ticklish, tikla, tiklosenta
tide, tajdo
tie, ligi, ligilo; kravato
tiger, tigro
tight, streĉita, rigida, fiksa; -fitting, strikta
till, kaso; ĝis; kulturi
timber, ligno
time, tempo; horo; sezono; epoko; (mus.) takto; -ly, oportuna, frua; -table, hortabelo, horaro; at the same —, samtempe
tin, stano, stanumi; (sheet-iron coated) lado
tiny, eta

tip, pinto; dankmono, trinkmono; on -toe, piedpinte
tire, radringo; lacigi, tedi, enuigi; -d, laca; -some, enuiga, teda
title, titolo; rajto
to, al; ĝis; por; — and fro, tien kaj reen
toad, bufo; -stool, fungo (venena)
toast, rostita pano; (drink health) tosti, tosto
tobacco, tabako
today, hodiaŭ
toe, piedfingro
together, kune
toil, labori, laboregi, laboro; -some, laciga
toilet, necesejo; tualeto
tomato, tomato
tomb, tombo
tomorrow, morgaŭ; day after —, postmorgaŭ
ton, tuno
tone, tono; — down, moderigi
tongue, lango; (language) lingvo; hold your —! silentu!
tonight, hodiaŭ nokte, hodiaŭ vespere
too, ankaŭ, tro; — much, tro, tro multe
tool, ilo
tooth, dento
top, supro, supra; pinto; superi; (toy) turbo; -coat, surtuto; -heavy, falema
topic, temo; -al events, aktualajoj
torch, torĉo
tornado, uragano
torpedo, torpedo
total, tuta, tuto; absoluta; sumo, sumigi
touch, tuŝi, tuŝo; palpi; koncerni, rilati al; -ing, kortuŝa
tough, malmola; malcedema; malfacila, peniga
tour, rondvojaĝo; -ist, turisto
toward(s), al, en la direkto al, -n
towel, tuko, viŝtuko

tower, turo; altiĝi, altleviĝi
town, urbo; -council, konsilantaro;
 -hall, urbdomo
toy, ludilo
track, post-signo; post-sekvi; vojeto
trade, komerci, komerco; metio; -r,
 komercisto, negocisto; -mark, fab-
 rikmarko
traffic, trafiko; komercado
tragedy, tragedio
train, vagonaro; eduki; disciplini;
 ekzerci; (animals) dresi
tram, tramo; -way, tramvojo
trans-, trans-
transform, transformi, aliformigi
translate, traduki
transmission, transsendo; transmit,
 transsendi; transmitter, sendilo
transport, transporti, transporto
trap, kapti, kaptilo; klapo; -door,
 klap-pordo
travel, vojaĝi, vojaĝado; (by vehicle) veturi
tray, pleto
treachery, perfido
treason, perfido; ŝtatperfido
treasure, trezoro; -r, kasisto
treat, pritrakti; (doctor) kuraci; -ise,
 traktajo
tree, arbo
tremble, tremi
trench, trancêo
trial, provo, ekzameno; tento; juĝ-
 ado; sufero
triangle, triangulo
tribe, gento
tribunal, tribunalo
tried, elprovita, sperta
trip, ekskurso; fali, faligi
triumph, triumfo, triumfi
troop, bando, anaro; (mil.) trupo
trot, troti, trotado
trouble, ĝeni, ĝeno; ĉagreni, ĉagreno; aflikti, aflikto; peno
trousers, pantalono
truck, ŝarĝvagono

true, vera; certa; fidela; sincera;
 truly, vere
trunk, (body) torso; (tree) trunko;
 (elephant) rostro; (box) kesto,
 kofro
trust, fidi, fido; (entrust) konfidi;
 (com.) kredito; (fin.) sindikato
truth, vero; -ful, verema
try, peni; provi; juĝi; tenti; -ing,
 severa, ĝena
tub, kuvo
tube, tubo
tuberculosis, tuberkulozo
Tuesday, mardo
tulip, tulipo
tune, ario; akordo; akordigi; -ful,
 harmonia
tunnel, tunelo
turkey, meleagro
turn, turni, turniĝi; vico; (by lathe)
 torni; — out, rezulti; by -s,
 laŭvice; in —, siavice
twelve, dek-du; twelfth, dek-dua
twenty, dudek; twentieth, dudeka
twenty-one, dudek-unu
twice, duoble; dufoje
twilight, krepusko
twin, ĝemelo
twine, ŝnureto; interplekti, interplek-
 tigi
twist, tordi, tordo
two, du; -fold, duobla, duoble
type, tipo; speco; preslitero; -writer,
 skribmaŝino; typical, tipa; typist,
 maŝinskribisto
tyrant, tirano

U
udder, bestmamo
ugly, malbela
ulcer, ulcero; -ate, ulceriĝi
umbrella, ombrelo
un-, ne-, mal-, sen-
unanimous, unuanima
uncle, onklo

under, sub, sube; malpli ol; **-go,** suferi, toleri; **-hand,** sekreta, ruza; **-ling,** subulo; **-neath,** sub; **-stand,** kompreni; **-take,** entrepreni; **-wear,** subvesto

undress, senvestigi, senvestiĝi, senvestigi sin

unearth, elterigi; **-ly,** netera, supernatura

unemployed, senokupa, senlaboru

unfailingly, nepre

uniform, sama, unuforma; (costume) uniformo

unify, unuigi

union, unuigo, unuiĝo; kuniĝo, unio; harmonio

unison, unuvoĉe, unusoneco

unite, unuigi, unuiĝi; **United States,** Unuiĝintaj Statoj, Usono

universe, universo

university, universitato

unless, se . . . ne, kun la escepto de

unoccupied, neokupita, vakanta, libera

unpleasant, neagrabla

unsafe, danĝera

until, ĝis

untold, nedirita; netaksebla

up, supre; **-bringing,** edukado; **-hold** subteni; **-on,** sur; **-roar,** tumulto, bruego; **-set,** renversi; ĝeni; **-sidedown,** renverse; **-stairs,** supre(n); **— to,** ĝis; **-wards,** supren

uranium, uranio

urban, urba

urchin, bubo

urge, instigi; antaŭenpuŝi; **-nt,** urĝa

urine, urino; **urinate,** urini

us, ni, nin

use, uzi, uzo; kutimo; **-ful,** utila; **-less,** senutila; **— up,** foruzi; konsumi; **be of —,** utili

usual, kutima, ordinara; **-ly,** ĝenerale, ordinare

uterus, utero

utmost, plej lasta; pleja; **to the —,** ĝis la fino, limo

V

vacant, vaka, vakanta; **to be —,** vaki; **vacate,** vakigi; **vacate office,** eksiĝi

vacuum, vakejo, malpleno

vague, malpreciza, necerta, nedifinita

vain, (conceited) vanta; malmodesta; (futile) vana; **in —,** vane

valet, lakeo

valiant, brava

valid, valida, valora; laŭleĝa

valise, valizo

valley, valo

value, valoro; estimi, ŝati; (be worth) valori; (estimate) taksi; **valuable,** multvalora

valve, klapo; (bot., rad., zool.) valvo

vanish, malaperi

vapor, vaporo

varied, diversa; **variety,** diverseco

varnish, lako, laki

vase, vazo

vast, vasta, granda

vegetable, vegetajo; (edible) legomo; **vegetarian,** vegetarano

veil, vualo; kovrajo; kaŝi; maskı

vein, vejno

velvet, veluro

venereal, venera

vent, aerfluejo; kamentubo

venture, kuraĝi; riski; entrepreno

veranda, verando

verb, verbo

verse, strofo; versaĵo, poeziaĵo

version, traduko; raporto; opinło

very, tre; **— much,** tre (multe)

vest, veŝto

veteran, veterano

via, laŭ

vibrate, vibri

vice, malvirto; (as prefix) vic-

vicinity, proksimeco

victim, viktimo; (sacrifice) oferito

victor, venkinto; **-y,** venko

view, vidi, vido; rigardi; opinio; **have in —,** celi, **-point,** vidpunkto; **in — of,** pro

village, vilaĝo; **-r,** vilaĝano
vine, vinberarbo; **-yard,** vinberejo
vinegar, vinagro
violate, profani; perforti; malobei; violence, perforto
violin, violono
virgin, virgulino
virtue, virto; **virtuous,** virta
vision, vidpovo; vizio
visit, viziti, vizito
vivid, brilega; vivsimila
vocal, voĉa
voice, voĉo; esprimi
volt, volto
volume, amplekso; (book) volumo; (geom.) volumeno
voluntary, laŭvola, propravola; nedeviga
vomit, vomi
vote, voĉdoni, voĉdono; baloti
vow, ĵurpromesi, ĵurpromeso
vowel, vokalo
voyage, (mar) vojaĝi, vojaĝo

W

wade, vadi
wage, salajro
wagon, vagono; ŝarĝvagono
waist, talio; **-coat,** veŝto
wait, atendi; **-er,** kelnero
wake, veki, vekiĝi; mortfesteno; **-ful,** maldormema
walk, marŝi, piediri; promeni, promeno
wall, muro; **-paper,** tapeto
wallet, (Amer.) monujo; pendsaketo
waltz, valsi, valso
wander, vagi; (in mind) deliri
want, deziri; (need) bezoni, bezono; (lack) manko; **be -ing,** manki
war, milito, militi; **-like,** militema
ward, gardi; zorgato; kvartalo; (hospital) fako; **-en,** gardisto; **-robe,** vestejo
warm, varma, varmigi, varmiĝi; fervora; **-th,** varmeco

warn, averti; **-ing,** averto
was estis
wash, lavi, lavi sin, lavado; **-er-woman,** lavistino
waste, senutila, senutilaĵo; dezerto; malŝpari; **-paper-basket,** paperkorbo
watch, poŝhorloĝo; gardi; observi; atenti; **-dog,** gardhundo; **— out!** atentu!
water, akvo, akvumi; (cattle) trinkigi; **-fall,** akvofalo; **-proof,** kontraŭpluva
wave, ondo, ondi; flirti; mansigni, mansigno; **— length** (rad.) ondlongeco; **wavy,** ondforma
wax, vakso
way, vojo; kutimo; maniero, **-ward,** kaprica; **by the —,** pasante: **in any —,** iel ajn; **in every —;** ĉiel; **in such a —,** tiamaniere; **in that —,** tiel; **in what —,** kiel, kiamaniere; **on the —,** survoje
we, ni
weak, malforta; **-en,** malfortigi, malfortiĝi
weapon, armilo, batalilo
wear, porti; **— out,** eluzi
weather, vetero
weave, teksi
wed, edz(in)igi, edz(in)iĝi; **-ding,** geedziĝo; **-lock,** edzeco
Wednesday, merkredo
weed, kreskaĵaĉo; **to —,** sarki
week, semajno; **-ly,** semajne, ĉiusemajne
weep, plori
weigh, (tr.) pesi; (intr.) pezi; pripensi; **-t.** ŝarĝo; graveco; pezo; pezilo, pezeco
welcome, bonvena, bonveno; bonvenigi
well, sana, bonfarta; bone, tre; nu; (water) puto; **-bred,** bonedukita; **— done!** brave! **-earned,** meritita; **-informed,** klera: **-off, -to-do,** bonhava: **as — as,** tiel bone kiel

[243

went, iris
were, estis
west, okcidento, okcidenta
wet, malseka, malsekigi; pluva
whale, baleno
what (thing) kio, kion; tio kio; (kind of) kia; -ever, kio ajn; -'s the matter? Kio estas?
wheat, tritiko
wheel, rado; (helm) direktilo; -barrow, puŝveturilo
when, kiam; -ever, kiam ajn
where, kie, kien; -abouts, apud kie, proksime al kio; -as, ĉar, tial ke, pro tio ke; -to, kien, al kie
whether, ĉu
which, (one) kiu; (thing) kio
while, dum; kvankam; — away, pasigi; a little — ago, antaŭnelonge
whip, vipo, vipi; (cream, etc.) kirli
whiskers, vangharoj
whiskey, viskio
whisper, flustri, flustro
whist, visto
whistle, fajfi, fajfo, fajfilo
white, blanka, blanko; blankulo; -n, blankigi, blankiĝi
whither, kien
who, kiu, kiun; -ever, kiu ajn
whole, tuta, tuto; ĉiom; sendifekta; sana; -sale, pogrande; amase; -some, saniga; bona; on the —, entute
whore, malĉastulino; publikulino
whose, kies
why, kial; pro kio
wicked, malbonega; malvirta; peka
wide, larĝa, vasta; -awake, vigla, maldorma; -spread, ĝenerala
widow, vidvino; -er, vidvo
wife, edzino
wig, peruko
wild, sovaĝa, necivilizita; senkultura; fantazia; furioza; diboĉema
will, (end. future tense) -os; volo; testamento, testamenti; -ing, vol-

onta, komplezema; -ingly, volonte; against one's —, kontraŭvole; at —, laŭvole, be -ing, voli
wilt, velki
win, gajni, gajno; atingi; venki
wind, vento; -ward, kontraŭventa
wind, vindi, tordi; serpentumi; (watch etc.) streĉi
window, fenestro
wine, vino
wing, flugilo; (of building) flankajo
wink, palpebrumi, palpebrumo
winter, vintro; travintri
wipe, viŝi; — out, forviŝi
wire, metalfadeno, drato; telegrafi, telegramo
wisdom, saĝo, saĝeco
wise, saĝa
wish, deziri, deziro; voli
wit, sprito, spriteco; spritulo; komprenemo; -ticism, spritajo
with, kun; per; pri; por; -draw, retiri, eltiri; eliĝi; -hold, deteni; -out, sen; ekstere; -stand, kontraŭstari, rezisti
witness, atesti, atesto, atestanto; eye-, vidinto
wobbly, ŝanceliĝa
woe, mizero, malĝojo; malbono; —! Ho, ve!
wolf, lupo
woman, virino; -ly, virina, virineca
womb, utero
wonder, miri, mirindaĵo; -ful, mirinda, miriga; I — whether, mi scivolas ĉu
woo, amindumi
wood, ligno; arbareto; -en, ligna; -pile, ŝtiparo
wool, lano; -len, lana
word, vorto; (uttered) parolo; promeso; -building, vortfarado; — for —, laŭvorte; -y, multvorta, parolema; in a —, unuvorte; in one's own -s, propravorte
work, labori, laboro; efiki; (lit., mus.) verki, verko; (machine)

244]

funkcii, funkciigi; **-ing-classes**, laboristaro; **-s**, (of clock, etc.), mekanikajo; **out of —**, senokupa, senlabora

world, mondo; tero; **-ly** mondeca; **-wide**, tutmonda

worm, vermo

worry, turmenti, turmentiĝi; ĉagreno, ĉagreni

worship, adori, adorado

worst, plej malbona, plej malbone; venki

worth, valoro, indeco; **-less**, senvalora, sentaŭga; **-y**, inda

would, volus; (end. conditional) -us

wound, vundi, vundo

wrap, kunvolvi, envolvi, kunfaldi; ŝalo

wreck, (ŝip)pereo; perei; detrui, ruinigi

wrestle, lukti

wring, premtordi; **-er**, elpremilo; **— out**, elpremi

wrinkle, sulketo, sulkigi, sulkiĝi

wrist, man-radiko; **-band**, manumo; **-watch**, manumhorloĝo

write, skribi; (compose as author, musician) verki; **-r**, verkisto

wrong, erara; malprava; neĝusta; maljusta; malbonfaro; **be —**, malpravi; erari

X

X-ray, rentgen-radio

xylophone, ksilofono

Y

yacht, jakto

yard, korto; (3 feet) jardo; **-stick**, mezurilo

yarn, ŝpinajo; rakonto

yawn, oscedi

year, jaro; **-ly**, ĉiujara, ĉiujare

yearn, sopiri (je)

yeast, fermentilo

yellow, flava

yes, jes

yesterday, hieraŭ; **the day before —**, antaŭhieraŭ

yet, ankoraŭ; tamen

yield, cedi; fleksiĝi; produkti, produkto

you, vi, vin; **-r(s)**, via; **-rself**, vi mem

young, juna; idaro; **— lady**, fraŭlino, junulino; **-ster**, junulo; **with —**, graveda

youth, juneco, junulo, junularo; **-ful**, juna, juneca, junula

Yule, Kristnasko

Z

zeal, fervorego

zebra, zebro

zero, nulo

zigzag, zigzagi, zigzaga

zinc, zinko

zone, zono; kvartalo

zoology, zoologio; **zoologist**, zoologo

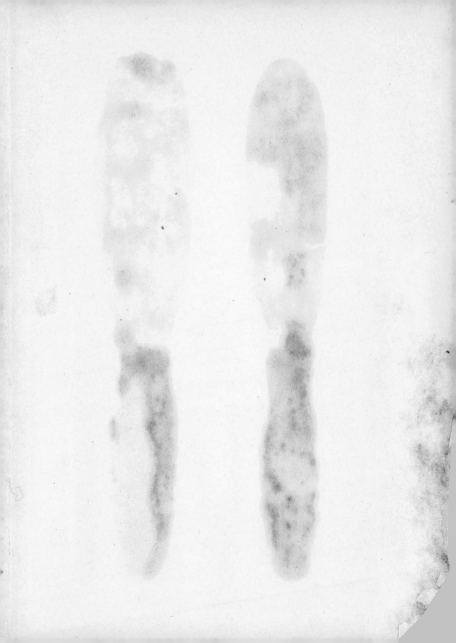

DATE DUE
